Towards a New Day

Towards a New Day

A Monk's Story

Father Ralph Martin SSM

DARTON · LONGMAN + TODD

First published in 2015 by
Darton, Longman and Todd Ltd
1 Spencer Court
140 – 142 Wandsworth High Street
London   SW18 4JJ

ISBN 978-0-232-53163-3

A catalogue record for this book is available from the British Library

Printed and bound in Great Britain by Bell & Bain, Glasgow

Dedication

To the memory of Herbert Hamilton Kelly
SSM, with thanksgiving for his vision, and
in hope and expectation that this vision,
re-imagined and re-formed, will continue
to contribute to the mission of the church
in tomorrow's world.

*Almighty and eternal God, from whose
presence the angels go forth to do your will:
grant that in obedience we may serve to the
glory of your name, and overshadowed by
your protection, receive at last the crown of
life, through Jesus Christ our Lord.*

Ad gloriam Dei in eius voluntate

Contents

List of illustrations

1. Ralph, Mom, Bill, Gerry, Dad and Albert, Canada, 1937.
2. The SSM at Kelham.
3. Ralph on his profession day, 1960.
4. Fr Malcolm Broadhead SSM and Fr Francis Horner SSM on Ralph's profession day.
5. Christmas Day football match at Kelham, 1962. Professed v. Novices.
6. Israel Qwelane from South Africa, John Ackon from Ghana and Ito Maitin from South Africa as students at Kelham in 1961.
7. Ralph in Japan with Fr Edmund Wheat SSM and Fr Moses Kimata SSM (right).
8. Percussion centre of chapel at St Nicholas. KK and Acheampong.
9. Graduation Class at St Nicholas, 1988, with Sister Joyce at centre.
10. Auntie Ekuwah in the college kitchen.
11. Fr Tanki Mofama SSM blessing Ralph after Tanki's ordination to the priesthood.
12. Fr Tanki Mofama SSM (standing left), Bishop John Lewis SSM, Ralph, Fr Michael Lapsley SSM and Fr Christopher Myers SSM.
13. Ralph with Ralph Martin Allen in 1996; one of the many children Ralph baptized who were named in his honour .

14. Ralph's departure from Ghana; pictured with Robert Okine, a former Kelham student, then Bishop of Koforidua.
15. At the launch of Ralph's book on John Moschus at All Saints Convent, Oxford, 2012. From left to right: Fr Colin Griffiths SSM; Bishop Christopher Morgan, former student; Ralph; Canon Vincent Strudwick; the Revd Barry Collins, also a former student.

Acknowledgements

My thanks to Mr and Mrs William Martin and Mr and Mrs Albert Martin for keeping my letters and encouraging me to share them.

To the Society of the Sacred Mission, brothers, sisters, associates, companions and my friends who made the journeying possible.

To those who accompanied me at different times on the way.

To Canon Vincent Strudwick for editing this book.

To Judith Longman, who freely gave her time and expertise to make the publication possible.

To David Moloney at Darton, Longman and Todd for producing the book and enabling it to reach a larger and much wider audience.

Preface

The story that follows is not an official history of the Society of the Sacred Mission; rather it is the story of one member of the Society, as the title suggests. However, that story can only be understood in the context of the Society to which he belonged.

Ralph Martin, a Canadian, heard about the Society of the Sacred Mission in Toronto, and came to England to explore joining it. Already a priest, he was a novice for three years and then was professed, that is, he made his promises of 'poverty, chastity and obedience' to become a full member of the Society at Michaelmas 1960. He remained initially at the Mother House of the Society at Kelham and taught in the theological college that it ran until the college closed in 1973. Then, with a developing vision for the future, Ralph, having been elected 'Provincial' (that is the member in charge of all the brothers in England) responded to a series of opportunities that planted seeds for the SSM to contribute to society and the church in a time of rapid and potentially cataclysmic change.

The whole story of the SSM had been part of the unfolding of a great idea, envisaged by a Church of England priest at the end of the nineteenth century. It had begun as a missionary brotherhood. Herbert Hamilton Kelly,[1] born in 1860 and son of a parson, wrote that he was 'haunted by the dream of organised power, concentrating upon the attainment of one common aim'. Having been an army cadet at Woolwich, then at Queen's College Oxford, he was ordained and obsessed with how, in that Victorian world of opportunity, the aim of glorifying God might be tackled in a less haphazard way than the Church of England generally employed.

'Brotherhoods' were an increasingly popular way of getting things done, and when Kelly was invited to provide and train priests and laymen for service in Corea,[2] he formed the Corean Missionary Brotherhood, laying down three conditions:

> A man must be ready to work without pay;
> therefore he must intend to live unmarried.
> He must come simply to serve Christ, and be ready
> to work in whatever place or role to which he is assigned.

From small beginnings the Brotherhood evolved into a full blown religious community, in many ways (like a few other groups of men and a large number of sisterhoods in the second half of the nineteenth century) copying the great Roman Catholic Orders, with a full round of corporate daily prayer and a missionary, educational or nursing purpose. The early years were at the church of St John the Divine, Kennington in London; then Kelly moved to Mildenhall in Suffolk, and, as SSM grew, the Mother House and college finally moved in 1903 to the large St Pancras-like mansion built by Giles Gilbert Scott at Kelham, on the banks of the Trent, in Nottinghamshire.

However, by the early twentieth century, the majority of the Society's members were in Africa, where although committed to the same round of prayer and community life, they engaged in more 'friar-like'[3] missionary and educational ministries.

In 1947, the Society was invited to serve in Australia and opened a theological college on the lines of Kelham, with a growing number of (mainly ex-service) professed brothers.

This was a high point in the history of the Society. At the beginning of the sixties there were 85 professed members, and Ralph joined nine other men at Kelham preparing for membership in the novitiate.

As a member of the seminary staff, chaplain to some students and visiting preacher to many parishes and institutions, Ralph became a valued friend to many; but it was as the global shifts in cultural perceptions in the wider society began to challenge the way Kelly's idea was institutionalised, and many brothers left the Society, that Ralph came into a leadership role. Struggling at first, he sought to identify the Society's enduring vision, and re-shape it to serve a future that was unfolding.

The first part of the story is written as a narrative, giving Ralph's perspective on the Society's life as he perceived and experienced it. This is not how all experienced it, and so is a personal history. For example, Richard Holloway in his *Leaving Alexandria* tells his story in the years at Kelham just before Ralph came;[4] there are of course common threads, and both have their place in helping to understand the place and its grip on peoples formation; but they are different. Ralph's ends with leaving Kelham and the beginning of his ideas to re-found the Society in this new world and culture.

In 1987, perhaps because I had been with the Society at Kelham, and then at the beginning of the re-founding as an Associate at Willen, I was asked to contribute a chapter on the role of religious communities in the renewal of the church in a book to prepare bishops and others for the coming Lambeth conference of 1988[5]. In addition to my experience with Anglican Communities, I had been arrested by the thinking of two Roman Catholics. One was Fr Paul Collins, and the other Fr Gerard Arbuckle.

It was Collins who introduced the idea of re-founding, which he described as a 'mutation' in which there is both disjunction and continuity; something that has happened in the church from time to time since the moment the early Christians struggled to disentangle themselves from their Jewish matrix. It is time to do it again he argued, if the religious life – and indeed the church – is to emerge from crisis and chaos.

Arbuckle, in an article in *The Tablet*, says that communities have to discern members of the calibre to be leaders in this process, and asks 'Are we prepared to discover these rather rare people, support them and respond to their creative leadership?'[6]

SSM discovered and elected Ralph Martin, which launched the whole Society on a pilgrimage, full of ups and downs, described in the following chapters.

The second part of 'A Monk's Story' was written as a 'log' at the time. It is kept in that form so that the day to day immediacy and liveliness is preserved, but with editorial comment and explanation to ensure the log is read in the context of what was happening in church and society.

In telling his story, Ralph is characteristically modest about his own academic achievements. However, he is a considerable scholar, and during his years 'in the land of Oz' as he calls them, while having a pastoral role he returned to scholarship, and translated a sixth century Greek text, written by John Moschus, a monk from one of the many monasteries in the neighbourhood of Jerusalem[7].

He translated all the stories that Moschus collected on his tour of North Africa, Egypt, Palestine and Turkey in a collection called *The Spiritual Meadow*. In 2012 an anthology of Ralph's translation, together with an introduction, was published by the Sisters of the Love of God at Fairacres, Oxford.

This introduction gives us a clue which will help us understand Ralph's own story and motivation, as he toured different parts of the modern world. Speaking of John Moschus he writes:

'He set out not to sell anything or to preach the latest brand of orthodoxy but to gather evidence to support his underlying conviction that heroic deeds and unselfish sacrifice were not all that uncommon in this world, and were not to be found exclusively in the great and famous. He thought that such spiritual treasures could be found in abundance in the lives of ordinary men and women of all classes, and all occupations.'

So his journal includes hermits and saints, but also sailors, prostitutes and even animals, and he records their stories, struggles, defeats and victories against all the odds. There is much in this approach that can be recognised in Ralph Martin's own attitudes as he tells his story – another monk, fourteen hundred years later in a very different world. And yet what is revealed in his story is that what appeared to be the slow death of a Community in the form in which it had flourished in the twentieth century, was an opportunity for the transformation of Kelly's idea, carrying his principles and spirituality into new forms which could illuminate and enliven what has been described as 'the rumour of God' in different places in a changing world; ordinary people, men, women, saints and sinners, capable of hearing a call and responding.

At Michaelmas 2014, fifty four years after Ralph's profession, a new brother of SSM was professed at the church of St John the Divine at Kennington where SSM began. The Rood from Kelham chapel is now there, and in the presence of a large congregation of professed – men and women, English, Australian and African – and associates from 'The Well', former students from Kelham and others touched by SSM's new ministries, the old and the new forms of Kelly's vision were tangible.

Like Kelly, Ralph Martin is a visionary. His beautifully written journal (letters to his siblings Bill and Albert) tells his story and that of the Society of the Sacred Mission. It is a compelling read for all, inside the church or outside, who puzzle about the church in modern society. Ralph is a man who in his calling dared to try to interpret a religious idea, and re-incarnate it in different ways, for a changing world.

His story follows in his own words, from his recollections, diaries and letters as it unfolded.

Vincent Strudwick
December 2014

The Revd Canon Dr Vincent Strudwick is an Honorary Fellow of Kellogg College in the University of Oxford.

Journeying: Introduction

Becoming a disciple and entering a pilgrim's path was apparently much simpler in the early days of Christianity. All that seems to have been involved, in at least one case, was two men, hard at work, looking up to see this stranger called Jesus standing on the shore next to their boat and looking squarely at them. 'Follow me' he said, and they did. They walked with him and became part of the group who accompanied him for the rest of his life, and when his life was over the spirit of the man became embodied in them at Pentecost and they carried his message and his presence to the ends of the world. The joining may have been simple, but walking with Jesus was never an easy ride because this man was first and foremost a boundary-breaker. He broke down so many of the rules and regulations that had, up until then, defined their lives as Jewish believers. He healed people on the Sabbath regularly and when his group was hungry and weary he encouraged them to pluck ears of corn on the Sabbath. He held up a Samaritan (of all people!) as an example of a man who truly obeyed God's laws even if he could not have recited them. He healed the servant of a Roman centurion and the daughter of a woman from Syro-Phoenicia. He was ready to talk to anyone he met and he accepted dinner invitations from tax collectors (collaborators with the occupying power) and other such 'no-goods' and 'no accounts' as well as from Pharisees and lawyers. So in these and many other ways he split open the traditional faith of these ordinary fishermen.

In due course they became aware that he was more than a boundary-breaker. He was also a healer and a joy-giver who could change lives, and change them for the better. He changed the lives of the deaf, the blind and the crippled. He changed them all into whole human beings, able at last to take a full part in human affairs. As a result, in their walk with him, the new disciples felt they were on a journey of liberation, setting men and women free, free to be whole and to be human wherever they went because that was another boundary he regularly broke; the age-old boundary that defined and confined the lives of men and women and kept them as separate categories. He, for his part, always treated women as people and discussed theology with a woman he happened to meet at a well near Samaria; in fact she became his first recorded missionary long before any of the others.

Boundary-breaker, joy-giver, yes, but in the end they came to realise that the whole meaning and purpose of his life was to bring unity to humankind. He lived so that we all might become one item. By the love that he taught them so generously, and by the Spirit of love that he gave them so freely at Pentecost (or Whitsun) to reside forever in the hearts of each one of them, he transformed that little band of individual disciples into a single family, a loving family, now for the first time open and welcoming to non-Jews of every colour and culture; a loving family where strangers could be turned into brothers and sisters, where the wounded could find healing, where the joys of the Jesus- style life could be accessed and could expand, forever growing and forever a new thing.

All that happened a long time ago and since then the world has expanded and changed exponentially, but the basic pattern of discipleship remains the same. You still become a Christian not by glancing down the catalogue of churches operating in your area at the present time and choosing for yourself the one with the longest pedigree, or the largest attendance, or what seems in your eyes to be the most accurate and convincing theology. Nor do you become a Christian by casting a critical eye over the pages of the New Testament with its commentaries and asking yourself, 'How much of all this do I still believe? Do I still believe in the virgin birth? Do I still believe he walked across the waters? Do

I still believe he walked out of the tomb three days after he had died? Do I still believe all or any of that? In fact could I pass any examination in the basics of faith? Have I even got enough faith to be called an ordinary Christian or should I just fall back amongst the hangers-on? 'But NO! The pattern today remains the same as it was at the start. You become a Christian in only one way, by somewhere, somehow encountering Jesus Christ and, at his kind invitation, falling in behind him. After all, this is the way all those early seekers became Christians; the way Saul the persecutor became Paul the apostle, and centuries later Francis the playboy became Francis the poor man, and in our own day Romero the arch-conservative bishop became Romero the martyred bishop who gave his life for the poor. Nor is this 'walking after the Lord' any easier for people now than it was for people then, because Jesus does not accompany us like a pet dog on a lead. We accompany him on his world-changing, never-look-back mission.

I suppose that every brother in SSM joined the Society in the conviction that God was calling him and that was why he left home, went to Kelham and joined that community. He was responding to a gracious and wonderful invitation. However, once he arrived at Kelham there was no longer any question of what you should do next or where you should go. The prior who was the Queen Bee of that particular hive, by means of the direct line of communication he purportedly had with God, was well able to answer any queries you might raise. 'I am not sure', 'You may be right', 'I just don't know', were words never heard on his lips. Certainty, wisdom and decisions were the stuff of his days and he never hesitated. As a result the house at Kelham was a complex network of inter-locking boundaries which, with a wonderful clarity, marked out for you where you were in the pecking order, where you should be and what you should be doing at any hour of the day. Such dependable boundaries around you gave life cathedralesque proportions. It felt safe, it felt holy, it felt permanent, very reassuring and secure – and it certainly was, until that day when the one who walked slightly ahead of us gave men the permission to blow the place sky high. Why he did that, who knows? We never knew and still don't know, but it all went up in the air with a bang and a boom in a cloud of dust; the 130 room Gilbert Scott mansion, the theological college and its students, the library, the awesome chapel, the orchard, the pigs, the football pitches, the tennis courts as well as some brothers – all blown into a million tiny fragments never to be reassembled in this world or in this life. In fact the devastation couldn't have been more total if we had planted a tea chest stuffed with TNT in the cellars of Kelham Hall and pushed home the plunger.

So what was our part in this dramatic explosion? For we did indeed have a part to play. We are not reduced to mere passive victims unless we choose to be, but it took some time, years even, for us to recognise our part, and even when we did we were often (always?) in two minds (at least) about embracing it. Our part, put simply, was to let go, to cease clinging to Kelham Hall and clutching at its history and its habits. Our part was to let go of all that as graciously as we could, and to step out boldly into the flat new landscape where nearly all the old boundaries had disappeared.

However, instead of stepping out boldly we were more often tempted into indulging in a certain amount of whimpering, echoing the words of the psalmist, 'How long O Lord will you forget me? Forever?' or 'Why should the nations now say "Where is now their God?"' I doubt whether the nations ever said any such thing or were even aware of our plight, but it was certainly a question we often put to ourselves, 'Where is the God we worshipped for so long on the Kelham rood?'[8] That triumphant, winning, even slightly arrogant God? However that was a strange question, even a slightly foolish question for any Christian disciple to ask, let alone those who were priests, scholars, and monks. God was exactly where he had always been from the beginning. He had never been blown up or gone away. He was, he remained, inside us, in our hearts and in our guts, because everyone has a little piece of God inside them. Etty Hillesum, a maverick Dutch secular Jew and scholar who kept a diary, encountered 'God' in a prison camp, and died in Auschwitz. She wrote of those who will give God space inside their heart, and then defend that space fiercely against all the forces of disillusion, cynicism, humiliation and despair, weariness and boredom. She wrote 'I realise, God,

4

that you can't help us very much, or change this situation very much, but I can help you, and must help you by providing you with a space in the heart of this chaos, a space where a loving, gentle defenceless God may still be named, loved and worshipped, when everyone else has deleted you.'

Of course our situation and circumstances bore no relation to the undiluted horror this woman lived through, but the lessons she learned in that extremity became for me of universal application for every Christian. For what carried us through all those turbulent years of upheaval, was the God who remained inside us to guide and to cheer us and to provide us with endless gifts. He was our hidden treasure, our pearl of great price.

It was in those years that we began to experience our companion with whom we walked, as the great healer and joy-giver, for he began at once to change things and endless were the gifts he bestowed on us over the next years. For those who went to Willen in Milton Keynes new town, the first gift was the beautiful Willen parish church, built in 1680, which became our priory chapel. Even better, was the congregation ably shepherded and led by two great women, Susan Nickless and Bet Morgan, who became our dearest friends and most loyal supporters. Next came the new priory building, not a Victorian mansion half-heartedly adapted for a religious community, but a new and modern building which we had helped the architect to plan. Then the Hospice of Our Lady and St John was built in Willen and we connected with it through Fr Francis Horner, who had been a New Testament tutor at Kelham. We also connected with St Etheldreda's children's home in Bedford and three sisters belonging to the Deaconess Community of St Andrew: Sisters Joyce, Hazel and Muriel. Beyond Milton Keynes we were given work in several urban parishes in Sheffield through the new priory Edmund Wheat was leading there, assisted by Gordon Holroyd, who had spent many years in South Africa. At Quernmore Park near Lancaster, Hilary Greenwood and Gregory Wilkins, both former tutors from 1976, made the main role of the priory to be a 'Christian Institute' to provide theological education for lay people in short courses and seminars.

Apart from these fresh works, our life began to change its texture as we slowly, and perhaps a little reluctantly, made space in our life and work in Milton Keynes and Sheffield for women to join us. Mary Hartwell, Margaret Dewey and Bridget Brooke joined us as associate members. Then, after the coming of the women as 'associates' we were greatly blessed when three families, the Webbers, Lionel, Jean and daughter Anne, the Strudwicks, Vincent (a former member of SSM), Nina and daughters Becky, Alice and Martha, and the Davis family. John, Linda and children Arthur, Emily and Irene decided, at great cost to themselves, to uproot from their homes and jobs and to throw in their lot with us. Our community, for the first time, was now composed of men, women, families and children. All this involved many adjustments for the newcomers and for us and these adjustments were sometimes painful. I can't say that the inclusion of women and families was without difficulties and tensions; but what is clear now is whatever the problems, these women, these couples and their children altered the flavour of our community life forever. As one who was present through the whole process, I would say that at the end of this time we were less monastic, less self-conscious, and more human than we had been at the beginning. I count those as gains, though not all did. Still another dimension came to our ministry in the 1980s when the Society committed itself to the mission of the church overseas in Ghana, where one of our brothers, Richard Roseveare had been one time bishop and from where several students had been sent to train for the ministry at Kelham. The Society now made a large donation for the purchase of accommodation which was to become St Nicholas theological college in Cape Coast, training Africans in their own environment and country. I was to be Principal, living and working there for eight happy years.

All these things took place within the ten year period 1973-83 and they were all projects that were completely new to us, areas in which none of us had had any previous experience; but it was in the doing of these fresh projects that we regained a little of our lost confidence and developed a new image of what SSM might be, and that is why I say that they all came our way as gifts from our companion in the way, Jesus the joy-giver.

By the end of the period we might almost have sung, though we never did, the words of that old hymn,

> Be still my soul, for Jesus will repay
> From his own fullness, all he takes away.

Slowly, gradually, we found ourselves moving into a third place as we began to walk with Jesus the Unity-maker. For many years, even decades after the closure of Kelham Theological College and the sale of Kelham Hall we, the members of the Society who were left behind, felt that our main goal in life, the objective of all our activities, was survival. We were desperately concerned that the name SSM should not disappear from the pages of the Anglican story, that this name should still be heard in the corridors of ecclesiastical power. It took a long time for a different truth to break the surface; that when you are walking with Jesus, he never calls anyone just to survive, he calls us to a journey, an odyssey made in company with him as he journeys towards the fullness of humanity, a home that knows no barriers or prejudices, a home that lies beyond racial differences, gender differences, and religious differences. In this home there is a God who is not bound and confined by human creeds and needs, a God present in the Sikh community, in the Muslim community, in the Jewish community; in other words the God of the global village. That is the destination and the objective towards which our pilgrimage has unwittingly been bound and the only way by which we will arrive at that destination is by growing beyond those barriers we put up in the past to guard and protect our lives, and accepting those whom lately we feared, and welcoming those whom lately we rejected. And the only thing that will give us the power to move forwards along this difficult and dangerous path is love, the love we receive from Jesus by means of our brothers and sisters in community and the love we share with those who are outside our community. It is, after all, love which called us into life in the first place and love which can heal our wounds and give us the courage to come out of our safe hiding places and step out along the world. Only love can enable us to transcend our limits and move into the open exposed country beyond our barriers, and it is Jesus our companion, the one who dwells, and has always dwelt, within our hearts who shows us what his love is and invites us to participate in it.

Having reached this point, we then had to search for signs to confirm that we were on the true pilgrim way. In my story as it unfolded, there were convincing ones. The first was at Willen in the new city of Milton Keynes in the 1970s, the second was in Ghana in the 1980s and the third was in Maseru capital city of Lesotho in Southern Africa in the 1990s. Each is still a work in progress.

At Maseru priory we have seen a remarkable transformation. An SSM community that for over a hundred years had been entirely white, English, and yes, racist, embodied in colonial culture, was transformed into a largely Basotho community led by its own Basotho men and deeply involved in the HIV-AIDS mission of the church in that place, as well as being fully committed to differing pastoral and parochial ministries. It has now become for the first time an African community set for growth in the new South Africa facing the problems and opportunities of the new century.

At Willen, and forty years on from our arrival there, the process is still going on, and we see another priory undergoing an equally radical transformation. Beginning as a traditional religious community, all male, Anglo-Catholic, white and in traditional monks habits, it has grown into a multi-racial, multi-faith community made up of single and partnered men and women who come looking for a new way of living in community and being of service to the thriving city of Milton Keynes. It is only theoretically multi-faith at present though there has been one Buddhist candidate for membership as an associate. What they have already achieved is a greater unity of professed brothers, marrieds and singles, which we aimed for but never reached in the 1970s. The priory in this new shape has taken for itself a new name, 'The Well', expressing the wish to be a place of encounter with Jesus and encounter with the stranger as well as being a place of renewal and refreshment. All is summed up in the icon of Jesus conversing with the Samaritan woman at the well, the icon which we feel, better than any other, depicts their story and their meaning. They have adopted as their five core values, Spirituality, Hospitality, Inclusiveness, Peace and Justice, and Sustainability.

In Ghana, there is no longer an SSM presence, but the influence of the foundation persists at the college, and in the quality of its graduating students.

The two priories, one in Lesotho and one in the UK, are signs to me that we have not parted company with the Jesus who called us. We are still following after him, journeying on to a new world, a surprising world that lies beyond this divided, contentious and fearful world in which we were born. Perhaps the last word can best be left to Etty Hillesum who from her prison camp wrote:

'What really mattered most was to be truly inwardly happy, to accept God's world and to enjoy it without turning away from all the suffering there is…There is so much to relish, life is rich even though it has to be conquered from minute to minute.'

It is in that spirit that we may look forward to a new day.

Ralph Martin
December 2014

1

As We Were: Kelham 1957 – 1962

My story begins on July 16, 1957, a day which found me sitting on the train, gazing out the window as I hurtled down the line from Leeds towards Kelham and SSM. I was frozen stiff with alarm and foreboding at the position I had put myself in. The only thing I knew about SSM was the article I had read in Peter Anson's *The Call of the Cloister* which I had picked up by chance in the Anglican Book Room on Jarvis Street in Toronto, and I had briefly met the strangely habited Father Theodore Smith, the Warden of the Society's Theological College at Kelham, when he visited Toronto to interview me about my application to join the Society. What made me think I wanted the religious life? What was the religious life? I was afraid to even open that can of worms. So why had I turned my back on Canada and my family and plunged into a completely unknown society? Even now after nearly sixty years I have not satisfactorily answered those questions though these days I usually reply by means of another question. 'Why did you marry your present partner? Was there some clear advantage to be gained by it? Was it part of your plans for your career? Or was it because you fell in love? An irrational, inexplicable, not always sensible but always risky thing to do? Were you moved simply by the powers of attraction to do what seemed to make some kind of sense at the time and which has made life, on the whole, enjoyable ever since?' Something like that was why I was on that train. When we left Retford they announced that the next stop would be Newark and my tension increased. I contemplated staying on the train and travelling through to London where I could get the next ship back to Canada, but I couldn't face the unpleasant confrontations when I was discovered to be travelling without a proper ticket. Down I got at Newark and crossed over the line by the bridge, and standing there on the platform I saw two figures in cassocks and cowls, Fr Theodore, whom I had met before in January, and Fr Marcus, the Novice Master. We drove back to Kelham (about twenty-five minutes), where Theodore said good-bye to me, and never spoke to me again until Christmas. Meanwhile Marcus took me into the kitchen for a cup of tea. The kitchen was a large busy room crowded with stoves and equipment, with a stone-flagged floor where a young novice, John Packwood, was flying about in the last stages of preparing supper for a house of about 160 hungry men.

The Kelham that they brought me to that day was a bizarre building which housed a unique community. The main house was an enormous red brick, gothic, baronial mansion built in about 1851 by the Manners-Sutton family, who reduced themselves to bankruptcy before they were able to complete it, leaving behind in the unfinished house great empty spaces where grand staircases were meant to have been and many empty bases where marble pillars were meant to have stood. The architect was Giles Gilbert Scott, the man who built St Pancras station in London. In fact Kelham Hall was even known by some as St Pancras by the Trent, the river running down the edge of the garden. To this lofty pile had been added between the wars, when the college peaked numerically, two wings to provide the maximum student accommodation at minimal cost, looking as if they had been lifted out of a London suburb, and on the fourth wing of the courtyard a magnificent chapel which was neither Gothic nor suburban but completely in its own style and very beautiful. Life in that house at that time was very basic and simple, with no central heating in student rooms, no dishwashers, no floor polishers or sophisticated equipment of any kind. It was only twelve years since the end of the Second World War, rationing and ration books had only recently disappeared, and the country as a whole was still emerging from the hardships of those years. The community within this conglomeration of styles was doubly unique. It was unique as a religious community and unique as a theological college. This religious community of around thirty men took into their home as temporary members over a hundred men who lived with them for four to six years, as well as a 'junior' seminary of thirty to forty boys between sixteen and eighteen in a separate regime known as 'The Cottage'. No other community would have contemplated submitting to such a swamping of their way of life and their activities, and no other theological college could have contemplated submitting themselves to all the rules, customs and restrictions of those vowed to the religious life. Here the students completely shaped the life of the community and the community completely shaped the lives of the students. It was 'The Principles'[9] of the Society which were instilled into every member of that house. These 'Principles', which I shall quote throughout this section, were written in the very earliest days of the Society by Fr Kelly our founder. They were read aloud in the refectory during every retreat. The first 'principle' was:

By this you were created – the will of God, and to this end – the praise of his glory.

And our life went on from that starting point.

If we ask why any young man, even one who wanted to be a priest, would submit himself to living as a monk during the years of his training, making a promise of at least temporary celibacy, pledging obedience to the House Rule and to all the 'superiors' placed over him, the answer would be that for most of the years of the college's existence, from 1893–1946, the men who came to Kelham had no other option for most of them came from working class homes where a university education was far beyond what their parents could ever provide. The Society had come into existence largely to take on such men who could, in the ordinary way of things, never have become priests. The Society undertook to feed, clothe, and educate them for ministry with no fees charged. This was the Society's offering to the church for nearly eighty years. All this began slowly but inevitably to come apart after World War II with the passing of the Butler Education Act guaranteeing children of all classes an education suitable to their abilities with sufficient bursaries and scholarships provided. By 1957 nearly all the students at Kelham were receiving government grants of one kind or another but they had still chosen to come because they believed that the monastic life was the best context in which they could prepare for the ministry. However the fact remained that they were now financially independent of the Society. In fact the Society was becoming dependent on them, and if they should find the monastic round grew a little tedious, or if they should fall in love (always a peril with the young) they could fairly easily arrange a transfer to another college without too much trouble or embarrassment.

Cold showers

It is perhaps best to begin where every day at Kelham, summer or winter, began – in the cold showers.

Obey gladly, even if that cannot be, at least hide your unwillingness.

There were two common bathrooms with showers at one end and sinks at the other. In fact it was a very democratic way to begin the day with everyone, old and young, tutors and students, monks and novices, all together, all stripped of any distinguishing marks of rank or signs of religious status, shivering and naked as they passed at top speed through those icy waters, hoping to leave time for a quick shave before the bell rang for morning prayer in chapel. This strand of democracy ran all through the patterns of the day. There was no senior common room to which the elders might retire, no separate table in the refectory where the tutors might gather for 'high-table talk' and refrain from engaging with the students, no special wing in the building which could form an SSM ghetto. All tasks assigned, whether in the garden or in the kitchen or at sports, were assigned randomly to all alike. Of course in the class room, some were lecturers, some learners; in the chapel each group sat in its own block, but no privileges or benefits were conferred by where you sat in chapel; and in practice all differences between individuals were blurred and modified by the memory of where that day had begun, with both of you shivering and naked side by side in the cold showers.

If you have given your whole life to God why should you prefer to lose it in this way rather than in that?

If your work weary you, if it overpass your strength, do it first; you may think about rest afterwards.

If it cost you your life, what better could you ask than that the time of trial be very short, since the reward is the same?

The Chapel

Since alike through the envy of the evil one and the frailty of human nature the life of absolute devotion is of especial difficulty and temptation, it is therefore of proportionate necessity that the soul should be restrained and fortified therein by the calm of systematic and perfected worship. Constitution IV

In other words, the chapel certainly dominated our day. We filed in and out of there at least four times a day for morning prayer, silent prayer, and Mass before breakfast, for the service of Sext before lunch, for Evensong which was always before dinner and then to finish the day, Compline before bedtime. If you were a professed member of the Society, three extra short services were thrown in to make the day complete: Prime, immediately before morning prayer, Terce, before lectures began in the morning, and None, before tea in the afternoon. Thus it was arranged, whether by chance or by design, that knees must be bent in prayer before any food could cross our lips. In total this all added up to about two hours fifteen minutes for a student, and almost three hours for a brother per day because our services were by no means light-weight affairs made up of hymns and inspiration. In the course of this daily round throughout the year we read through publicly almost the whole of the Old Testament, and the New Testament twice, and in addition said or sung our way through the 150 psalms each and every month, and in addition said all 176 verses of psalm 119 at Prime, Terce, Sext, and None each and every day. When asked whether we did not find this oft-repeated filing in and out of chapel each day tedious or boring, I can only reply that, to the best of my recollection, we seldom found it irksome although we sometimes quoted that mythical nun whose single solitary sin in confession was: 'I felt a passing disinclination to attend None on Friday'. No, all those services were just 'what they did' at Kelham, like washing up, playing football, or polishing the corridors, and it was seldom questioned. Looking back over the years it seems to me that this regular gathering of the members of the house into the chapel at key points in the day to focus for a few minutes on an end not our own, and then as regularly scattering each to his own work or study, was almost like the breathing of an institution continually inhaling and exhaling.

Certainly in the chapel we ran through the whole gamut of emotions in the course of the year, from the gentle mourning days of Lent when it seemed all the hymns were in a minor key and when, in addition to all else, we said just above a whisper the whole seven penitential psalms on our knees each day, one at the end of each service, to the great festivals when we triumphantly processed around the chapel in one long parade behind the cross and candles amidst clouds of incense and singing at the top of our lungs 'Hail thee festival day, blest day that art hallowed for ever.' Then in between these extremes came all the ordinary days, the green days, which provided a framework and a context for our daily study and work. The chapel seemed to bring out the best in us and the 'systematic and perfected worship' referred to in the Constitution translated into a zero tolerance for any shoddiness, sloppiness or unpreparedness. I don't think any Guards' Regiment did more in their preparations for the changing of the guard than we did in our preparations for the High Mass. If you were down to take part, the rehearsals were endless, the Master of Ceremonies was meticulous, the Sacristan was merciless. For each and every minute the mass lasted there was one point and one point only where your feet should be standing on the sanctuary carpet, one position and one position only which your hands and arms should be holding. Then for all the others there were practices for the recitation of the psalms to keep us all together, with no dominant, no out-of-step, no silent voices, not too loud, not too soft. It might now seem a little extreme but at the time it reflected the importance we attached to the worship we were performing and the seriousness with which we played our part in it.

If your life is not your own, your time belongs to God.

Daily Life

Life at Kelham was made up of four quite separate parts and everyone who lived there, without exception, was involved every day in all four parts. There was chapel, there was physical work, there was study, and there was recreation.

Once we had emerged from chapel in the morning, and after a substantial breakfast where bacon, beans, kippers, fried bread and plenty of coffee all featured on the menu, we were ready to begin the first session of physical work. This item was not on the time-table for any theoretical reason or because Saint Benedict had recommended that monks should do some hard work each day. It was on the timetable because in a household of about 170 men, there was not one hired man. Rather strangely for an institution of this size, salaries never appeared on the annual budget. Whatever needed to be done was done by professed, novices and students alike, and it was done by setting aside about an hour between breakfast and the start of classes for cleaning and tidying up the house – this was called 'Departments' – and then an hour and half in the afternoon after lunch for outside jobs and the bigger jobs. This slot was known as House List. So, what was involved?

Even in the most menial offices it is well when possible humbly to ask permission to help. There is a great danger of cumbering people with services which are bred of our own presumption.

1. Departments.[10]
    During this hour everyone was assigned a housekeeping task, sweeping, polishing, dusting corridors, common rooms, lecture rooms, two libraries, and the chapel. Or you may be on 'Grub' (so called) responsible with your team members for carrying the food from the kitchen to the tables, washing up the dishes at the end of the meal, laying the tables ready for the next meal, or you may be down for 'Spuds', peeling and preparing the potatoes and vegetables in the back kitchen for the evening meal, or you may be carrying the swill from the kitchen to feed the pigs (until this was stopped by the Health & Safety people) or you may be fetching the post from the village post-office and distributing it out on the refectory tables at the appropriate places before grace was said at breakfast. If you were on 'Boilers' (there were three heating boilers and two for hot water) you would be tending one of the five boilers which kept the whole plant luke-warm at best and that only on a sunny day. That was heavy work. In the morning you had to remove all clinker from the fire, rake out the ashes and then barrow them down to the ash tip, and then fill up the hopper on those boilers that had automatic feed with fresh coal; otherwise you had to make up the fire with your shovel. This job entitled you to coffee at elevenses and a drink of hot milk after compline, a privilege extended to few others. All these jobs had to be completed within the hour of Departments, efficiently and at top speed, to enable you to return to your room, tend to the stove there, have a shave if you had got up too late to have one before morning prayer, and be ready, bright and wide awake, for your first class. Departments had a grand change in the personnel twice a term so as to enable everyone to try everything.

He who is permitted to work receives a favour and confers none. You have then no claim either to gratitude or praise. A servant in reality, whether of God or God's children, has no ground to anticipate great consideration or polite request.

2. House List

This was the second burst of physical work, it occupied about an hour and a half between lunch and afternoon tea. After lunch you sauntered down to the common room and checked a board which had every man's name inscribed on it, and in a square next to it, a number or a letter indicating what job had been assigned to you that afternoon. You might find yourself on your knees in company with the person who had been trying to teach you Greek in the morning, scrubbing the stone flags of the kitchen floor with a bucket, a scrubbing brush and a bar of carbolic soap. You might be laying wax in the chapel or in one of the corridors and then bringing it to a high polish with the aid of one of those long-handled weights, sitting on a piece of old blanket and swung vigorously back and forth. Sometime you might find yourself in the cemetery under Brother Edward, the brother funeral-man, scrubbing the moss off the grave stones or even, when necessary, digging a new grave because all the brothers working in England were buried in our cemetery next to the village churchyard. Once a week the letter F would appear opposite your name and you would don football shorts, collected from Stores with a pair of scruffy boots, and head out to the football pitch. The possibilities were almost endless and they were nearly all done in small teams whose leaders were appropriate to the task in hand, not to any place they might have in the pecking order. So the man who had appeared so thick in the history lecture in the morning might have his lecturer under him in the stump-clearing exercise in the garden in the afternoon. The important point to notice is that the element of choice had been almost entirely eliminated from the area of physical work. Those jobs were not there for your entertainment or to kill a little time for you, or to develop your native skills, though all these things could and did happen. They were there because they needed doing and there was no one else to do them. It made no difference whether you enjoyed the job or hated the job, all you had to do was to report on time and get the job done. Personal preferences did not enter into the equation, although of course they sometimes snuck in by the back door, in disguise, and unseen by those in authority.

Behind this approach was the hope that later on when considering what to do with the rest of your life, when Kelham days were over, you wouldn't automatically choose the thing you liked most to do, or what was to your greatest advantage, but would choose what was most needed; the mission station in Africa, the slum in an English town, the prison chaplaincy, the places where things were toughest and where the volunteers were most scarce.

So until 3.30 the house and grounds was a hive or purposeful activity, and then all repaired to the showers (hot this time!) while the brothers went first to the chapel for the service of None and all reached the common room by four o' clock where tea was dispensed from large copper urns with door-step slices of bread and marmalade, but no margarine. Never could you have both on the same slice!

Concerning choice of Work. You may not choose your work; indeed count not yourself worthy of any work. You may prefer, however, that which is most dangerous, least notable, least popular. There will generally be room for you here.

Studies

Although the main reason for the students to be at Kelham was to study theology, and the main reason for the college to be there was to provide these men with the training they needed if they were to be ordained, yet the study of theology, in a strange way, was not the heart of our life there. The heart of our life there was the sacred mission of Christ in this world and the study of theology was just one of the tools necessary for the carrying out of that mission. In addition to this were several factors that made the doing of theology at Kelham fairly distinctive.

The first was the length of the course, it was a full four years and if you had entered the Cottage (our junior section) as a sixteen year old you would have been there for five or six years, a long time and a formative time in any man's growth to maturity. The length was determined not by how long it took to get a man ready to pass the twelve papers of the General Ordination Examination set by the Church of England, but on what was the minimum time, in SSM's view, it took before a man could be shaped and readied to exercise an effective and evangelical priesthood. This longer period of time allowed a steadier less rushed progress through the required subjects and gave the student more time to digest what he had taken in. Many men in their fourth year were surprised at how many of the enthusiasms of their first year they had jettisoned as time went by.

However many things it may be useful to know, the first object of study is to discipline the mind to hold nothing either rashly or vainly, but on the other hand to seek patiently and to behold reverently, since only that which is without is reached easily, but that which is within is of God.

In most theological colleges, lectures, essays and seminars constitute almost the whole life of the college and at the end of term the college 'breaks up' and staff and students are free to pursue non-academic pursuits until it is time to re-assemble. But at Kelham there were an important number of non-academic matters that were fed into the mix. Perhaps the most important was the lay brothers of the Society, non-ordained professed members. In my time, apart from Brother George Every, there were no lay brothers lecturing on the course, but they were a vital part of the house and so influenced the students. There was Brother James Berry who was in charge of the SSM Press housed in a long shed down near the main gate. Here the SSM quarterly magazine was produced twice a year as well as various booklets for liturgical or propaganda purposes and so students were often sent to the Press on House List to aid in the final stages of production. I can still hear Brother Jimmy's voice booming out as soon as you opened the Press door, 'Come in thou blessed of the Lord!' Jimmy had lived for nearly fifty years at Kelham, he had been a great cricketer and tennis player in his time and he had observed generations of students with the kindly but not uncritical eye of a rather dour Lancashire man. He never preached, never complained, never criticised, but he lived by clear if unspoken standards of his own and he was much loved and respected. Without saying much he showed us how a servant of the Lord should conduct himself. The same could be said of Brother Aiden who was in charge of the kitchen and who, with the Housemaster, planned and supervised the whole modernising of the kitchen and its facilities in the early 1960s. He was also the Infirmarius and so your first port of call if you felt unwell. He always received you with gentle laconic humour, he certainly never panicked! In all these ways these men played an important part in our corporate life, as did Brother Noel who was for many years the Director's private secretary, steward and postmaster, until he was sent off to Accra in Ghana to be the secretary to Bishop Richard Roseveare and the diocese of Accra. He produced and directed several plays at Kelham, *The Shoemaker's Holiday* was one, for which he made most of the costumes himself. He then produced with the local youth group a version of the York Mystery Plays in Accra Cathedral, and later, *A Midsummer Night's Dream* at St Agnes' Mission, Teyateyaneng in Lesotho.

When work is committed to you remember your responsibility is for getting it done, not for providing the reasons why it was not done: nor is it sufficient that you used the proper means. You cannot expect often to be really of use, and when an opportunity is given you, concentrate yourself wholly upon that one thing.

Your work lies in what you have done, not in how many things you have attempted.

Many of those who were tutors and lecturers on the course were slightly different from the normal staff in a theological college. I know in my own case I taught in succession over the years Latin, Greek, Old Testament, Paul's epistles, the gospels, and dogmatic theology – a wide range of subjects, not because I was an authority on all or even on any of these, but rather to fill in the gaps in the time-table left behind by departing brothers. I was always an earnest amateur rather than an aspiring academic theologian and I think some others were in the same position. We were on the college staff because we had been assigned to that position, to help the young men wrestle with all the questions posed by St Paul, or modern life, or the contemporary church, but we could just as well have been assigned to a mission station in Lesotho or to the Teacher Training College at Modderpoort and some were. Our main loyalty remained to the Society and its mission rather than to academic theology. To some degree these attitudes were reflected on the students. No degrees were conferred on them when they completed the course. All that happened was that the Society recommended them, after they had passed the General Ordination Examination, to some priest in need of an assistant, and to some bishop, as men ready for ordination who would serve the church well.

In the service of God's glory it will be of very little help that you should yourself be counted learned and be had in repute among men. Be not anxious therefore about human tests and judgements. One has said, 'I would rather feel compunction than know its definition.'

The student body always had a global dimension through the number of overseas students we always had in residence from Ghana, Japan, South Africa, the West Indies and other places. These men were slotted into the student body, sharing rooms, football, work, worship along with everyone else, and while more could and should have been done to help them with the challenges of exposure to an alien culture and a strange language, they still made big impact on our life by the friendships they formed, the experience they brought from distant shores and their constant reminder that the church stretched far beyond the Church of England in this little island.

There was always a lot of movement in our house with brothers departing to or coming from Africa, foreign student returning home, and our own students leaving the house for ordination and their first parish work. Departures were not casual affairs. Before anyone left the house they were given a missionary benediction. This took place right after breakfast in the chapel with the taxi waiting in the drive outside to speed the man away to pastures new. There were some, it's true, we saw depart from us with a sigh of relief, but for the most part there was sense of loss and sadness that prevailed. But of course, being British, whatever we felt was kept under wraps with no provision made for charismatic prayers hugs or songs. A psalm was sung, a few collects said, the prior blessed the departing brothers and led them to the back door where their mates hoisted them onto their shoulders and carried them out like football heroes to loud cheers and clapping as the taxi disappeared down the driveway.

You may have much to bear, most people have, but it is not well to make everybody bear it. There is always someone whose burden is heavier than yours. Find him out and if you can, help him. Bear one another's burdens.

In most respects the day to day life of the college was no different from that of any college. Every student attended one or two lectures a day, wrote an essay once a week which would then be discussed with the tutor who set it, and spent some hours in discussing, arguing, confronting one another and their tutors in the class room, in their own rooms, in the common room and while working in the garden. After all these were young guys with lively minds meeting some insoluble problems to which they usually had some perfectly obvious solution; if only their obtuse colleagues could be persuaded to see it. But of course the training for the priesthood was more than academic courses and discussions, and it was in order to foster growth in the spirit and to encourage the personal development of the men, that each class of students had its own chaplain appointed from among the priest brothers in the house. Chaplains were expected to make time for an informal chat at least once a term to check that all was well, to hear their confessions as required, receive reports on any misdemeanours and be on hand for any personal or family crisis. This system did not always work well. Sometimes chaplains were a little too zealous in their caring, sometimes a little too nonchalant. Sometimes students had serious matters on their agenda which they were unwilling to share, such as having a girlfriend to whom they were deeply committed but whose existence, if it became known to the authorities, would lead to their transfer to another college. Kelham men were expected to be celibate during their training and were encouraged to take a pledge of celibacy for the first five years of their ministry; a pledge which was seldom, almost never, taken. So there were some unhappy times between chaplains and their charges but there were also other times and other ways when a chaplain and a student over the years built up such a reserve of mutual trust and respect, even with some affection added, that those years became the foundation of a lifelong friendship.

Do not despair about yourself, for that has ruined many souls and vocations. God who is infinite holiness has borne with you a long time; you may well bear with yourself a little till his grace shall have done its perfect work. Blessed the one who has here lived well and who has reached a satisfactory end.

Recreation

Unfortunately, or maybe fortunately, Fr Kelly, the founder of SSM, and his immediate successors had very serious reservations about recreation. They were not happy with the concept. They subscribed wholeheartedly to the old adage that Satan found work for idle hands to do, and the idea of young men sitting around at leisure in easy chairs, chewing the fat, and discussing whatever idea might drift through their empty heads, made them shudder with alarm. Hence it was that in drawing up the daily time-table, every minute was occupied with study, work, or prayer and the only free time when they were able to do as they pleased was the half hour that intervened between the end of dinner and the bell for Evensong, if you were not on Grub. It was almost as if they were out to produce a generation of workaholics, and for better or worse that is what they often did in fact produce.

Learn to occupy every moment, and in the best way. Pray, meditate, study, do some act of charity. 'The night comes when no one can work.'

Let your recreation be what is right yet, so far as is possible, useful and energizing. You may not waste God's time upon prolonged pleasure which profits nothing.

Always keep clearly in your mind what you have to do, that you may instantly find some object which is of use, even for five minutes.

In line with this, it may come as a surprise to us today to realise that in a house of so many men, mostly young and all single, there was only one telephone ('Newark 350') situated in the front hall. This instrument could only be used with permission, and permission was not granted lightly for anything less than a death in the family or some equivalent disaster. It sounds impossible today but it made for a much less interrupted day! There was also only one radio in the house, situated on the mantelpiece in the downstairs lecture room and that was only switched on for the midday news or matters of national importance; not for entertainment. Three newspapers were brought in, the London *Times*, the *Manchester Guardian*, and the *Newark Advertiser*. These were brought out and laid on a table in the Common Room after lunch where anyone interested could read them.

The one exception to this fairly rigorist approach was football. Football was even provided for in the Principles and could be a source of joy and pleasure.

In regard to outer things, first it is necessary that you should so exercise yourself in self-mastery that there shall be nothing which you cannot easily lay aside. You must leave all one day whether you will or not.

Notwithstanding, detachment is not inconsistent with the enjoyment of anything God has made to be enjoyed and permits us to have.

All those who showed any talent for the game were drafted into the first or second eleven who challenged local teams to a match in our grounds every Saturday afternoon from Michaelmas until Easter. The visitors were invited into the house after the match for showers and then tea with the rest of the community. If you were not on the House team, you were expected to attend the matches on Saturday afternoons, and cheer your brothers on with shouts of 'House! House!' but never any player's name!

But football was not just for the fanatics; everyone under thirty (and that was the vast majority) had to play at least once a week. This was done, not in the expectation that we would all make first class players, but because it provided fresh air, exercise, and a safety valve for the daily frustrations and rages of everyday life at almost no expense. All that was necessary were boots and shorts and an old T-shirt, all available from House Stores and handed down from generation to generation. The whole student body was divided into teams which played through the term for their own House Cup – a cardboard, gilded, home-made affair which old Fr Leslie Pearce presented amid much hilarity at the end of term. These teams were given various slightly derogatory names, notably The Daffodils, The Buttercups, The Tulips, etc. These names reflected the attitude of the football captain and his mates to us once-a-week amateurs. However the names also indicated that we approached our weekly game somewhat light-heartedly with an absence of pressure and competition. It was just a good run-around and any prowess gained on the field in no way affected your status or standing in the house. Yet, in those years, I did what I had never done in my life before, I enjoyed playing a sport. In the summer term there was cricket, but there was not the same pressure here to enrol everyone, and those totally ignorant of the game were allowed to play tennis which I learned, and also learned to enjoy after I got there.

Of course not every student was a sportsman even though everyone participated in sport, and, as in any large self-contained community various sub-cultures formed, disintegrated and was transformed as one class after another of students arrived, passed through and departed. Keen footballers, members of the first and second XI along with their fans, often congregated around the stove in the football captain's room to discuss the beautiful game in all its manifestations both local and international. This group was at times referred to as 'The Men's Club'.

Do not lament the smallness of your capacities. Such complaints come either of laziness, or of affectation, or of ambition. Everybody is clever enough for what God wants of him, and strong enough for what he is set to do, if not for what he would like to be.

Apart from football there were two occasions in the course of the year which were given over to entertainment. The first was the play produced on the evening of the feast of the Dedication of the Chapel, and the second was the Pantomime put on for the last night of the Michaelmas term, before the students left the next morning for the Christmas holidays. The Dedication fell on November 21, and this was the more serious effort. *The Importance of Being Earnest*, *The Mikado*, *Twelfth Night* and an Agatha Christie were the sort of productions they staged. As well as those who enjoyed acting, there was a host of men who were keen on stagecraft and scenery and over the years a large store of costumes had been built up with fresh items added each year by the sewing room. One end of the two-storey high Common Room was blocked off for the stage and a quite high standard of drama was reached. However there were two major drawbacks that were never entirely solved. First there was a Cinderella aspect to the whole thing. After such an enormous amount of preparation, and practicing, involving every minute of spare time for months and demanding innumerable imaginative solutions to impossible problems, there was never more than one performance, and that for an audience of students and brothers only with perhaps the addition of our doctor or the local farmer. As no women could possibly be admitted to the house, even happily-married couples were ruled out. The second problem was that as time went on and the culture changed in single sex schools and colleges, so did we also begin to feel increasingly uncomfortable with men playing the women's parts and this greatly restricted our choice of works to perform. We did find one or two with an all-male cast of characters but they were rare and nearly always war drama. We did think of bringing in some lady friends from outside, but officially we were not even supposed to have lady friends and the prior was always nervous about what such relaxations of the rule might lead to. However the Dedication play was one of the highlights of our year and was greatly appreciated by everyone who was crowded into what was left of space in the Common Room, the prior and senior brothers along the front row with pipes alight and a cloud of tobacco smoke hovering over us all. Light refreshments were brought out at the end and Compline could even be delayed by as much as half an hour. What greater excesses could be demanded?

Be subject the one to the other says the apostle. It is easy to obey superiors, but he who would learn humility should love to submit himself to those who are least esteemed.

The pantomime on the last night of the Michaelmas term was in the best traditions of English music hall Christmas pantomimes. It was always based on a nursery tale, burlesqued and sung as a kind of comic opera. The text and songs were written each year by one of the brothers or students and adapted to whatever events had transpired during the year, all fitted out with appropriate music. Ours was of course a very closed community. We had lived together twenty-four hours a day, seven days a week from the

September before, and from all the year preceding that. We had discussed theology in groups, eaten in one refectory, worked in squads, played in teams, worshipped in choir with only minimal breaks or time off. Hence there was bound to emerge over the months a bulge of swollen irritants made up of countless incidents when someone had committed a public gaffe, or had unblushingly tread upon your toes, or had played some crudely insensitive practical joke. Then there were the various idiosyncrasies, ticks and twitches, facial grimaces, peculiar personal habits of us all but more particularly of the tutorial brothers whose behaviour fell daily under the hawk-eyed observation of a host of students, and all of the above made grist for the pantomime writer's mill. An actor could bring the house down merely by walking on the stage mimicking the walk, imitating the grin, echoing the favourite phrase or word of one of the brothers. Then too it was performed on the night before they left for the Christmas holidays and so they arrived already 'high' and more than ready to find the whole performance hysterically funny. To an outsider who wandered in for the evening and who had not been part of the preceding months, it would for the most part have made less, maybe even no, sense. Those who wrote the script were all the time walking the razor's edge between offending the prior and the brothers on the one hand and boring the students on the other. Offending authorities was not something lightly done. Before my time there had been a famous occasion when, early on in the second act after several sharp jabs at authority and some rather unkind laughs, the prior Fr Stephen Bedale rose from his seat on the front row and said through clenched teeth, 'Thank you gentlemen, we all appreciate your efforts, and now we will have Compline in chapel in fifteen minutes.' And in those days they would all have been in their places in chapel in fifteen minutes with never a man missing. It was not for nothing that the students nick-named Fr Stephen 'Yahweh'. However that is the only such disaster on record. For the rest the Pantomime acted as a mild end of term blow-out, a release of long suppressed annoyances, and a hilarious evening. While a novice, Vincent Strudwick produced the pantomime, *Sinbad the Sailor*. Sinbad was played by a student named Eric Smart. Wrecked on his desert island, he was captured by the islanders and put in a pot to cook. While doing a sand dance, the chorus sang (to the tune of a movement from Alexandre Luigin's nineteenth-century *Ballet Egyptien*):

> 'Of the way of cooking an obstreperous young man
> This is the neatest one.
> (Don't forget to add a little pepper
> When the upper side of the meat is done)
> He'll make quite a tantalising entrée
> When we've finished with the pilchards and the smaller fry,
> What is left will go into the pantry
> With carrots and the turnips for the cottage pie.
> A tasty pasty!
> A smarty party!
> Sinbad for supper
> What price this culinary art?
> How d'you dish up a
> Legumerie of Eric Smart?
> What do you expect to see
> Set in the Refectory?
> Sinbad stew?
> Spoons will do!'

Having a go at the College cuisine, with a passing reference to 'Domestici', together with a chorus of 'damsels' in palm leaf skirts, while very 'schoolboy' was enough to prepare happily for the Christmas vacation.

These few reminiscences should provide at least a sketch of what Kelham was up to until the mid-sixties. We now turn to look at some of the reasons why in three short years, 1970–1973, the whole place with all its real estate, its manpower and its traditions disappeared in the twinkling of an eye. The college closed, the house sold, and a greatly reduced community dispersed to different parts of the country.

2

Decade of Change: 1962–1972

Living through the years 1962–1972 was like living through a world-wide earthquake which shattered the foundations of society although, oddly enough, at first we were hardly aware of what was happening to us and around us. Or, if you prefer a political analogy, it was the equivalent of having lived through the Russian Revolution, although this was a revolution that eventually brought us more of life than of death. The benefits of the National Health Service became accessible to all, slums were torn down and better housing, if still not altogether satisfactory, replaced them. Unemployment went down and the standard of living rose consistently; central heating, TV and paid holidays, all became commonplace. The armies of workers clocking in at 'the works' or 'the Pit' became armies of tourists bound for Spain or Thailand in sporty gear, with no flat caps or hob-nailed boots! You could hardly think of all this as an earthquake at all and yet, as time went by when you looked around, fewer and fewer of the ancient landmarks which had stood beside our early lives and the lives of our Moms and Dads were left still standing. For example: Sheffield was known world-wide for the quality of the steel it produced, Tyneside for the ships they turned out onto the seas, the north-east and Wales for the coal they produced to heat the country and drive its industry, the north-east coast for the herring they harvested from the sea. Now, when you looked around, all that was gone. The factories stood idle, the winding gear had been taken away from the pit-heads, the slag heaps had been grassed over and made into social amenities, and the herring for smoking were now imported from Norway. Along with the disappearance of so many visible markers, many less tangible things had gone as well, such as the vital necessity of the hard physical labour of a few, along with their sacrifice and sweat. All the country's former producers had become consumers, and the workers had now been asked to run theme parks to instruct the younger generation on what our life had once been like. It is interesting to compare the recruiting posters for the 1914-18 War with Lord Kitchener with piercing gaze, heavy moustache, and accusing finger saying, 'Your Country Needs You', with recruitment advertisements for the armed forces in glossy magazines in the 1970s enticing young people in with promises of career training and travel abroad.

One result is that when this mighty earthquake paused, as it did from time to time, and people emerged from their new homes to look around, they found themselves in a new and different landscape amongst a different kind of people who spoke a different kind of language. It is in this context, against this background that we must now go on to consider what happened to the Society of the Sacred Mission and Kelham Theological College in these same years. And if you think that the monks lived in a separate enclosed world insulated from all the storms that were sweeping across the whole country, you are mistaken. Some of the monks themselves may have imagined that they were living apart from the world and safe from its pressures but they were not; although it took some decades before the truth of this got through to them.

Just to reinforce this point that the monks at Kelham were a small, but integral part of British society, it is worth noticing the surprising number of parallels there are between the community at Kelham and the coal-mining industry even though there was no direct link between the two except for one or two students who had worked in the mines before coming to college, or were the sons of miners – and that visiting a local pit was included in the college curriculum.

To begin with, at the start of this period, in the 1950's both the miners and the Kelham monks felt complete confidence in what they were doing and complete security in their place in society. Both occupied entrenched positions – the miners had been a part of the economy of the country for hundreds of years, and the monks had been turning young men into mission priests for the Anglican Communion for well over fifty years. Consequently, they both assumed without question that their future would be an expansion of their past. If anyone had told them that within twenty years Kelham, and within thirty years the majority of pits, would have disappeared from the life of the country, they would not, could not, have comprehended the message.

The miners worked hard, they paid a heavy price in sweat, and in dangerous working conditions, and they had often been constrained to enter and remain in their jobs by family and social pressures. However what these sacrifices produced was the coal that kept us warm and kept industry humming. The monks, for their part, also led a rigorous life, they too paid a price in celibacy, poverty, and obedience, and were constrained by what they felt was their calling, and the consequent vows they had taken to remain where they were. What their sacrifice produced was an opening into ministry for many who had no other chance and the opening of fresh mission stations with attendant schools and clinics in remote parts of Southern Africa.

Miners were an all-male working-class group and often worked in the mines where their fathers had worked before them. It was a self-contained group bound closely together by their dependence on one another, their membership of the union, and their own brand of humour. A man's mates were as important to him as his family. Kelham too was an all-male group, no woman was allowed in the House, except in the gallery of the chapel. It was mostly working class, unlike the majority of theological colleges in the Church of England which always had a whiff of Oxford hanging about them. The men at Kelham were also bound closely together by shared experience during a critical period of their lives, a shared faith, and shared aims in life, and not least, by their own brand of humour. Endless were the laughs arising when mates gathered in front of the fire or over the coffee cups, and the laughter echoed down through the succeeding years. It was a self-contained society with few outsiders coming in and we were encouraged to find our friendship within our own ranks, for did not our 'Principles' tell us, *'Be not anxious to look for friends outside for here is that fulfilled – there is no one who has left home or brothers or children for my sake, who will not receive a hundredfold in return even in this present age.'*

By the 1970s much had changed for both groups. The tide of money and affluence was rising all the time, bringing in higher wages, higher prices and making former luxuries today's necessities. Sacrifice had become an outmoded idea. It was no longer necessary in the post war world; it was even felt to be a slightly kinky perversion. Enclosed communities, especially all-male ones, were objects more of suspicion than of admiration, while many of the old class distinctions had become blurred by the increasing prosperity of all. These signs indicated the movements below the surface that were making our foundations tremble, and both of these groups fell apart within a few years of each other. Kelham Theological College, after a public confrontation with the bishops at the General Synod in London in 1971, was closed in 1972 and the House sold in 1973. The miners, after a long and bitter strike in 1984 which the Prime Minister Margaret Thatcher used to break them, wound down pretty rapidly as she continued with her policy of closing pits.

The purpose of this somewhat lengthy digression is to demonstrate the power and the extent of this earthquake. If the mining industry, rooted in the economy and finances of the country, and built on generations of loyal service and hard work, was still unable to stand against its shocks what chance a religious community rooted in the life of the Church of England, founded on a vision and built up on generations of loyal service? The community, whatever it may have claimed, was cemented into life in the modern changing world and so was gripped by all the pressures that that world exerted, just as much as Shackelton's ship in Antarctica was gripped by the pack-ice.

When I arrived at Kelham in the summer of 1957 I found a place that was bursting with life. There were twenty-four men in the novitiate, about thirty professed brothers stationed in the

House, and about a hundred students, divided into four classes, preparing for ministry. With another thirty lads, sixteen to eighteen, in a separate section preparing to enter the theological course. 'The Cottage' formed a separate, but related, community. Those were the years when the Society had reached its peak, with about eighty fully professed members working in the UK, Southern Africa and Australia. These were also the days before *Honest to God* appeared and before the Second Vatican Council had been called by Pope John XXIII, days when the whole church was beginning at last to recover from the turmoil and horrors of the war years and in reaction was experiencing sensations of triumph and confidence, maybe even over-confidence. We were happy with all the details of our present situation, though our worship, our thinking, our customs were almost entirely what we had inherited from the 'between the wars' period and which most of us followed faithfully, unthinking, unblinking, feeling no great need to change in any way; we would have said 'If it doesn't itch, don't scratch it!' although we were in fact just cruising along on the interest piled up by the faith and hard work invested by the men who had gone before us many years ago. The result of this was that we felt at the time as though we were living through the days of springtime, looking forward to years of continuous growth and expansion in all our works and ways. The Director was frequently asking the novice-master 'How many men can you let me have by next year? The next year? So that I can plan to deploy them wisely.' Whereas the truth was that we were living through the days of St Luke's summer, or Indian summer, enjoying deceptively warm breezes before the cold blasts of winter arrived on our doorstep.

The first sign of the coming winter, which we noticed but were not unduly worried by, was the steady drop in the number of applications for entry to the college from the mid 60's onwards.[11] For us this meant an equal drop in the number of men who were applying to enter the novitiate of the Society, since pretty well all our novices came from the student body at Kelham. We found each succeeding year that instead of being faced with an army of applicants from which we could select the best, we were faced with a shrinking band, nearly all of whom we were obliged to accept if we wished the college to remain viable. However this was not a private problem for the SSM, this was a world-wide problem, as every year the number of men who were seeking ordination declined as did the number of those seeking a life in the religious communities.

Then appeared *Honest to God* by Bishop John Robinson. In it he asked some hard questions about how we had been talking about God, and could we continue to go on talking in those same old ways. It seemed like an average Ivory Tower subject, of interest mostly to professional Christians, but to the surprise of everyone it struck a resounding chord in the hearts, particularly of young people who felt that the bishop had shattered completely and for all time all that they had been taught in Sunday school in the days of their innocent childhood. The book initiated a long and passionate debate both inside and outside the church though it is not clear how much connection that debate had with another phenomenon we noticed during those years. Young people, our children, our nieces and nephews, quietly, politely, without any fuss or palaver, just disappeared from our pews. Our congregations came more and more to be composed of the 'silver-tops'. The young no longer seemed to find our customary presentation of the faith plausible. I heard this well described once by the RC bishop of Los Angeles preaching in Magdalene College Chapel. He was referring, as an illustration of his main point (which I have now forgotten), to the difficulties he experienced in trying to talk about Christian beliefs and values to his own nieces and nephews. He said, 'I find them gazing earnestly and sympathetically at me, with their heads bent slightly to one side, much in the way my dog gazes at me when I play the fool in front of him to tease and befuddle him.' What we had to say now was incomprehensible, or unbelievable, and certainly irrelevant to the lives our young folks were living and the choices they had to make. Why was it so? No one in any church, Catholic or Protestant, knew the answer. Religious communities that clung ever more obsessively to every jot and tittle of the ancient traditions and customs were in decline. Religious communities that eagerly jettisoned every last shredded shibboleth in order to get aboard the latest bandwagon were in decline.

We in SSM, in a truly Anglican spirit, did both. We got rid of the old and we invented the new, but we still declined. We tore down the old washing-up room and imported a new electric dish-washer, we replaced the old bumpers that had slid across our floors for generations and bought brand new electric polishers, We began to say mass from behind the altar, reduced the number of daily services from seven to four, and gave permission to discard the habit when not on duty. What more could anyone do in order to be abreast of the times?

Then came the charismatic movement. This movement had originated in the USA and had now reached our shores and the result for us was that, in addition to the regular round of liturgical services in chapel, prayer circles were formed where an assorted collection of individuals, professed and students from all classes, met and prayed together, usually with a candle burning in the middle of the circle, with choruses rising up and hands held high. It was even whispered that some participants had also begun to speak in tongues – the furthest reach of charismatic prayer. Suddenly emotions and feelings were on the surface and in the middle in a way they had never been before; some people developed an aptitude for free prayer although, as Anglicans, we had probably never in our lives heard a prayer said or ourselves used a prayer in church that was not printed on the page in front of us and flanked with rubrics which told you when and how it could be used. Anglicans don't do extempore prayer. So perhaps it was time for us to get a little freed up in our corporate prayer life and many experienced it as a kind of intoxication, but others found it excruciatingly embarrassing and subversive of our way of life. To some it was a great 'breakthrough' to others a great 'breakdown'. 'Let it all hang out' was the motto of those days but it was not a motto everyone could follow so that in the end charismatic prayer was a divisive force within the community dividing individual members from one another. We hoped that it would deepen and intensify our life of prayer but we never really learned how to integrate the new freedom and confidence of charismatic prayer with the liturgical round of offices and mass which were still at the hub of our daily life.

Then, as charismatic prayer lost its first impetus, we came upon encounter groups. Encounter groups, at least as we understood them at the time after the prior and few brothers had been away to experience them in courses set up by the Church of England's Board of Education, was a way to break through the formality and the inhibitions that marked our community life where, apart from your mates, you always addressed people as 'father' or 'brother'. Where you kept to your own place in refectory and chapel, and only the prior was allowed to propose agenda for our weekly chapter. We were now going to be open, honest and free with each other. Up until now we had dealt with hiccups between brothers by a weekly meeting called the Fault Chapter at which we gathered in chapel, said a psalm, and each in turn stood up and apologised for the common rules he had broken that week. In practice the faults were standard and routine and made up of a limited list from which you made a suitable selection and offered them to the brothers. It was in fact a session of mutual apology for failures to uphold the common life but it was a bloodless routine from which the spirit had long since drained away. Now the Fault Chapter was replaced with sessions in the common room in easy chairs with coffee and cigarettes. The old Fault Chapter statements such as 'on Tuesday I broke a cup' and 'on Wednesday I slept in and was absent from mass' or 'Friday after Compline I broke the greater silence and had a long chat with my room mates' were no longer satisfactory. All these and others like were now replaced with a new type of question: 'Why have you never liked me?' 'Do you realise how your casual remark yesterday cut me to the quick?' 'Could you not be quiet for a minute and listen to what I am trying to say to you?' 'Why do you never listen?'

Now it is true that you could live side by side with a brother in the same house for fifteen or twenty years and still have no more idea of what was going on in his inner life than you would have about any neighbour that lived across the road from you at home; and so we hoped to break through some of the formality and unreality which then marked large swathes of our relationships with one another and get to know one another better. It was a worthy objective, but for many reasons this particular solution never worked; in fact some people were seriously damaged by it all and the rest of us soon learned the correct responses at the meetings which would indicate our willingness to co-operate while still guarding our tender spots.

It seems a little strange now that that in those years we were driven to try things we had never done before and which had never been a part of our tradition. Why was that? Perhaps it was a sign of our uncertainty and our anxiety about the future. We were aware that our future was going to be very different and that it would make great demands upon us, and that we needed to change radically if we were going to meet those demands; we knew that the new electric dish-washer and the alterations to the chapel time-table were not going to be enough, but what that future might be and what changes were going to be necessary we could not even begin to imagine, and so in our perplexity we scrambled about ready to try anything that came along.

One thing that greatly increased our anxiety all through this time as a series of recurring earth tremors, was the steady departure of brothers from the Society. I will give you twelve examples; not that this is an exhaustive list, but these were the most significant because of the length of time each one had served and the importance of the position each held at the time:

1. Matthew Shaw was pro-provincial, university lecturer, and the first prior of the newly opened priory at Lancaster.
2. Giles Ambrose was pro-provincial and had been novice-master for some years at Kelham.
3. Vincent Strudwick was sub-warden of the college, lecturer in church history, and well-spring of sanity, common sense and humour.
4. Simon Mein was provincial and prior at Kelham, the warden of the college and the driving force behind all our innovations.
5. Marcus Stephens had been novice-master at Kelham for many years and was provincial of the Southern African province at the time.

6. George Every was lecturer in Church History for many years, author, poet and the brother most widely known in the ecumenical world.

7. Theodore Smith had been provincial prior and warden of the college at Kelham which he had ruled autocratically for many years.

8. Malcolm Broadhead was formerly a lecturer at Kelham and was then prior of Quernmore Park. He was very active in our outreach programme.

9. Nigel Kinsella.

10. Peter Adkins.

11. Dominic Tye.

These last three were all recent graduates of Lancaster University and took over most of the lecturing at Kelham after the departure of the previous staff. They were, briefly, the hope of the future.

12. Douglas Brown is really outside this period, but he had been provincial of Australia and England and had lectured in philosophy at both Kelham and St Michael's House.

Each of these men made a serious, life-changing and conscientious decision, and any comment on such would be inappropriate and beside the point. However, taken as a group, we might ask what they were saying to and about the society. It might be appropriate even now to listen to their unspoken message to us which we were not very willing to hear at the time.

First of all their decision to leave the Society was certainly not due to any loss of faith in God or the church since all but two of them carried on with their vocation in a new setting; some doing even more valuable work than they had been free to do in the Society.

Perhaps their decision expresses more serious doubts about the Society, whether it (and particularly the college) continued to have a clear and unique role within the church by opening up ministry for those who would not otherwise be used. Was the Society any longer necessary?

Then too, they obviously had serious doubts about celibacy as a necessary condition for their own ministry within the church. The position of women had been changing all through these years; they were now taking their place as valued colleagues rather than problematical adjuncts, and all male communities were felt to be somewhat less than 'normal' or 'natural' or even 'healthy'. Of these twelve, eight married and two more entered committed partnerships. There was no longer the same impulse to remain celibate.

Neither would it be true to say that the departure of these twelve greatly hastened the collapse of the Society. We could certainly have done at that time with one or two elder statesmen who could have provided us with a bit of ballast and steadied our wandering thoughts with the wisdom stored up from ages of experience, but no such elder statesmen were there to be had. We had two leaders, a younger one who was in the vanguard of every latest experiment and was as excitable as the rest of us, and an older one who, as soon as the closure of the college became clear and inevitable, lost all faith in himself, in the Society and perhaps even in God.

However even if all twelve had stayed, it is hard to see how they could have changed the situation very significantly. These departures were like cracks and fissures appearing in the walls and ramparts denoting the movement of the ground beneath the foundations. For all their varied skills and gifts it is doubtful that these men could have long preserved the Society or ring-fenced the College from the impact of the new values and new life-styles that were rising up beneath us and whose true worth we have only now begun to evaluate forty years later. At the time we were at first swept along by the waves of progress and later swept under by them. Meanwhile, all around us events were fast marching forward.

There were in the 1960s about forty theological colleges in the UK, all with extensive buildings and falling numbers, and all increasingly subsidised from central church funds. This at a time when, after heavy losses on the market, central church funds were diminishing rapidly. Every college had its own history and its own tradition and between them they represented every possible shade and gradation of theology and ritual in the Anglican Communion. Those responsible for training people for the ministry in the church, harassed themselves by the latest financial constraints, were anxious to find a less wasteful way of financing their programmes and at the same time of making the whole training programme more coherent and less idio-rhythmic – ominous adjectives! The immediate aim was to cut expenses by closing some of the colleges but which ones? Who would volunteer to walk the plank when each college felt that it had been entrusted with an invaluable and unique tradition? As often happens in these cases, a Commission was appointed and commissioners were charged and sent off on circuit around the colleges to inspect them and report back on them, but inspectors are only human and brought face to face with our students and tutors in action at Kelham, all putting their best foot forward, they could not bring themselves to do more than suggest some tentative improvements which we might consider. They had nothing to say that made us feel in danger, in fact they commended us. But we were in danger nonetheless. The crunch came in January 1971 when the final report on all the theological colleges appeared, about two weeks before the meeting of the General Synod at Westminster where it would be received and passed. Unfortunately the appearance of the report coincided with a six week postal strike which made the distribution of the report almost impossible. Hence it was that one day in mid-January, about ten days before the Synod met, a leather-clad courier sped on his motor bike up the front drive and dropped a mimeographed version of the report on our door step. When Fr Hilary Greenwood, who was then the college Warden, thumbed feverishly through to check that we were still OK, he was speechless to find in the last pages that four theological colleges would no longer be recognised by the bishops, nor would the bishops any longer accept men trained there for ordination. One of the deleted colleges was Kelham.[12]

I would like to think, though this could well be mere wishful dreaming on my part, that if instead of a mimeographed report dropped through our letter box, one of the bishops had taken the time to drive up the A1 to Kelham, to sit down with the brothers, explain the predicament that the bishops and the whole church was in, and to ask for our co-operation and help, that we would have risen to the occasion and responded in a positive, even if heart-broken, way in the spirit of our seventeenth Principle:

He who works for his own pleasure will work as he chooses, as well as at what he prefers. He who does God's will for God's glory alone must be ready to go on or to stop, to take up or lay down, to rule or to serve, to continue or to change, without hesitation.

As you accept the work or office to which God calls, so be prepared instantly to lay it down if a better or more capable person be sent by him.

But, confronted with a death sentence like a bolt from the blue, a sentence to be passed by the Synod in ten days' time, and with no way, because of the strike, of informing our old students and friends of what was happening to us, we resorted to panic and hysteria. Brother James's press was humming late into the night as we rushed through a special edition of the SSM News carrying on page one a lovely picture of the high altar in the chapel above a caption reading: 'For sale: One chapel', and filled with other material in similar vein, including a picture of all brothers who were college tutors standing in a row over the caption: 'Now amongst the unemployed'. Copies of this edition we rushed around to as many of the old students as we could reach to stir them up to battle. All the facts this SSM News contained were true enough, but it was also offensive, and counter-productive; it lost us more friends than it gained; it was more than a little foolish.

It is now clear to most people, even in SSM, that the decision of the bishops to close the college was inevitable and the right thing to do. The day had long gone by when we, and more particularly we the tutors who were left after all the departures, should have been entrusted with a college preparing people for ministry in the ever-changing modern world. But that is one of those lessons that only become clear with the passage of time and with the benefit of hindsight. At the time, when the Synod met, such were

45

the emotions aroused, largely by our newsletter and by our old students, that the recommendations of the report were partly reversed and Kelham was allowed to remain open with a ceiling of twenty-five students, supplemented with overseas students while the freed-up space in the house could be used for a programme of conferences and seminars. This was hailed as a great victory on the day but it proved very soon to be only a prolongation of the misery. The doubts and divisions of the college tutors retained their potency, and there was no one amongst our number with the imagination, the flair or the drive to innovate an eye-catching conference programme. Hilary tried several weekend seminars but none of them were successful and by Easter 1972 the tutors were ready to announce that they were unwilling to go on with the college and Hilary was ready to bow to their intransigence. Of course the college tutors had no authority to close the college; that had to be deferred until the Great Chapter of the Society which was due to meet the next August. In the meantime Father Martin Knight, the Bursar, went about saying that the tutors were suffering a 'rough patch' and the Chapter would soon sort them out – wishful dreaming on his part! The Great Chapter when it met was faced with a group of tutors who had lost all desire to teach, and realised that we were at the end of the road, but being unwilling to pull the plug themselves. They referred it back to the English Provincial Chapter. This body convened a week after the Great Chapter had closed and only one outcome was possible. In September 1972 Kelham Theological College was closed except for the last class of students who moved over to the Red House, the Society Guest House across the road, with Fr Hilary and Fr Francis to finish off their course.

It is hard to measure the impact that the closure had on every brother in the Province, especially as we soon realised that the closure of the college must soon lead to moving from Kelham Hall. Two examples of the impact will have to do. Fr Martin Night had come to Kelham in 1919 after discharge from the army and had been in the Society ever since. He was Society Bursar for many years and had worked in Southern Africa. He was a short man with perhaps little imagination but with a tenacious loyalty.

He would often with great pride say, 'Kelham is our Citeaux, our Monte Casino, and our Assisi' (his grip on reality was always a bit tenuous!). He was in hospital that August with chest complications but when he heard the news of what the chapter had done, he turned his face to the wall, spiritually if not physically, and died. He was buried between the final sessions of the chapter, one of the last of the old brigade to go into the Society cemetery. Then there was Brother James Berry. He had worked faithfully and loyally in the printing press since he was a twenty year old, turning out edition after edition of the SSM Quarterly. When we told him of the closure, he didn't say much, and when we opened the house at Willen he came with us as requested, but he didn't understand what we were doing there or why we had come or what was his new role. A humble lay brother of the old school, he had always left all the big decisions to what he called, with a wry smile, 'the brains department' of the Society, the tutors and office holders, and now they had let him down. He too died soon after settling down at Willen and was the first of ours to be buried in Willen churchyard.

The Society of the Sacred Mission and Kelham Theological College had lived in a form of symbiosis from the day of their foundation, rather like a pair of Siamese twins joined at the hip. The big question that now arose immediately was whether the Society could survive the death of the College.

The year 1972 thus marks a very critical turning point in the life of the community and by way of conclusion to these tumultuous years and we had to ask: 'What have we learned from these last ten years? Do they teach us any lessons for the future?' Perhaps what they taught us is the hard lesson that there is no known way of stopping an earthquake from happening and there are precious few defences against it when the earth begins to shift. The brute strength and the iron determination of the miners did not save the mines from closures or preserve their jobs. Neither did the prayers and high ideals of the monks of Kelham preserve their home and keep safe their college. It would almost seem that no intelligence, or dedication or even love can stave off the losses that earthquakes bring in their wake. So that in the end maybe the only wisdom was to wait patiently until the last tremor died away and the dust settled, and then to sally forth and start again with whatever bits and pieces were left. Certainly, if you follow that course, God will not fail you. At least that has been my experience.

After the closure and the chapter, at which I had been appointed Provincial for England, we were faced with three questions: a) Did we have to leave Kelham? b) What were we going to do? c) Where should we do it?

a. In some respects the first one was the easiest. Our experience of the last eighteen months, trying to run the place with twenty-five students supplemented by conferences had shown us that if we stayed at Kelham our future would be dictated and shaped by those buildings. We could only do those things which would utilise 130 rooms in a Victorian Gothic mansion deep in Nottinghamshire, plus fifty acres of parkland. It was beyond us by far. About this time too, George Every, Alex Adkins, and Malcolm Broadhead left us so that even the numbers we had were shrinking. We (I?) also felt that we needed a fresh start in a new place where we would no longer be 'the Kelham Fathers'. We needed to do what we had never done before, things that people of our capabilities were capable of doing, and do it in a place where we were unknown. If we stayed at Kelham the ghosts of past brothers and their achievements would continually haunt us, maybe even devour us.

b. I have described the impact of these events on two brothers but it would be true to say that all of us, from the youngest to the oldest, were suffering from what would now be called post-traumatic stress. The symptoms of this disorder were that we couldn't focus on, or feel any enthusiasm for, new ventures of any kind; we had been stripped of the self-confidence necessary to explore new avenues, and we wallowed in the slough of despond. Partly this centred on Gregory and Hilary who radiated defeat and disillusion, but they weren't the cause of it, rather its foremost victims. However having Dunstan

McKee, an Australian, elected as our new Director was a great stimulus for us; he did more than anyone to rescue the province. Trained at St Michael's House, he had never been to Kelham. He had ideas, and, even more important, he was willing to listen to and work with other people's ideas.

My first job as Provincial was to go around and have a chat with each brother, and after that I saw as my chief challenge the meeting of this emptiness of heart, this lack of conviction, and this I hoped to do by finding those projects which could enkindle some enthusiasm, evoke some commitment in each brother so that he could feel again that he was doing something he believed in and so re-establishing his worth and, in time rebuilding the Society. In my interviews with brothers I found, or thought I found three areas that were still attractive to brothers.

i.   There were those like Gregory and Hilary and Nigel who were most devoted to the college and 'Kelham Theology'. They wanted most of all to insure that the intellectual tradition of the Society, Fr Kelly's understanding of the gospel of God, did not disappear with the chapel.

ii. Then there was another group who were certainly non-intellectual, if not anti. They wanted to be involved with ordinary people at the parish level.

iii. There was a group who felt that the community had been almost throttled by the pressures of running a college, and they wanted a chance to live the SSM life in a house not dominated by any large institution or task. This later acquired, when they went to Milton Keynes, the description of a 'Still Centre', a term not everyone was pleased with.

Of course the boundaries between these three groups were not clearly defined and brothers moved freely from one to the other, sometimes within the hour, and would then go on to suggest several new categories.

However at one of the early provincial chapters in my first year, after a morning-long discussion of all these and other possibilities, I announced that after lunch the chapter would reassemble in three groups in three separate rooms. Those who wanted to pursue academic interests in room A, those who wanted to work in a parish in room B, and those wanting to explore SSM community life on its own in room C. This meant that everyone had, at least tentatively, to declare their interest and make some sort of token commitment to some actual form of future SSM life before they could take part in the next session. There was a certain amount of criticism of this approach later, but the choices made that day were not final or binding and this decision did take us a little way forward. Each group achieved some kind of definition. They knew who was going to throw in their lot with them, and they could now begin to make plans for their future.

  c. We were then faced with the question of where we were going to live once Kelham Hall had been sold. As the parish group was made up of Norman Jacobson, Philip Kench, Rodney Hart, Chad Payne and Leonard Melville, it was clear that they needed a leader and, with great difficulty, I persuaded Edmund to resign his job as chaplain of St Martin's, Lancaster and assume the leadership of this group. The choice of place then was largely left to Edmund, who wanted to return to South Yorkshire and to Sheffield. He was a friend of the rector of St Mark's and so we ended up buying a house in that parish and this group eventually went on their way. They were fairly soon joined by Lawrence Eyers from Australia though this was not a great success!

The group whose interests were mainly academic were Gregory, Hilary, Nigel and Alex and Malcolm at first, though the last two soon left them. Lancaster seemed the obvious place for this group as there was already a good library and the Priory had many good contacts with the university. This group then did a Swiss Family Robinson around Kelham Hall and went on their way in due course.

The third group, the community oriented group, had to find some new place where they could 'do their thing'. I had at first wondered if it could be combined with what was planned at Lancaster but had a swift letter from their chapter saying there was not sufficient space for both of us. The next step was to contact a real estate agent, whom we followed around the countryside for the first six months of 1973 looking at empty country houses in a variety of settings but usually rural. I returned from each trip, ever more depressed. Some of the houses were attractive and historic but I wondered, 'Why? Why go to this place? What would we do when we got here?' Our break came when Dominic was in retreat at Fairacres, the convent of the Anglican Community of the Love of God in Oxford. The Urban Dean of the new city of Milton Keynes, which was only just emerging from the drawing boards, had approached these Sisters asking them to come and establish a priory in the new city to be a centre of prayer and Christian community. The sisters did not have the resources to go themselves but they asked Dominic if we would be interested. Right from the start I had the feeling that this perhaps was the sign we had been waiting for. It was an invitation, a request from the church. The Urban Dean wanted us, so he said, to be a religious community within the new city, a reference point, a spiritual resource on which others could draw; and this all fitted very neatly with the ideas that had been evolving with us. A motto popular amongst us in those early days was: 'Don't just do something – stand there!' We thus hoped that in the context of this new city we could be useful to others and helpful while remaining rooted in our own base. We met Christopher Newton, the Urban Dean, at Fortes on the M1 just outside Newport Pagnell. His enthusiasm for all aspects of the new city and especially for us was overwhelming. He swept away any remaining hesitations of ours over sausage and chips and before the coffee arrived it was a done deal. He took us immediately to the village of Willen, showed us the beautiful church which we could use as our chapel, introduced us to Bet Morgan and Mrs Nickless, the two power sources in the parish, and then took us across to look at the rectory where we could move in as soon as we wished. In August 1973 Dominic, Chad, Sydney and I moved into the Rectory and the priory began.

In large part inspired and encouraged by the enthusiasm of Christopher Newton, we found the atmosphere of the new city to be confident, exciting, expansionist and optimistic, the very things we were looking for and a wonderful restorative after the battering we had taken in the previous two years. Here was something which the church had confidently asked us to do and which we were capable of doing. Of course we were far from clear and far from united on what would be an appropriate response to this new situation, but I think the one thing that was clear from the beginning was our desire to contribute to the work and witness of the church in the new city, while at the same time refounding and rebuilding a new version of SSM in the post-Kelham chapter of our history into which we had now been thrust willy-nilly. Perhaps we can see what sort of ideas and ideals we had at that time more clearly in the buildings we put up at Willen Priory than in any resolutions we passed at provincial chapter or in any of the articles we wrote for various magazines.

Before the building began, before even any plans were drawn up, all those involved in the new house met together with the architect for several interesting meetings. He started by telling us that every building reflected the aspirations and values of the people who put it up. Therefore he needed to know: What sort of house did we want? What sort of community did we intend to be? What would be our life-style? How would we relate to outsiders? In short, what would be our mission? Not easy questions for any group to answer at any time but particularly difficult for that group to answer at that time. In fact we responded to the architect, after lengthy discussion amongst ourselves, with a series of negatives, and that in itself says a lot about where we were at the time. We were fairly clear on what we didn't want, while still remaining hazy on what we did want!

We didn't want a building that looked like a monastery, or even looked churchy. We wanted it to look secular, ordinary, and not noticeably different from all the other homes going up in Milton Keynes at that time, so no Gothic doorways or stained-glass windows. Neither did we want it to look institutional, imposing and overwhelming to first-time visitors as Kelham Hall had been. We wanted it built on a domestic scale with the same sized rooms as most other people in Milton Keynes had in their homes. We wanted to create a homely, welcoming atmosphere where strangers would feel at ease, so no long echoing corridors, magnificent staircases or lengthy roof-lines. We at first suggested a series of smallish houses scattered around the property, but the architect, while sympathetic to our reasoning, said it would be much more economical to put the houses together as a terrace. We accepted his suggestion because this would make it possible to sell off the units as private houses when we moved on, for from the beginning we knew that the whole project must be stamped with provisionality; the day of our departure would come sooner or later. We had thought that Kelham was permanent, immovable, and that had been a large part of our problem; from now on our plans must be provisional and adaptable. We also said it was not to be a house built for a single-style monolithic community such as we had lived in up to that point. We wanted a house that could provide for a variety of styles of community living; in other words, we wanted a flexible community that could from time to time readjust its customs and rules as might be required for new types of mission in a new city. Therefore we wanted a variety of units with clusters of rooms around a refectory and common room, single rooms, double rooms, rooms that were isolated. Bert wanted space to pursue his gardening interests, a vegetable garden, a pond for his ducks and geese, a private garden where members of the community could be private and grounds that would be open to the public. (This accounts for the siting of the house kitty-corner across the property cutting off a small section of the garden and privatising it. Though that plan was foiled when Bert decided to take that bit for his vegetables!). Then there should be space for the printing press which we planned to bring down from Kelham, though that plan too was foiled when Br Saul, Jimmy's apprentice, decided his vocation was to the priesthood! Flexibility was the watchword and to some extent we achieved this. Within a few years we were admitting women to the community, and then married couples, while we also found a separate space for two brothers who wanted to be contemplatives and for brothers who wanted to take on a secular job.

We wanted a community geared to change. As Dunstan said at the time, 'If up until now the Society has been constructed out of sheets of plastic with brothers jammed into whatever squares or holes the construction left vacant whatever the shape or size of the brother might be, from now on the Society would be fashioned from plasticine, taking its shape from the members it contained.'

Our overall vision at the time was to bring about the rebirth of the SSM charisma in a new setting with a new people, tackling new problems. Everything would no doubt be different but the charisma, that SSM combination of sacrifice and humour, would remain the same. Nor were our interests exclusively to do with SSM. These were days when all religious communities, Anglican and Roman that had been founded in Victorian times, found themselves on a steep Gadarene slope heading towards decline and extinction. We wanted to explore and discover, while some life was still left to us, what sort or style of community could, while remaining true to the gospel, still be in tune with the times, be attractive to a new generation, and be set for growth.

Suffice it to say that we were more successful at embodying our vision in bricks and mortar than we were in lives and ministries. There are several factors which may at least partially explain this, but my own personal opinion centres on two areas.

For many of the brothers, though not all, who lived in the priory in those early days Willen was a fault de mieux. They didn't come so much because they had been caught up in a vision, more because they desperately needed a place to live after the closing of Kelham. This meant that whenever changes were discussed they were minimalists from the start. They wanted, as far as was humanly possible, the life at Willen to duplicate the old life at Kelham; hence in the beginning we continued to wear the habit daily. After all Syd, Jimmie, Bert were old men by this time; they had been formed over decades of living by the Kelham house rule, so that while they were willing to discuss and to give conditional consent to women associates, married associates with their children, they could never really in their heart see these innovations as anything but so many dubious compromises with the SSM principles they had been taught. They might yield to the prior's pressure but they could never want what he wanted or see why he wanted it. So particularly our married associates were made to feel tolerated rather than warmly accepted, neighbours not family.[13]

Secondly, we did not have people with the skills, and I include myself here, to promote the priory and the services it might offer to the clergy and people of Milton Keynes. We could have done with a few more extraverts but we were rather weighted towards introversion and self-preservation. Hence that description of the priory as 'Still Centre' sometimes came to mean a 'hide' from behind which we peered out cautiously at the surging life of Milton Keynes buzzing around us. We related well to the parish, to the Hospice in its founding days, to the children's home in Bedford, and the Webbers and the Strudwicks when they moved in with us made good contacts for us in the wider community, but we never managed to open our doors as widely as we had hoped, until the advent of Dilly Baker and the Well community replaced us many years later.

The story of Quernmore Park and Sheffield are different stories. I have told this one in some detail as I was part of it.

3

New City: New Start 1973–1981

These years were very critical ones in the life of SSM, when the focus and effort of every brother and every chapter was on how to re-define the Society, how to re-imagine what shape the Society would take once it had broken out of the chrysalis of Kelham Hall.

The Big Move began in the first week of August 1973 when Bert, Dominic, novice Gerald Martin and I moved into Willen vicarage, arriving with a pantechnicon full of treasure which we had plundered from the sinking Kelham, although we were moving from a 130 room mansion into an eight room 1947 post-war austerity vicarage. We had to exercise a good deal of discretion in what we took and what we left behind. Nevertheless the van was crammed with furniture, furnishings, pots, pans, several tea chests full of library books, all the office equipment, garden tools, mowers, shovels, plates (the steel ones!), cutlery, beds and bedding; a place had to be found for everything and even for things for which no place could as yet be found, such as the books for the not-yet-existent library which were stacked for the time being in the empty garage.

Exhausted but excited, we felt as we trundled down the M1 that we had been given a new start, a new chance at a new job, one on a greatly reduced scale, and so one which we felt confident and eager to tackle as we turned off the motorway at Junction 14 and made for the village of Willen. But perhaps the feelings of the brothers in those days are best captured by Fr Sydney in an article he wrote, entitled:

Keeping up with the angels

Late on Michaelmas day we returned home to Milton Keynes from our final Eucharist of thanksgiving in our chapel at Kelham. At Kelham we met about a thousand of our friends who had helped us through the years with their prayers and fellowship. Together with them we thanked God for past blessings, and we prayed for guidance and grace as we go into a new future. The occasion was both sad and joyful.

That morning I celebrated my golden jubilee of profession, and, looking back on fifty years or more I see two things that have always impressed me about that chapel. One, the shafts of sunlight slanting on the altar at the Eucharist, and secondly, the deep evening shadows in contrast with the flood-lit crucifix, revealing Christ in his glory on the cross. Below in the shadows and silence were men who had either brought their troubles to the Lord or were whispering to him of their love and dedication.

As well as saying good-bye to the splendour of the house and chapel, many people were out in the grounds. Perhaps like me they also were saying good-bye to the giant plane tree by the garden wall, and the sycamore and cherry trees and copper beech – I touched them in passing because they had been old friends of mine for years.

Looking back I can hear the clip-clop of a horse bringing some of us in a cab from the station to Kelham. We approached slowly and gently one sunny warm afternoon in June, but that was more than fifty years ago. The other day we left the house with a rush down the great M1, carrying with us the Kelham plate and the Principles. Like the Principles of the Society our tableware of stainless steel will endure for a long time.

Is it wise to be in such a rush to leave the old home? Do we really

know what we want to do? Stop! Look! And think again! Oh dear!
Discussion and prayer have been our concern for months and
besides all that, we are under the protection of the angels and these
imperious beings are apt to drive us on without delay. Angels have
always been like that. One angel gave Peter a thump on his side,
saying, 'Get up! Let's go!' and bewildered Peter had to get up and
go at once. So with us who dare to claim the help and protection
of the angels; a pantechnicon van and two other vehicles stood on
the terrace of the house. 'Come on! Let's go!' said someone and off
we went with surprising speed down the great highway to Milton
Keynes Bucks. You know what? It's a great exciting business trying to
keep up with the angels, especially when in old age you might have
dreamed of retiring in quiet and obscurity amid the splendours of
Kelham.[14]

At the last Eucharist which Sydney mentions in his article,
the preacher was the bishop of Southwell, Denis Wakeling, who
reminded us that 'to worship the Lord in the beauty of holiness'
was an ideal for which this chapel and our Society had always
stood, but now the time had come when the Society had decided
that it was time to leave behind what was good and precious in
order to find something better and the brothers were leaving
behind Kelham with its magnificent chapel to find new life in new
circumstances. As often before, Denis Wakeling managed to hit
the nail squarely on the head for all of us.

Keeping up with the angels, looking for new life in new
circumstances, that was all very intoxicating stuff, but, as usual,
those circumstances turned out to be not quite like what we were
expecting and nothing like we had ever met before. There were
two matters in particular that we had not reckoned on and over
which we had no control whatsoever:

1. We came to work in the new city but the new city did
    not arrive at Willen until almost ten years after we had
    moved in. As a consequence, although we could hear
    the massive earth-movers digging out Willen Lake and
    then piling up the dirt in small hills across the road to
    form part of the new Linear Park, and while we could see

on the horizon the cranes nodding and bobbing as they erected the steel work for the City Centre, and while our own little plot was turned into a construction site as the new priory took shape, yet, in spite of all this we were still living surrounded by fields of wheat where birds were singing in the mornings and we were ministering to a parish made up of a handful of farmers and retired folk who had been in that congregation for years and years. In fact it was not so very different from many an isolated rural parish anywhere in the country, except that this one was soon to be gobbled up by the ever-encroaching new city, whose relentless advances were observed with apprehension, awe and extreme distaste.

2. The second matter that differed from our hopes and plans was in the field of recruitment. We had hoped for, we needed, fresh recruits, young men who had not been formed at Kelham who could bring their fresh ideas and fresh vigour to help our slightly jaded efforts at implementing the vision of what SSM was to be. The recruits came alright but, with one exception, they were not men and were not very young. Instead, in these years, when no young man turned up to join the novitiate, four women came seeking to be associates, women in their mid-life in the midst of their chosen careers, Mary at the Job Centre in Bletchley, Irene at the Development Corporation, Margaret from work in Australia and now with the USPG, and Bridget in the Eye Clinic in Sheffield. Two moved into the priory and two lived alongside. In addition to these four, three families uprooted themselves and came to live near us and work with us. The Webbers, the Strudwicks, and the Davis's, all with young children.

These two 'unplanned' factors effectively rewrote our road map for the future, for, by accepting these particular recruits, the community was changed forever. However it took us some time to realise the implications of what we had done and some would say that during these years we never did solve the problems or even face the problems our new recruits represented.

The first group of people who were at hand and ready to be incorporated into the new community, were the parishioners of St Mary Magdalene's Church, Willen, and we met their representatives on the very first day when Christopher Newton called a meeting of Dunstan, Bert, Dominic, and me in Willen church to introduce us to the church wardens. The church itself was something of a shock. From the outside, as you walked up the path, it looked like an undistinguished red brick, Victorian building but when you entered through the west door a revelation awaited you. You found yourself in a 17th century church designed by Richard Hook and looking as if it had somehow strayed from the centre of London. Cherubs fluttered around the plastered ceiling, some holding up a plaque inscribed 1680. The whole interior was flooded with sunlight from the clear glass windows. Waiting for us inside was Mrs Nickless, who lived in the house next door to the church and was the parish council secretary. As soon as we were all seated the door flew open and Bet Morgan marched up the aisle with her copper-coloured hair, rosy cheeks, and an air of confidence which she assumed to hide her nervousness. These two women were great friends and were also the power base of the parish, and became the dear friends of all the brothers. They had been a little apprehensive about meeting a group of 'monks', goodness knows what they expected, but soon good humour prevailed over shyness and we ended up in complete concord drinking tea together in the antique splendours and faded glories of Mrs Nickless's sitting room.

We soon decided that to build a chapel when living next door to such a beautiful church would be a complete waste of money and so the chapel was dropped from our plans for the new priory and we now began every day in the church at 7.00am with morning prayer and Eucharist, with Midday Office at 12.45, Evensong at 7.00pm and Compline we said informally at 9.00pm in the common room. The congregation averaged about twelve on a Sunday morning but it gradually grew, not from folks moving into the new city but from people in the neighbourhood who had had connections with Willen Church in years gone by. Such were Jack and Annie Moore who had attended the village school between the wars. One Sunday Annie brought her ancient mother who had also grown up in Willen Village. She kept us all entranced at the coffee hour in the priory after service by telling us how when she was a little girl here, on the first of May they all went out to gather the May blossom. She then sang in her quavering voice the special song which the children sang as the gathered the May blossoms. Beautiful! I only regret that we did not tape it. But there are so many other memories of bitter cold December nights when a little band, bundled up to the ears, marched from house to house through the village singing carols for all, more especially for those families where there were children, and then scurrying down to Bet and Glen's farm to warm up on Bet's hot chicken soup in front of a fire that Glen had stoked up in advance. Then there were those parties we organised for the parish on St Mary Magdalen's day for which Mr Rees allowed using one of his empty barns. Bet and the women brought enough food to feed an army all to be washed down with generous helpings from the large punch bowl. A fiddler was also in attendance to play for us so we square-danced until the sweat ran down from our faces and we almost dropped from exhaustion. I don't think that barn had ever contained a happier crowd and they were certainly the happiest parties that I have ever attended.

At this time when many were predicting that the days of SSM were numbered now, or even that the religious life, as we had known it, no longer had any place in the church of the new millennium, the following article appeared in the Newsletter, entitled:

'A Double Jubilee'

We have been happy to celebrate within the last few months the golden jubilees of two brothers; Fr Peter at Michaelmas, and Br James on January 3rd. A lot has happened since 1923 when these two men made their profession. They themselves have changed and massive changes have taken place both in the world around and in the Society. If all the new House Rules (now instilling discipline, now implanting maturity) to which they have had to conform were gathered together, they would fill several tea chests. If all the new liturgical rites (now greatly enriched, now greatly simplified) were lined up they would fill a bookcase in the library. Peter once claimed that he felt he had been just a toad under the liturgical harrow! During their time dictators have come and gone in Europe, nations have emerged and submerged in Africa, priors have appeared and disappeared at Kelham, the college has blossomed and faded away, and in fact you might say that nothing remains of all that we had in 1923. But if you said that you would be wrong, because these two brothers remain. Day by day without fail for fifty years, amidst war, depression, and affluence, amidst innovations, reformations and counter-revolutions, they have got up when the bell went in the morning, got dressed, said their prayers in chapel, and gone to their work, Peter to his cabbage patch and James to his printing press, if not always without complaining, yet always without refusing, so that what remains today is these same two men with the same faith, hope and love they had in 1923 except perhaps somewhat deepened, richer and more stable. They are at once the bond with our past and the foundation of our future.

Two ordinary men with two unremarkable lives and yet they are perhaps the most convincing witnesses that we have to the genuine value, the usefulness, even the beauty of this style of life and they are our best pledge of its continuance into the future.

As Kelham was gradually emptied of furniture and people and the last class of students were preparing for graduation, Br James was moved down to the new Willen Priory. He came loyally and joined in with priory life and made friends in the parish but he never really grasped what we were trying to do. He died of a heart complaint about eighteen months after he arrived and was the first to be buried in Willen churchyard.

Br James death left us with an empty room and that was when we decided to invite Sir Almeric Rich to come and join us. Sir Almeric Rich was a genuine baronet with the appearance of a Colonel Blimp, walrus moustaches, red face, and a tendency to shout if you couldn't at first understand him but at heart he had the zeal and enthusiasm of a first year theological student and a passion for helping the needy. He had worked in borstals from the time they were introduced as a place of reformation rather than just a punishment for young offenders. He had ended his days as governor of Huntercombe Borstal. He was a frequent visitor and shrewd observer of all that we did at Kelham and as far as possible he replicated our life in his borstal. I was asked down one January to preach at the Feast of Dedication of the chapel. A feast that we kept with much pomp and ceremony in our magnificent chapel at Kelham and which he repeated in his Quonset hut chapel in the borstal. We started off with a procession, I in cope, flanked by two young lads in borstal uniform (navy-blue jackets and gray trousers) carrying candles, down the aisle singing 'Hail thee festival day' (as we did at Kelham) with great volume and almost no tune from a hut full of young lads recruited from the back streets of London and Birmingham. We processed down the aisle – no great distance – the thurible belching out smoke like a steam engine, circled round the red hot coal stove at the back just as a young lad sprang forward to throw open the back doors allowing us to march forth into the snow, make a circle and return up the aisle for a final assault on the altar. It is a service I will never forget. I don't know what it meant to the lads but it definitely meant something serious because it meant something serious to the Governor. If Almeric handed out any punishment e.g. up at 4.00am to do an hour's PT in the snow in gym kit, the offender would find beside him this little old man with knobbly knees going through the whole drill with him. He never assigned a punishment he did not share himself. After retirement he lived a sort of half-life in a residential hotel in Henley-on-Thames and he jumped at the chance to come and join us. The only clue he ever let fall as to his aristocratic background was when he was down to lead intercessions at the morning Eucharist. One of his favourite intercessions went, 'Let us give thanks for all our old friends who have been so patient with us over the years and have put up with us when we are tiresome.' The word 'tiresome' always conjured up for me visions of large Victorian nurseries, presided over by large Victorian nannies in white caps and aprons, who when a small boy refused to eat his porridge would say in chilling tones, 'Almeric! Don't be tiresome!' Willen was the only village in England whose morning papers were delivered daily by a baronet! He was the only person we ever invited to come and live with us but we thought that he had all the characteristics, all the humility and love that we hoped to build into the walls of SSM's new home and so shape our future.

Gradually the parish was developing, the priory was gathering and the plans for the new buildings were going ahead, but almost from the beginning we knew that we were facing a big and decisive question. Recruitment – who would join us? And under what conditions? As we have already noticed those who wanted to come and join us during the course of those early years were four women and three families so these courageous people forced us out of the realms of theory into facing practical questions. We were influenced too by Rosemary Haughton, an RC woman and herself the leader of a mixed community, who wrote an article for our newsletter which did much to nudge us forward.

There are endless different possible ways of associating the central, explicitly dedicated, group with those who need to share with it in some degree. That degree could vary from fully sharing the life for some years, but without vows, through sharing the buildings and some of the work and observances, to a loose association by occasional visits and help of various kinds ... A religious community which has, instead of a sharply defined circumference, a gradually spreading circle of members of various kinds and degrees is in touch with all kinds' problems ideas, and aspirations, not only as a helper but as sharing in them. Such a community reaches out into the very heart of contemporary life in its miseries and its heroisms, both practically and in prayer and love. .... At a time of much searching and much despair such communities can be centres of hope without arrogance, of certainty without smugness and can give to the struggling world something invaluable, something which, perhaps, no one else can give.

While we were listening to these voices around us, there were a significant number of brothers who felt that admitting women to membership in SSM would be a betrayal of Fr Kelly's vision and overthrow eighty years of our tradition. It was in reply to these fears that the following paper was circulated amongst the brothers at that time.

For Fr Kelly, all the structures of the religious life were simply methods of getting work done more effectively and so to the greater glory of God. All of these monastic traditions: the habit, the minor offices, life in priories and the rest were of value in so far as they helped to forward the work and for that reason only. They were expendable. Of course he did not even consider the question of women associates but he has left us the criteria with which to discuss the question. In considering whether or not to have women associates, we are neither to refuse it because it has no tradition behind it, nor to adopt it because it is congenial to the present day climate of opinion. A priory has simply to ask, is it to God's glory? In the sense of, will it make for efficiency and effectiveness in the service we are trying to render to the church in this place? So that in a new city like Milton Keynes, where the Society is trying to stand beside and assist all those agencies, forces, and people of good will who are working to make a new city into a new community, if the members feel that a community made up of both men and women would better serve this purpose then they are free to organise such a community, more than that, it is their duty to do so if they wish to remain loyal to the founding vision of SSM, because what Fr Kelly left to us his followers was most of all, freedom, freedom to adopt and adapt any rule or any custom if it allowed for the easier spread of the gospel of God, for, as long as the glory of God is secured, anything goes.

Long, long were the discussions in chapter and out of chapter and deep, deep were the divisions they revealed, but at last a loop hole was found, strangely enough, within the Society's Constitution. The Constitution had always provided from the beginning for a class of person who lived and worked in our priories for a time without ever becoming fully professed members of the Society. These people were called associates. Every student in our colleges was an associate. They were committed to the ideals of the Society, and lived by its rules 'for a season' and were a vital part of its work and witness. Here was our compromise ready to hand. Women could not be full members of SSM but they could be associates, live with us, work with us, and take the promises that associates took, and soon in the newsletter a small paragraph appeared announcing the arrival of Lionel and Jean Webber. Lionel was to be vicar of New Bradwell and chaplain to the Stantonbury campus, Jean was taking up a teaching job and Anne their daughter went into school at Stantonbury. Meanwhile at Sheffield, Bridget Brooke became an associate of the new priory there.

Sadly, as was to happen in the Church of England fifteen years later when women were first ordained to the priesthood, there were some in the Society who felt betrayed, let down, and frustrated by these developments. But it was Sydney who (perhaps unwittingly) reminded us very forcibly of what it really meant to be a member of SSM in the obituary notice he wrote at that time for Howard Preece, a brother in the Society with whom he had served, first as seamen in the Royal Navy in 1914-18, then for some years in the missions in South /Africa.

'Of your charity pray for the soul of Howard Preece of the SSM who died at Modderpoort OFS South Africa on November 10, 1974 aged 75 in the 50th year of his profession. Requiescat in pace.

Such are the bare facts of a lifetime spent within the Society of the Sacred Mission. It is a privilege to clothe these bare facts with a few details concerning one who was a sailor (RN) student, priest, school teacher, and school manager, missionary and church builder – and a lovable and steadfast member of our Society. His outward manner was quiet and courteous. He said very little and his silences could be embarrassing to those who did not know him. People were drawn to him because he was easy to live with, undemanding for himself and clear and helpful in what he had to say. He was a man of great strength, both physically and spiritually and he was unflappable in a crisis – a good man to have around in moments of fear and violence which occurred sometimes in our African schools,

Howard gave himself wholeheartedly to our missionary work in the Orange Free State. He was on the staff of our teachers' training college where he did a great work, having his place in a complicated time-table and yet never groaning that it was too much or too exhausting. The boys and girls respected him and, long after they had left the college, spoke of him with affection. He was an efficient manager of the large Bantu United School in Kroonstadt. This was a tremendous undertaking: there were teachers to appoint and schools to develop, and all were kept quietly and steadily under control. Wages were paid promptly: indeed, so regular and precise was Howard's wage-paying routine that it is a wonder that he was never robbed of the big sums of money he carried around in a well-known, battered attaché case. He was also a mission priest in whatever area he lived, and rarely failed to arrive at a lonely mission out-station, in spite of rain frequent floods and bad roads. He had an old suitcase made up into a church bag, which contained everything needed for a Holy Communion service, as well as registers, and rosaries and books for sale. He built three or four simple but adequate churches on a shoestring budget, without any fuss or tremendous fund-raising appeals and the altar space was always tastefully decorated with colours. I envied him very much when he pointed out to me a large shady tree which he had planted long ago in '29 at Modderpoort and under which he could now sit and relax.

As a member of our Society he was an unassuming example of poverty, obedience and celibacy. He never amassed any quantity of things. He had just what was sufficient and serviceable: a few books for teaching, a box of carpenter's tools for running repairs, and a church case for Sunday services. In addition there was his naval ditty-box, his seamanship manual, and his pipe and bag of smelly tobacco. His religious obedience was evident. Without fuss he laid down one job and took up another, as his superiors required, and carried on faithfully and thoroughly. Towards the end of his life he was sent up into the mountains of Lesotho, seven thousand feet above sea level. Blinko (his nickname in the Society) hated the cold, but managed to keep a hut warmed to well over seventy degrees. We said that it was a shame for a man of his age to be sent to so remote a place, but 'Blinko' never batted an eyelid and made that hut his Shangri-la. His vow of celibacy enabled him to give his love and skill to those whom he taught. Their lives were made richer on account of his friendship and care for them.

Howard was a man who, as a member of the SSM set out to give his life and his love to Christ and his church. He set a straight course for God. He was a good sailor, who made the most of whatever winds there were. As a good crewman he was easy to live and work with, and there was never the ego bulge about him. In the end he died quietly and unobtrusively, he cast off the moorings and went with the tide. We pray that the winds blow gently and that his sturdy craft sails straight on course and make a perfect landfall on the other side.

And that's what it's all about. That's what it means to be a member of SSM whether you are male or female, black or white, single or married, septuagenarian or novice. That's all there is to it.

Mary Hartwell was one of the first women who showed an interest in the priory and soon was thinking of making a commitment of her life through the priory. She lived locally. In April '77 she described her job in Bletchley Job Centre in the newsletter.

Milton Keynes is an area of diverse employment: cooked meats and caramel, tea-bags and toiletries, pianos and plastics are but a few of the products which have come to join the original industries of the town – Wolverton Carriage and Wagon Works (now British Rail Engineering and still the largest employer in North Bucks), printing and brick making. This has proved to be one of the great strengths of Milton Keynes in the last two years. Some new towns have been less fortunate, and a recession in one major industry has spelt unemployment for the whole area. In Milton Keynes however, a large spread of industry has ensured that when one door shuts another tends to open.

Opportunities for work are still good compared with most parts of the country, though here as elsewhere there is some concern about the young people who will be leaving school during the summer. Unemployment is at present estimated at 4.9 per cent which is low compared with other regions, though for each individual concerned it is 100 per cent. In Milton Keynes unemployment is largely the prerogative of the unskilled and there is still a shortage of skilled engineering workers.

The Training Services Agency has sited a new Skill Centre here and they will train people principally for the construction and allied trades, building, heavy vehicle maintenance and repair. A construction labour force is one of the essential requirements for building a new city. The trades are varied and include everyone from pipe-layers and road makers to dumper drivers and mechanics who keep the massive earth moving equipment in repair. There are at present 5000 men employed in construction in the new city.

During the past three or four years hundreds of these men have been housed by the Development Corporation. Many of them are people who have never before been able to have a settled home because no one site has been large enough to ensure continuity of work for a long time. But now, with the promise of a continuous building programme that will last till the end of the century, they have been able to settle down with their wives and families.

Take the case of Tom and Jean. When Tom first came to see me at the Job Centre he was rather desperate. He and his wife had been living with their three children in an eighth floor, two roomed, flat in central London. During the long summer holidays the children's enforced confinement to the flat had driven his wife near to mental collapse and the doctor had advised him to move. He had heard that if he could get work in Milton Keynes, the Development Corporation would let him a house. We eventually found him a suitable job, and because of his predicament he was allocated immediate housing. So he and his family moved to the new city. They had their three bedroom house and a garden for the children to play in. They were within easy walking distance of the local school and the children no longer needed to be escorted there and back. There was open countryside around them. The future looked very bright. But of course they had to furnish their house and to help them in this the Development

Corporation started a scheme called 'Tugboat' Under its auspices voluntary workers collect any sort of second hand furniture which can be purchased by newcomers at nominal rates.

Thus was Mary's day made up – an interesting parallel perhaps to the days of some of the brothers in the South African missions.

In addition to our own membership there appeared several groups who were interested in forming a link with us. The first of these was Dr Marjorie Reid who wanted to establish a hospice in the new city because, in her own words, *Despite the scientific and technological resources of modern medicine, there comes a time with certain patients when, although they have some months of life ahead of them, curative therapy has nothing more to offer. These patients now need very special care. They need relief of pain while being enabled to remain mentally alert; they need preservation of personal dignity, compassion, and often peace to find themselves. Both they and their families need spiritual care and support.*

For all these reasons Dr Reid chose to dedicate the hospice under the name of Our Lady and St John because these were the two that remained by the cross and loved our Lord through his dying and she also hoped to locate it in Willen where a dedicated community would be part of the background as a support for the staff upon whom great spiritual demands would be made. The foundation of the hospice was not without crises and setbacks as it soon became clear that with the astronomical rise in the cost of building they would not have enough money to erect a new building or even to begin one in the foreseeable future. At this point Manor Farm, next to the church came on the market following on the death of Harry Rees. This was just the sort of location they had been looking for and when their offer of £58000 was accepted they could hope to open their doors before public interest dwindled away. On the priory side Francis took up the cause with unbridled enthusiasm (not a common phenomenon in his life!) and was soon bicycling all over the county talking to groups of all shapes and sizes, in fact to anyone who would listen and so building public support as well as engaging in the long tedious work of fundraising. He represented the Society on the Hospice Board of Governors.

Another group came into view as a result of my undertaking weekly visiting in Bedford Jail. The chaplain told me to park my car at the St Etheldreda's Children's home just a block away. I had not parked there many times when I was accosted by Sr Hazel one evening who promptly took me inside and introduced me to Sr Joyce and Sr Muriel, the three sisters who were in charge of this home for children in care aged 2 to 19.

That marked the beginning of a lifelong friendship with Joyce and Hazel. Joyce was a woman of heroic dimensions. She kept together that home of 35 maladjusted children and 15, at times, wobbly staff and never really lost her cool. She never forgot what each child liked to eat and what each child did not like to eat, she listened to them and gave them individually a mother's love irrespective of how they responded. All of this could be seen at her funeral in a church packed with grieving young men and women who had grown up under her care. The sisters began by coming over to Willen for their infrequent time off but within a few years as it became clear that government policy was now to phase out residential children's homes and replace them by with foster families, we agreed to build a house for the three sisters on our paddock where they could come when St Eth's closed and in the expectation that these three experienced women would then be free to become vital part of the Willen team sharing fully in all our working, thinking and praying. Unfortunately by the time they were free to come, the makeup of the priory had changed and things did not work out as we had anticipated, but still the new house provided a good home for Joyce and Hazel in their retirement.

Another group we formed a connection with at this time were three Orthodox nuns who were living the other side of Newport Pagnell at Filgrave. Their leader was Mother Maria, a Swiss who had grown up as a Methodist and been converted to Orthodoxy in Paris during the war. She had lived for many years at St Mary's Abbey at West Malling in Kent where she had done her novitiate. She was joined there by Sr Thekla from a Russian émigré family, and then with Sr Catherine.

They were an indomitable trio of women who feared no priest, Anglican or orthodox, no bishop not even a patriarch. With some money Catherine had inherited they had privately printed a series of books they had themselves written under the title of the Library of Orthodox Theology which they now pedalled about among the book shops of England. Mother Maria was a warm maternal sort of person with a lovely sense of humour. As she lay slowly and painfully dying of cancer, she would say with a wry smile, 'I did think they might have managed things a little better than this!' Thekla was as strong as a Russian ox and grew enough vegetables to keep the table, bringing a Slavonic fervour to the garden as to all else in her life. Sr Catherine was a saintly soul who upheld the other two with her faith and prayer. We often went across to join in their services. It was a breath of the exotic wafted across distant centuries amidst the concrete, glass, and mud of the new city.

We were carried out even further on to the ecumenical circumference when a group of Japanese Buddhist monks applied and were given permission by the Development Corporation to build a Peace Pagoda in the park next to the priory. This particular sect of Buddhism had built these Peace Pagodas, all identical, in various parts of the world and each was staffed with a small band of monks. After the Development Corporation had accepted their application and given them permission to build, but before the first stone was laid, they convened a public meeting of all those living in the village or area. Ostensibly this was to give those who felt reservations or unhappiness about this project a democratic opportunity to object. The meeting took place at the priory and there was a good attendance, but my lasting memory is of Susan Nickless in her worn coat, tweed skirt, felt hat, and quivering high-pitched voice, protesting, 'But this is an English village and Buddhist pagodas have never been a part of our tradition.' She was ably backed up by Sydney who repeated her message at much greater length. He said he was greatly offended that after having spent most of his life converting the heathen, the heathen were now building new temples within spitting distance of his bedroom window. Nor were these two reconciled when the monks came beating their drums at the Christmas Eve midnight mass, and sat in the back pew throughout to share the feast with us. When the brothers pointed out to Syd that these monks building a Peace Pagoda in Milton Keynes was not so very different from him building all those Gothic churches through the villages of the Orange Free State he said, 'That's quite different!'

Meanwhile the community centred on the priory was increasing in numbers and variety, as the new buildings provided ample accommodation for us all. It was now largely through these newcomers that we were linked with the on-going life of the new city.

Irene Nunns kept us in touch with the action at the Development Corporation where she worked. Vincent Strudwick, Ecumenical Education Officer for the churches in the New City, was our link with the diocese. Nina Strudwick had gathered a group of women in the workshop who were interested in weaving, spinning and patchwork. Linda Davis, after she had qualified as a GP in this country, was in the Stantonbury Health Centre.

The children: Becky and Alice Strudwick, Emma, Arthur, and Irene Davis were our contacts in the local Primary Schools and Martha Strudwick was our first member to actually begin a new life in Willen. Mary was in touch with the Job Centre.

Liz Macy, once she had qualified, was a public health nurse in the Stantonbury area.

John Gowing, a priest nearing retirement, came to be an associate and continued with his life's work in adult education. Steve Little, the new Social Services officer for the city, was given an office in the priory. Margaret Dewey did much with her writing and her contacts through the USPG in London. Francis was our link with the Hospice.

Dunstan spent one or two terms working on the Stantonbury campus.

This meant that we were as a group very much focused on the city outside and this at a time when the tide of new housing had not yet reached Willen or even very close to it. But what about our common life? How well did we begin to cohere and grow towards unity? I think we all at that time shared a double goal, unity and mission, and I think we would also have agreed that we still had some way to go and some hard work to do before we achieved our goal. However, even in the now, we could frequently taste some of the sweet fruits that fell from that ultimate unity towards which we strived. As for example on a Sunday morning, after the service in Willen Church, when we all gathered around the table for our Sunday dinner together, cooked by one of us on a roster. Or perhaps on those evenings in the new common room where we tended to gather before Compline. The centre of most of these evenings was Sydney, who loved nothing better than to corral as many as possible into a game of 'Oh Hell', a form of whist which could be mastered in seconds by a person who had never before touched a card, and which yet provided us with hours and hours of pleasure, either the pleasure of beating Syd, or the more Christian pleasure of smarting under his triumphalist chuckles as he cantered out in front of the rest of us. What he enjoyed even more than cards was a session, preferably with a drink, around the fire telling stories (preferably his) about a lifetime of experience in the mission field. There was a whole collection of stories about Johnny-go-lightly, the wicked recalcitrant mission horse, wilful and uneducable in all his ways, until one Christmas day while the brothers were deep in siesta in Modderpoort priory, exhausted after all their labours, that horse wandered alone into the open unattended church and ate all the thatch off the Christmas crib and then drank up all the holy water in the stoup, and was thereafter as gentle as a lamb. Then there was the missionary bishop who, after instructing Sydney to take his soap and 'make the water cloudy' (they were sharing the high and capacious Bloemfontein Episcopal bath tub at the time) rang the servants' bell and at once Fanny his wife appeared with two brandies to refresh the weary missionaries.

What a gift the old man had for making us laugh and for drawing us together.

The coming of the women members and the families vastly increased the amount of mission work we were able to undertake, but their greatest and most important contribution was the effect they had on the Society itself. They changed the Society forever in those years, they made us more human. They, without a word spoken, enticed us to lay aside our former self-image of heroic monasticism, all cassocks, rules and plainsong, and accept ourselves as just human beings, battling our way along a rather baffling track through life like most other people, doing what we were able to do and daily reinvigorated by the love we drew from one another.

As we approached 1981, when my term as provincial expired, I naturally looked back over the path we had trod since we had left Kelham behind in 1973 and headed down the M1. The more I thought about it the less I was conscious of plans brilliantly conceived, or strategies consistently followed, or goals hard won and achieved. It didn't feel at all like that to me. I felt more as if we had all been engaged for nine years in a game of croquet, like the strange game described by Alice in Wonderland.

In that game that she played there, it seemed the croquet balls were hedgehogs all curled up in a ball and asleep, the hoops were formed by smart soldiers who doubled themselves over resting on both hands and toes, the mallets were living flamingos whose bodies you tucked under your arm and manoeuvred their heads into a position to knock the croquet ball on its way. However in that game it seemed that the hedgehogs would at times wake up, uncurl, and waddle off field, or the soldiers would hear the beat of a different drum and would march away to a different battle and the flamingos when you had them tucked neatly under your arm and were all ready to make your play would suddenly, without warning, twist their necks around until they were looking you in the eye with such a puzzled and piteous expression on their face, that you could not help but laugh. It seems that the main problem was that all the players were alive, and all played as if there were no rules and all played at once without waiting their turn.

Thus they were forever disagreeing, and beside all that the playing field was not a level. one. It was all ridges and valleys so no wonder that Alice found it a very difficult game indeed, as did we.

However it also appears that in Alice's croquet game there were no winners and no losers, nor were any scores kept. It was just an adventure Alice had as she progressed through Wonderland, and when the game was over she was ready to move on to the next day, which would doubtless bring equally amazing games to play. The new day that was coming up for me seemed to have an oriental tinge to it as the new provincial had suggested that I take a break from England and the English for a while and spend some time in our Japanese priory with the Japanese brothers at Kobe.

4

Japanese Foray

In November 1981 there were living in the priory at Tarumi, near Kobe, Moses, a close friend of mine who had been a novice with me at Kelham and was now the prior of the house, Andrew Muramatsu, who for most of the time that I was with them was on sabbatical leave in England, Simon Yamada, an older man who, after serving for ten years in the Imperial Japanese army during the war, on demobilisation had submitted himself for ordination. After serving in some parishes he had joined the SSJE (Society of St John the Evangelist) and, when they closed down their Japanese priory, he joined the SSM. The fourth and youngest member in the priory was Joshua Yoshinari a former sushi-chef; he had stood behind the counter in a big department store making a variety of sushi at top speed and placing them on the counter within easy reach of hungry customers. He was perhaps not the sharpest knife in the drawer but he had the widest smile and was the sweetest character. This was the group I joined after leaving Narita airport and being met by Moses who was the one and only familiar and welcoming face amongst the teeming millions that surged through Tokyo's arrival lounge.

However before I go any further I need to express my own reservations about anything I may write on the subject of Japanese life and culture, reservations I expressed in an article I wrote for the newsletter at that time.

Imagine a Japanese Shinto priest who speaks no English, on the popular 'Five Countries in Three Weeks' Japan Air Lines tour of Western Europe, during the two days allotted to England being hustled around St Paul's and Westminster Abbey one morning rather speedily so that after lunch at Macdonald's there would be time to do the Tower of London before catching the polar flight back to Tokyo in the late afternoon, and on the strength of this experience returning to Japan to write an article on 'The Church of England, its worship and its role in nuclear disarmament'. If you can imagine such a scenario, you will be aware of some of the limitations and impertinence of any article of mine on this subject. I was only in the country for eleven months, part of a tiny fragment of the miniscule Anglican church in Japan hidden away in the throbbing populations now of Kobe, now of Tokyo. I came away without having made any impact on the SSM or the Anglican Church in Japan but I was tremendously impressed with what I was able to observe of their life and culture, so totally different from anything that I had ever experienced before.

One of the first impressions that I had as soon as I stepped into the arrivals lounge at the airport, was that I had instantaneously been turned into a complete illiterate, roughly at the same level as a pre-school four year old. I was surrounded with signs of all sizes in garish colours and blazing lights eagerly pumping out information on all subjects, but none of them able to convey a scintilla of information to my muddled brain. Not even the exits, the entrances or the toilets were clear to me. The Japanese use no less than three different forms of writing. There are the pictograms called Kanji of which you need to know about three thousand before you can make any sense of a newspaper. Then there is the Hiragana, a set of some 75 signs which spell out the phonetic sound of any Japanese word, and Katakana, which give a parallel set 75 sounds used mostly to transliterate foreign or imported words. Like the pre-school child you are very dependent on 'those who know' since you yourself know nothing. You are free to observe all that is going on but your comprehension is, to say the least, limited.

Over the time that I was in Japan one of my strongest impressions was of the vitality, energy and enthusiasm for life of the people here. I don't think this impression is entirely due to the fact that I lived about half of my time in Japan on the campus of St Paul's Middle School (known as the Rykkio) in the centre of Tokyo where I had been invited by Robert Nishimura, formerly my next door neighbour at Trinity when we were both in Divinity, and now the headmaster of the Rykkio. He had asked me to come and teach a class in conversational Canadian to a bunch of his students who were bound for BC in Canada for a summer holiday in an exchange with a Canadian school. We practised how to order a hamburger, a hot dog, how to find the toilets, how to deal with busses and subways and other necessary hints for a young man abroad for the first time. But living thus on a student campus I saw from my windows every day from 6.30am until the sun went down students jogging, running, hopping and leapfrogging past my door and doing the most complicated and strenuous drills and exercises on the parking lot opposite to the beat of a drum or the chant of a school yell – all to keep fit or to hold a coveted place is some team or league or other. But apart from students, people's approach to life seems keener and more zealous. All local festivals seem to centre around hordes of semi-naked youths dragging enormous shrines down narrow streets as boisterously as possible; school yards are always fully occupied Saturdays and Sundays with endless drills and practices, trains are always crowded, streets are always full of people who have places to go, people to see and things to do.

I often felt that the Shinkanzen, the Bullet Train, was a good icon of life in modern Japan – up to date, fast, efficient and clean. However in spite of all this, or maybe because of it, one of the corner stones of life here is respect. When you meet a person for the first or even for the thousandth time, you don't grab them by the hand or slap them on the back or in any other way demand their attention and help; in fact you don't make any physical contact with them at all. Instead you put your hands neatly to your sides, your heels together and you bow to the person, whether a slight bending of the neck or a deep bowing of the spine, will depend on the number of steps higher or lower this person stands in relation to you on the ladder of society, because every person has their own set place on that ladder. But whether higher or lower your bow indicates that you are of less importance than they are and you stand ready to serve them and that is how you show your respect. If you live your life in a vast crowd, it is essential to observe all the boundaries and to never ever invade the other person's space. Otherwise daily life would soon become intolerable.

You not only show respect to individuals around you, you also show respect to any group you are a part of and you do this by fitting in modestly, quietly and without drawing undue attention to yourself. Often as I stood in the aisle of a packed train, my nose just about on a level with the tops of everyone else's head, I would gaze up and down the coach at a carpet of black haired heads, all bent over some small paperback or folded newspaper and all swaying gently with the rolling motion of the train. I got the feeling that it was as if we were all united in some great stage production, and we were about to join together in a chorus of song. As a result nonconformity, eccentricity and rebellion are less popular here and the received wisdom is to fit in, to conform and not to fuss. Again I may be partly influenced by my experience at the Rykkio School where I was sent for ten days to a summer camp with the boys up in the mountains. In the school generally, but in the camp especially, the emphasis is on working in harmony as a team for some clear end. From 6.30am till 9.30pm the boys ran from event to event unquestioningly and even with enthusiasm and then fell asleep at 9.40pm without even saying 'disco', leaving the weary teachers to refresh their souls with saki. But what surprised me most was the absence of complaint, dissension or revolt. If you wanted to stand out you did it by your contribution to what the team was scheduled to do. I'm sure the pressures and problems are not very different from what they are in the west but the reactions are not the same at all. I kept wondering if any of these boys ever said to their teacher or mother what Kate Beamish (our cook at Willen) reported her son Crispin at ten years old often saying to her, 'I am a person in my own right'.

I was told that in August 1945 when the atom bombs began to fall and Japan was on its knees in the last stages of exhaustion, there was some concern amongst both the allies and the Japanese about how to bring the vast war machine to a halt. After all, for over twenty-five years these people had been taught and had enthusiastically embraced the doctrine of giving all they had, even life itself for their country, and millions of soldiers and civilians had laid down their lives in obedience to this teaching. Would they ever understand or accept surrender? Or would the invasion forces be forced to fight street by street from Okinawa in the south to Hokkaido in the north? In fact it was simply done. The whole country and the armed forces were alerted to listen to the radio on a certain day when the Emperor would address the nation. They all gathered around their radios, old weather-beaten farmers in country villages, survivors in bombed-out cities, battered soldiers on war-torn islands and heard the Emperor's voice for the first time in their lives speaking in an archaic court dialect which they could scarcely understand, telling them that things had not turned out altogether propitiously or as they had expected and now they must lay down their arms and begin to bear what was unbearable and to endure what was unendurable. And they all did. They obeyed that divine voice. For them it could have happened in no other way, and in no other place could it have happened at all.

Religion is usually reckoned to play an even smaller part in the lives of modern Japanese than it does in the lives of modern Europeans, and yet Buddhist and Shinto shrines, large and small, imposing and home-made, continue to dot the Japanese landscape as commonplace a part of the scene as the parish churches of England but there the similarity ends for these shrines have no regular worship services, no priests attached to them, no enrolled congregations, no diocesan quotas, mission programmes or social concerns, and very little theology. What purpose then do they serve? There was a shrine near our priory at the intersection of the main roads by the Tarumi-Ginza shopping arcade. It was really just a few sheets of corrugated iron put up to keep the weather off a collection of little stone deities on shelves around a couple of home-made altars. Of no artistic merit, these humble little Woolworth style gods were just a good sized cylindrical stone, sometimes with a separate stone 'head' but generally without features. I often passed this shrine on my way to the train station and it was seldom empty. There is a bench inside where shoppers like to sit and wait for the bus; school children run through it playing tag; and quite often someone is praying in it. The little bell tinkles amidst the grinding of gears, incense from joss sticks mingles with traffic fumes, and a little god suddenly acquires a new red apron. It is all so humble and useful. It is not there because of any churchy mission or missionary, but simply because some people love it, perhaps because it supplies a need in their daily lives, a need still unsatisfied after all the groceries have been bought.

When you visit a shrine you stand there humbly, make a bow, ring the bell to get the god's attention, throw in your offering, a one yen or five yen piece will do it, the only use left for these particular coins in the modern city, and then you make your request and you are on your way. Shrine visits are a very private, individual activity and the purpose is to get a blessing for you and yours, or just to get 'good luck', but none the less important for that. It is popular to make such a visit on New Year's Day for a blessing on your year. It is estimated that 80 per cent of the population visit a shrine over the holiday, or you may make it the pretext for a visit into the country. When Bridget Brooke, a friend of SSM in Sheffield, came to visit us, I took her to a Buddhist shrine high in the mountains beyond Osaka. It took us three different trains to get there, the last one on a single track and more like a trolley than a train, but as Joshua went with us and bought all tickets we had no problems. This place was that rarity in Japan, a place with a feeling of isolation. Amongst a tall stand of cedars, almost like a Moderate Zone rain forest, there was a small village of holy shrines each with its Buddha within. The air was redolent of incense and pilgrims wended their way quietly to and fro. You felt you were in a place made holy by the prayers of so many ordinary people arising from their ordinary lives over the centuries.

You may think that religion plays such a minimal part in the lives of most people that it is completely without importance or significance, but that would be to make a mistake. It does play a very small part in the lives of most but it is a part which most are unwilling, maybe even unable, to leave behind. Even Mitsubishi engineers, after refitting an oil tanker with a new engine in Kobe Port, set up a small shrine in the engine room, lit candles, bowed low and poured saki before pulling the switch for the first time 'to make sure it works!' they explained to the mystified Scottish chief engineer from Glasgow. 'And it worked!' he reported, obviously impressed by such a practical, handy religion.

While living in the middle of Tokyo, I found that the priest of the near-by Anglican parish was Timothy Ogasawara who had studied for some years at Kelham. He and his wife and family now became good friends of mine. They were within walking distance of my place and I used to go over once a week to have an English conversation session with his daughter Miki, a lovely and vivacious young Japanese, who was about to embark on an exchange programme with a family in the USA. This arrangement opened for me a typical Japanese home and family and how I enjoyed those evening meals at that table, lovingly prepared by Mrs. O. When Pentecost came round Timothy insisted that I, like the first apostles, preach in my non-native tongue. In order to accomplish this, I gave him my sermon in advance which he translated and wrote out, not in Kanji but in English characters so I could read it. This joint production I stood up and preached at the appropriate time, not really knowing what I was saying, but Mrs. O. assured me afterwards 'wakarimas – wakarimas – we understood', and that's Japanese courtesy for you.

At that time also Bill and Marj, my brother and his wife, came to stay with me bringing a welcome breath of home. It was so good to have a place where I could put them up and we could spend time together. By that time I had mastered the shapes of enough Kanji so that we could venture out on our own on the subway and explore Tokyo and its treasures. On the day they left three of the teachers of the Rykkio, who had been with me on the camp, realizing that this day might be a low period for me took me with them out to the public baths. This is the Japanese way of relaxing par excellence. You start with a shower to get clean, and you are then given a small lightweight kimono, and you then join your friends to soak together in one of the large tubs of hot water. Being naked, sharing a tub, sipping saki or beer, exchanging one story after another with your mates, far from telephones and duties, is the perfect way to wind down. You then take up your kimono again and lounge around a low table drinking beer and munching on nibbles until two or three hours have slipped by and it is time for a closing cold shower and then back into your clothes and back into the working world. I have never forgotten the kindness of these three teachers on that day. It was a typical bit of Japanese sensitivity; maybe it is not the whole picture but it is a true bit of the picture none the less.

When the autumn returned it became time to think of my own return. When I was first asked to come out to Japan with Moses I admit that, like any pathetic addict, I still nourished deep in my heart the dream that Moses and I working together in a new situation could build up a new SSM foundation which, while rooted in the tradition, would bear fresh oriental fruits. As time went on I came to the conclusion that that was not likely to happen. One of the greatest Japanese hobbies is the cultivation of bonsai, those ancient trees that grow for centuries, nourished with love and pride by succeeding generations of a family. The art of bonsai cultivation is to keep the tree alive and healthy while making sure that it never outgrows its little pot, and this you do by lifting it out of the soil at regular intervals and snipping off any new roots that have sprouted below or any tender shoots that have appeared above and replanting it in the enriched ground. The more you love the plant the more careful you are to snip off any fresh growth. I thought that this might be the key to the Japanese SSM. The tradition of Father Kelly and his idea was greatly loved, even venerated by successive generations, and it still retained much of its original appearance though on a much smaller scale, but the way you now demonstrated your love and loyalty was by snipping off any fresh growth or variations which could alter the original shape.

Moses asked me what I would like for my farewell meal; and I chose sukiyaki. This is one of the traditional dishes cooked in a frying pan over a gas ring on the middle of the table. Leeks, mushrooms, tofu, shredded cabbage, Kobe beef are all thrown in and fried up in a sauce of soya and sugar, with fresh materials being added as those sitting around help themselves to what they fancy, dipping each item as they pick it out with their chop sticks into a beaten up raw egg in their individual soup bowls; all this against a steady background of saki, laughter and stories. That is how I like to remember my time in Japan, sitting together around a table sharing food and friendship.

During this year, in my spare time, I had been working on a retreat I was due to give to the sisters at Whitby on my return. This job had helped me to re-align my ideas about the Society and I now no longer thought that 'a still centre' was a good representation of what SSM was all about. I now thought of it as a base or centre for God's sacred mission of compassion and love such as we see that mission depicted in St John's gospel on which my retreat was to be based. So I did attain a little more inner clarity during my time in Japan in that beautiful land amidst these amazing people, and undoubtedly people who over the centuries have built up such wonderful customs of eating together from a common dish and bathing together in a common tub, have much they could teach us about community living.

On my return from Japan there followed some months of inner confusion and a general sense of lostness until one day through the letter-box came a letter from Christian Swayne, another classmate of mine at Trinity College in Toronto, who was now a member of the Order of the Holy Cross (USA) and was working with them out in Ghana where they were trying to build up a seminary where Ghanaians could prepare for the priesthood without leaving their native land. This had become all the more necessary since political instability, poverty and years of drought had made travel abroad far beyond their means. He wanted to know whether I would be willing to join them in this enterprise. As I read Christian's letter, my heart leapt up, the clouds rolled back and I packed my bags for I knew not exactly what.

5

A Ghanaian Tale

One day in Milton Keynes I received a letter from Christian Swayne, an old Trinity classmate of mine, now a member of the Order of the Holy Cross, and stationed in Ghana to where he had recently transported his little flock of novices from Liberia. He filled me in on the bishop's hopes and plans and invited me to come and join them in setting up the college. I could come as Rector, said the bishop, or, if I preferred a less exposed post, as a lecturer. This letter caught me at a propitious time. I had not long returned from a year in Japan with Moses at Kobe Priory, and was having some difficulty in finding a new job, or place in the English province. Edmund, our provincial had suggested that I live and work at the City Centre with the ecumenical team there, living with Liz Macy, but somehow I was not fitting into either the job or the place, and Christian's letter sounded in my ears like an answer to prayer. I counted both Christian and John Ackon personal friends and I had already visited Ghana for six weeks in 1964 when Richard Roseveares SSM was the bishop and Noel Welbourne SSM, his secretary, and I had found that a wonderful visit. I wrote back by return mail and said 'yes' by all means, though due to the collapsed state of Ghana Post the letter only arrived on the very day that my plane was due to land. In fact I was thrilled to go. I felt I would be with friends, doing a job I could do and one I whole-heartedly believed in. I always had got on very well with our Ghanaian students at Kelham although there I felt that we had not done as much for them as we might have done. The shortage of food, the economic collapse, the military regime, all these counted for nothing in my eyes – a little naïve, would you say?

Arriving at Kotoko Airport in Accra, Ghana, March 1983 was a descent into only occasionally contained chaos. There were at least four good reasons for this, of which the first and probably the most intractable was the world economic recession which had hit Ghana very hard. The serious imbalance of payments (they could export little and needed to import much) had swept most of the foreign currency from the country. In effect this meant that anything manufactured outside the country could not be bought with Ghanaian currency and was in any case only available in a few select shops. The result was that in hospitals no medicines or drugs were there to give to the sick, in schools no pencils or note-books to give to the children, in homes no light bulbs or cooking gas and in the shops no items except those manufactured in Ghana. This meant that to gather the material for the smallest task required gargantuan efforts. Getting water for a wash, charcoal for cooking breakfast, food for the table, a bus for work, paper for a letter, a stamp for the envelope, none of the above could be taken for granted; it was necessary to search them out from friends or friends of friends, under the counter, at the side door, all this had to be gone through before you could do your humdrum daily work.

In addition to the economic crisis, the country was in prolonged political torment. Since independence in 1957 there had been a series of coups, all more or less violent as, after the expulsion of Kwame Nkruma, one army general after another seized control of the government only to be shortly ousted by the next. The present incumbent was Major J. J. Rawlins who had already led one successful coup, ruled the country for a space and then handed power back to the elected representatives of the people, only to sack them later for corruption and incompetence and resume, with some bloodshed, dictatorial power for a second time. He was himself at this time a great admirer of Fidel Castro so a pinkish cloud hung above many of his policies such as his promise to clear the University of Cape Coast of its lay-about students and staff and turn the buildings into a holiday camp for the workers, or his promise to free the hospitals from the grip of the medicos and turn them all over to committees made up of the workers, gardeners and patients. At this point he had only just reassumed power and was busy putting down any remnants of opposition that were left.

Within this kaleidoscope of conflicting forces, the Anglican Church, not unexpectedly, was experiencing its own upheavals. Up until recently the whole of Ghana had been included in the one diocese of Accra, but then the diocese of Kumasi had been separated out of it for the Ashanti people, and less than two years before this four new dioceses had been created: Korforidua with Bishop Robert Okine (trained at Kelham in the 1960's) Cape Coast with Bishop John Ackon, Sunyane-Tamale with Bishop Joe Dadson, and Sekondi with Bishop Annobil. These four plus Kumasi with Bishop Arthur, plus the old diocese of Accra with Bishop Thompson (also trained at Kelham), now made up the six very young dioceses of the Anglican Church where six very new bishops were scrambling amidst the political chaos each to establish their own power base, administration and financial independence. The new bishop of Cape Coast, John Ackon was a gentle scholarly man who had prepared for his own ordination through four years of study in England at Kelham Theological College where I had been one of his tutors and, for a time, his chaplain. He now felt that he could best contribute to the building up of the Anglican Church of Ghana from his own little corner by taking the small group of young men whom he had gathered and was preparing for ordination, and who were now living with the boarders at Christ the King Anglican High School in Cape Coast and turning them into St Nicholas Theological College to provide a centre for the study of theology and a training school for ordinands for the whole of Ghana and whole church in West Africa. With this dream in mind, he pricked up his ears when he heard that the Order of the Holy Cross from West Park in New York now wished to move from Liberia where they had been working for the past fifty years and to come into Ghana and set up their novitiate there. The bishop contacted them and promised generous support if they would come to Cape Coast and build their monastery. In return they could help him establish the first Anglican theological college in the country, much as the Society of the Sacred Mission had been behind the establishment of Kelham Theological College many years before. Of the six new bishops, three had been trained at Kelham and one had been a resident there. Thus in their eyes to have an SSM professed brother associated with the new college gave it an authenticity that silenced any potential opposition. What they all were looking for most of all was a place where the men that came to them seeking the priesthood could be prepared within their own culture and tradition for ministry in the villages and cities of Ghana without unreasonable expense. It's true that there was already an ecumenical theological college in Legon in Accra, but there Anglican students were restricted to 10 per cent of the student body (about twelve out of one hundred and twenty), a number irrevocably fixed by the size of the Anglican contribution to the foundation of the college in the first place. Thus the college at Legon could at the most produce four new priests each year, a number that was completely inadequate for the six new expanding dioceses. In addition, the ethos at Legon was an overwhelming combination of Methodist and Presbyterian traditions which made a poor preparation for ministry in a church which had a long solidly entrenched and unquestioned Anglo-Catholic past going back to the monks of Nashdom who had set up a short-lived seminary in Kumasi in the 1920s. 'Is it true,' the students would later ask me, 'that there are churches in England where incense is not used?' Also in Ghana in the 1980s there was not a trace of any money available for the luxury of sending untried men overseas for alternative training in better places.

The final contributing cause to the chaos level at our beginnings was nature itself, or herself. For several years there had been a complete drought so that it was impossible to grow food, and the shops and markets were stripped bare. They used to say, 'A hungry man is an angry man!', well certainly a tense man, and such were the majority of that crowd milling about in the airport that night.

What met me when I came across the tarmac into the terminal were swarms of soldiers in worn out uniforms armed with Kalashnikovs, with only one bulb in ten functioning in the light fixtures which cast a dim religious light over the scene, while the heat seemed almost overwhelming. In fact when I first came down from the plane I thought I must be standing in the path of the jet exhaust, so strong and so muggy was the heat, but no, it was just the Ghanaian norm where the temperature seldom varies from 35-40C night or day, winter or summer. All luggage was dumped randomly over the floor, and each person had to scrabble for their own, and then find a customs officer who, after a perfunctory glance and with the help of a small dash, would mark your bag with blue chalk, after which a horde of small boys descended like a swarm of mosquitoes clambering for a bag to carry.

So that was the welcome: heat, humidity, strange smells, armed soldiers, baggage boys, much pushing and shoving in the semi-darkness, a huddle of stunned arrivals, and an exuberant welcome. And in the light of all these aforesaid disasters, economic, political, ecclesiastical and natural we could have been forgiven for thinking that this was not the most suitable time or the most suitable place to be launching a new venture such as a theological college. But none of us thought that at the time. Ghanaians are not given much to negative thinking. Instead I remembered the story Fr Gregory Wilkins (our former Director) used to tell of the time he too arrived at this very airport in the midst of some previous coup when he met all the same things that we were meeting. As he stood there, baffled and anxious and in his habit, he was slightly alarmed as he noticed a very large and very black young man in combat fatigues, carrying his Kalashnikov at the ready edging up closer and closer to him and leaning over to whisper in his ear. Poor Gregory was expecting to hear, 'White imperialist! Now is the time for our old colonial masters and exploiters of the masses to perish!' But what the young man said was, 'Father, I am a server at the cathedral.' Gregory weakly congratulated him, and moved on. Luckily for me, standing there as helpless and clueless as Gregory, Christian Swayne in Holy Cross habit stepped out of the crowd followed by John Ackon. They rushed me off to the parking lot and the bishop's car as we had to be back at Cape Coast before 10.00pm when the curfew began, after which not a dog could move his tongue – except, of course, the military dogs. We were soon hurtling through the night in the midst of a bevy of ancient cars, all minus headlights, minus windows, minus wings, skilfully weaving back and forth to dodge each other and the enormous pot-holes, known locally as pot-wells – you might well have thought you had got caught up in a stock-car rally. We were stopped three times in the ninety mile trip at police barriers across the road, but, blessed with the presence of a bishop in a white cassock in the front seat, we were speedily waved on.

We arrived in Cape Coast within ten minutes of the curfew at 10.00pm, to find all the streets empty and deserted. We dropped the bishop at his home and raced out to Akotakyre on the edge of town where the Holy Cross brothers and novices, six of them, were living in the servants' quarters of a well-to-do house. The brothers Vincent, Timothy, Thomas, Boniface, Charles, and Emmanuel, were all sitting in the garden in shorts and T-shirts and gave us a great welcome. 'Akwaba, Akwaba' was heard on every side but later when Christian and I retired to the room we shared and he asked me how long I would be able to stay with them, I was flummoxed. Would I be able to stand life in the tropics, beginning at 53, living on their meagre diet, with the country trembling on the verge of armed rebellion? Was I capable of giving an adequate theological training to these men, knowing in my heart, as I did that I was not a high powered academic, and neither was Christian – Sunday School teachers, gospel preachers maybe, but not professors. Would the OHC venture into African monasticism survive even? Would SSM agree for me to stay out here for a lengthy period? Such questions and many others hovered above my head like so many flies and mosquitoes so all I said was, 'Let's leave that one open-ended for now. We can see how things develop.' I was unwilling to make any big commitment to such a frail and fragile venture!

Next morning with a blazing sun rising in the clear blue sky everything looked more cheerful. We were all up by 5.30 and said Matins sitting on garden chairs in the only open space provided in the house, part kitchen, part dining space where we breakfasted on black tea and boiled rice. Later Christian took me into town to be formally greeted by the bishop and to meet the students, all twelve of them. They were at the end of their second term in their first year. Christian on Old Testament and the bishop on canon law had been giving them some classes, and they attended three sessions a week at the university where two friendly lecturers on African traditional religion and philosophy had allowed them to sit in on their classes. They also went once a week to the St Peter's Seminary up the road for some classes on Canon Law (Roman Catholic – that is!). That day Christian exhorted them all to be in good spirits, but that was unnecessary. They were in the best of spirits already. They were about to leave next day for their Easter break. They had an assured place in a college, no matter how tin-pot, Mickey Mouse or ad-hoc that college might be it was a college that led to ordination to the priesthood and now it had its own Rector and so looked even more feasible in their eyes. These were opportunities they had never had before and to which there were for them no alternatives, a chance to study, a chance to be a priest and have a life that was universally respected. So, there were many smiles, many more 'akwaba's and much laughter to welcome me into their midst.

When the men returned from their Easter holiday, we began in earnest to prepare the foundations of our new college of St Nicholas, but our starting point in fact was a long way behind the starting line. We had no buildings, no library, no text books, tables, chairs, stationery, no kitchen, and like everyone else in Ghana that year, very little food. We couldn't expect much if any support from the local people. We were living in a bankrupt world where it was a hard struggle to provide sufficient food for one's own family with no left overs. We had twelve men who had for two terms been living in the boarders' accommodation in the Anglican High School. Each man had brought with him his Bible, Prayer Book (1662) bound up with Hymns Ancient and Modern – Standard Edition, his mosquito net, and a bucket in which to wash himself and his clothes and nothing else. They also brought a great enthusiasm to press on with their studies regardless of how spartan the accommodation seemed in my eyes. There was never a word of complaint, on the contrary they felt they were the lucky ones for whom an unexpected door of opportunity had opened. Yet even so, as the food dished out at dinner time continued to shrink in quantity and increase in price, it soon became clear that we would not be able to keep open until the end of term, the students were starving and, along with several other institutions in Cape Coast, we sent everyone home one month early to find their own food as best they could. Meanwhile at Holy Cross, Br Boniface, a Muslim convert to Christianity, from the north, and a wheeler-dealer by nature from his mother's womb spent his whole time cruising the countryside searching for diesel for the vehicle and rice, cassava, dried fish, and garden eggs (i.e. aubergines) for the brothers.

Our first term was thus a short one, but there were still big decisions to be made in it regarding our future. One question to be resolved was on the matter of enrolment. Should we continue with the present twelve students for another two years and then, when they had completed their course send them out and take on the next class or should we add a new class in October and again in the following year until we had a three year college curriculum? The bishop favoured the former but Christian and I the latter and we prevailed so that before the term broke up, still in temporary accommodation, we were busy interviewing hopefuls and by the end we had gathered a second class of nine new students for October.

The longer break also gave me a bit of extra time to consider what I would teach when they all returned. I realised of course, that the lectures I had prepared and used at Kelham were not appropriate here. While all the men were fluent in spoken English, English was their second language and they found any technical theological vocabulary, not to say jargon, tripped them up, though later on I noticed that some of them showed a remarkable skill at mastering theological jargon as a kind of third language and learned to use it with some effect! Fortunately for me at the time, Margaret Dewey who was the librarian at Willen made me aware of SPCK's Library of Theology. This series covered a wide range of subjects and was written specifically for students such as ours all over the third world. In fact it tried to relate the subject under scrutiny to third world problems and also contained a number of excellent photographs; in other words the books were attractive.

I took this series as my basic text and with this help we began to work our way through the main books of the Bible. This series continued to meet most of our academic needs for many years and as money became more available we provided the students with copies to take home with them.

A further delay came in the September of that year, when I had to return to Toronto to take a retreat for the SSJD sisters which I had promised to do long before I had ever heard of the existence of St Nicholas Cape Coast. I took the opportunity while in Canada to lay in as many supplies of cutlery, plates, kettles and food as I could manage to carry in my luggage. When I got back to Ghana I found that the bishop had been busy and had managed to find us a house. He had rented a large house on the edge of town, overlooking a large lagoon where fishermen cast their nets all the day long, and beyond that was a fringe of palms bordering the south Atlantic and facing towards the South Pole. The house had about fourteen rooms, a large open garage-like space behind it, a row of three smaller rooms(servants' quarters), at the side and a good-sized though rather dilapidated annexe across the small courtyard. This would provide ample room for us, the only snag being that it was at present occupied by three families. Fortunately the family in the servants' quarters moved out almost at once so that I was able to take up residence there and the students then moved their beds from their former accommodation into the annexe. On the day we moved in Auntie Ekuwa also arrived, found for us by Bishop Ackon, complete with two large cooking kettles such as missionaries are boiled in, in *New Yorker* cartoon style, plus a wooden paddle. These with three stones set up in a corner of the courtyard as a tripod for the kettle, and a bit of firewood were all the equipment she required or asked for, and with that she went on to cook three meals a day for a college of around about thirty men for the next twenty-five years, though later we did provide her corner with a roof of thatch to keep her dry and a water barrel. What a treasure she was with no tantrums no cheating, a valued member of the community who got on well with both staff and students.

Right from day one we laid out the pattern of the day as we meant to go on. The model in the forefront of my mind was the one I had known and loved at Kelham Theological College for the sixteen years I was there, and in that sense St Nicholas was a direct child of Kelham. We began each day with Morning Prayer sung at 6.00am, followed by Mass, then by breakfast. The rest of the morning was then given over to classes until dinner at midday. The afternoons were for private study, or work around the grounds or for the washing of clothes which went on without ceasing. Evening Prayer came at 6.00pm, followed by supper. All the services were sung and sung vigorously with two or three hymns from Ancient and Modern since no Ghanaian could conceive of any worship without a generous sprinkling of hymnody. At first both classes and worship were in the garage space, but this brought the unexpected blessing of encouraging the two remaining families to find alternative accommodation. Apparently they didn't like living as an adjunct to the church!

Once we moved into the new house, the first problem that faced us was finance. How were we going to pay for it all? Each diocese paid fees for the students it sent to us but these were hardly sufficient to cover the rent for the house. There were a series of local fund-raising events but these were perhaps more effective in raising our spirits than in raising cash.

What made the college viable in those early days was the support and help we received from friends overseas in addition to what we could raise in Ghana. I had already placed an appeal in the SSM newsletter asking for anyone who would like to sponsor a student. We reckoned that for £300.00 we could cover the boarding and tuition costs of one student for a year, and the money could be sent to our priory bursar, Br Bert at Willen. We had a good response to this from individuals and parishes from as far away as St Catherine's Ontario where friends of mine, Bill and Marian Blott were in the parish of the Transfiguration, and then through Fr Moses from the St Michael's International School in Kobe as well as the Diocese of Oxford in England.

The Order of the Holy Cross had undertaken to provide us with a library free of charge, or, more accurately Fr Bonnell

Spencer OHC had taken this on as his project, writing around to his many contacts in the world of colleges and seminaries in the USA begging for books. These large parcels of books had begun to arrive by October and Fr Spencer (known to us as Bonnie) was himself in place in a frenzy of cataloguing and setting up the library so he would himself be ready when term opened to begin lecturing in Church History, and all this when he was far advanced into his 60's! Later on when we had the opportunity of purchasing the house for £65, 000 SSM contributed half the price and the other half was met by a grant from Anglicans in Mission (A. I. M.) the outreach work of the Anglican Church in Canada where John Rye was at the desk, an old college friend of both Christian's and mine. There were many other ways over the years, too numerous to count, whereby we received interest, sympathy, and financial support from all over the Anglican world from those who had faith in Africa and in its young people.

Of course the money was indispensable, but more basic to the whole enterprise was the people who came to make up the teaching community. Christian and Bishop John Ackon had been doing much of the teaching before I arrived and Christian continued until he was transferred to Kumasi. OHC also contributed Fr Bonnell Spencer to gather and then preside over the library and to lead church history classes. Later on Fr Nicholas was with us for a year, and Vincent Shamo, Boniface Adams and Leonard Abba, all OHC and all enrolled as students, played a big part from within the student body. On the local scene, the students went once a week to the University of Cape Coast (only about half an hour away) to receive lectures from Mr Anti on African Traditional Religion, West African church history and comparative religion. From these they returned complaining of the treatment they had of old received from the missionaries who had treated Africans as a 'tabula rasa', on which to write their various messages. It is not impossible that some traces of such missionary attitudes might still have lingered on, even at St Nicholas! They also attended Dr Ansah on philosophy and ethics. Once a week too they hiked up to St Peter's seminary where they joined the students in classes on canon law, the only fruit of which I ever perceived was the bandying about of the phrase 'motu proprio' at frequent inappropriate intervals in our daily routine. More effective were the games of soccer we had with the seminary from time to time though I am afraid we seldom were victorious, nevertheless the building up of links of friendship between two groups of men who would frequently find themselves neighbours in later life was an inestimable benefit. Then there came from overseas long series of people who paid their own way out and back, received a pittance for spending money, kept the time-table of classes adequately filled, and the administrative machinery well oiled. Michael Rawson during his gap year, which he stretched to two, was of exceptional help in organising our office and Nicholas Hammersley followed after him as driver and was also a great help and companion to me. Fr Murray Belway a college mate of Christian and me came and lectured as often as he could obtain Leave of Absence from his High School in Pembroke Ontario, and has now in fact retired in Ghana. Sister Jean came from the Order of St Helena and lectured in New Testament and Liturgics, Fr Cecil King who had been working for the SPCK in Zambia and was an omni-competent who was ready and able to plug any holes in the academic programme, Fr Daniel Allotey, a priest of the diocese of Cape Coast, and later to be the College Rector and later still the bishop of Cape Coast lectured regularly all through these years and helped us in many other ways with his advice and support.

All the above persons made up a frequently changing but generally harmonious and friendly community at the centre of our life which provided support for the ex-pats and for me and gave the college life some stability and forward movement. When the students turned up they found a group of slightly, or even much, older people in place, all of whom had had some experience of life and education overseas in a variety of places and who were all committed to Africa and its church.

The downside of this was the question we often asked ourselves of what sort of academic standard did we actually reach? It certainly wasn't near university level but then neither was it completely elementary even though we did put it all together as we went along. The students arrived from a very patchy primary and secondary school education, all of them having been at school during the times of the political upheavals and then English was a second, if not third, language for all of them, so that most of them had a hard struggle fitting into the routine of note-taking and research and essay writing. On the other side we staff were recruited from those who were available at the time and we all taught whatever we knew best in the ways to which we were accustomed. We set our own exams, marked them, and made our own judgements. It was all rather amateurish on our part, but in every case the bishop concerned had already made up his mind to ordain the man before he sent him, we were just to do what we could – which we did. I only remember once in seven years when we asked a student to leave because he failed every exam set and appeared to us to be uneducable, but for this great was the wrath of the bishop against us. We had humiliated the man before his family and in the face of his diocese. I was greatly helped by an old saying, 'If a job is worth doing, it is worth doing badly' i.e. even if you can't do it perfectly you should still make an imperfect effort. I also had much in mind the Kelham system which I had known in the UK. There men were prepared for the priesthood not just by academic study; that was considered to be only one third of the whole. They were also trained by living the common life – by worshipping together in a disciplined way in the chapel where everyone had his assigned role, by working together in small teams in the garden, the house, on the football pitch and as a result of this process carried on over several years they often succeeded in knocking the rougher corners off one another. That Kelham system, which goes back to Fr Kelly our SSM founder, we did manage in an outlandish way to reproduce at St Nicholas and we found that to a certain degree it worked there. Hence it also follows that in telling the story of the college, we must consider what happened outside the classroom. What we did, what happened to us, is as important as what we studied.

Ralph's Log
Our friends and supporters in the Cathedral congregation organised a 'Service of Song' to raise some money for the

college. These services of song are very popular here. They work by assembling a variety of local choirs: the Mothers Union, the Shepherds, the Sacred Heart, the Anglican Women's Fellowship, the Methodist and R. C. churches, even the prison has its choir. When assembled one choir after another stands up randomly and begins to sing some local song or chorus, always in Fante (the local language), accompanied by drums and percussion, with a heavy rhythm. This just sets all feet a-twitching and a-dancing, so everyone surges out into the aisles to sing and dance their way up to the large basket set on the chancel steps where they throw in their contribution. Everyone comes prepared with a pocket full of the smallest coins so as to be able to dance up that aisle again and again. This is indeed worship as recreation! However, on one occasion, just minutes before the service began, all lights went out – one of the effects of prolonged drought was the reduction of the water level in the Akosombo Dam to an all-time low, making electricity cuts very frequent and unpredictable. While a first-world congregation in such a crisis might have simply packed up and gone home in clouds of righteous rage or deep depression, these people were completely un-phased. Two candles were speedily produced and set up by the collection baskets and everything went ahead as planned; after all everyone knew a hundred or more choruses by heart and no books were necessary. It was an unforgettable sight, that large and murky cathedral, with drums throbbing, the huge congregation filling the air with their lilting melodies and accompanying the songs with their rhythmic steps, apparently without a care in the world. It was a religion which set us free, while God the Father from the mural above the chancel arch, benignly looked down, larger than life, peering out of the shadows with his hands raised in blessing – or was it surrender? A wonderful occasion.

One morning I sallied forth with my pockets stuffed with the money Marian Blott sent me to buy some furniture for the college so that we would be ready for our students in the new term in October. I reckoned that pretty basic for any student would be a desk on which to write, a chair on which to sit. I took Br Boniface with me as interpreter and market-mentor, and at the side of the road into town we saw a carpenter hard at work outside his two room house under a spreading mango tree, with some of his workmanship scattered around, chairs, tables and plain coffins – not the elaborate ones in favour with many here, made to look like a formula one racing car or a large whale. Therefore we felt this must be a sensible man and he greeted us from his bench in shirt and shorts with a big grin as we told him what we wanted. No problem as long as we could pay a deposit to enable him to buy some wood. So, the deposit paid, he promised to have 24 desks and 24 chairs ready by September (and they were!). That was a good start.

———•—

Sometime later in the year Fr Bonell Spencer OHC joined us to build up our library out of all the books he had solicited from various seminaries in the USA. At that time he wrote the following hymn for us that we sang at all graduations and other big ceremonies to a tune from Ancient & Modern:

As we assemble
  We may fear and tremble
  That we, unworthy, seek the priestly life,
  With you beside us
  Nicholas to guide us,
  May God uphold us in that holy strife.

Lord we adore you
  And we now implore you
  To give us wisdom and that wisdom's grace,
  That we may know you and may always show you
  To be the Saviour of the human race.

Give us compassion and our lives so fashion
  That we may serve you in all those who need;
  Bind up the wounded,

Comfort those confounded,
Absolve the sinner and the hungry feed.

To church and nation, now the revelation
Of your true kingdom may we clearly give;
That we may serve you
And may all deserve you
And in your presence may forever live.

Christian, whom the bishop appointed Provost of the Cathedral a few months ago, was made Regional Co-ordinator for the Council of Churches Relief Programme, as the plan was to distribute food sent in for the relief of famine, through the churches. Christian was very cheered to find that this was the first region in the country to begin distribution. Mostly rice, oil, and dried fish, but it was wonderfully encouraging to know that Christians in Canada and the US knew of our plight and were trying to do something. The actual distributions were done from trucks sent by the Christian Council, and around them raged many scenes of bitter recriminations, scrambles, and fist-shaking. The saying 'a hungry man is an angry man' was borne out every day. We in the priory were nearly all able-bodied people and so never actually went to bed hungry but on a diet of almost entirely rice, dried fish, and a few aubergines, we were constantly on the lookout for something to eat! Those who suffer most were those who could not get out and scramble for themselves and push to the head of every queue, for example, the old and infirm and the prisoners in the jails who were at the bottom of every pecking order. If there was not enough to go around, these were the ones whose plates remained empty, and many old people and some prisoners were dying of malnutrition every day.

A letter from Christian Swayne to Bill Blott of St Catherine's Ontario read: "What we are doing here is as much crazy as creative, but I guess that's normal for anything creative. We stagger from crisis to crisis but somehow we manage – but only just. As an example, we have been living about five miles out of the city centre, but yesterday we moved into town to a former convent, and that very day gas oil (diesel fuel) in the city ran out, but no problem because we can now walk to work as it is nearby. It looks like we will definitely get our house for the seminary – possession is likely in about fourteen days before the students arrive, so we are still in business."

I've just been made Regional Co-ordinator for the Council of Churches Relief Programme which has been driving me a bit wild but we are managing and we are (here I am boasting!) the first region in the nation to actually begin food distribution. We got organised within five days of notification of the programme – a miracle in Ghana today. My 'thing' is based on the feeding of the 5, 000. If you start with what is at hand, miracles will happen. We began feeding local prisoners in Cape Coast prison (at the parish's expense!) and within a month we are now distributing, for Christian Council Relief, for all the prisons in the Central Region. I don't know that we need the headache but it does prove that God will provide. The Relief Aid is still, of course, hopelessly inadequate but it gives people hope and that is as important as food really. People die of despair as often as of actual starvation. It's wonderfully encouraging to our people here when I can show them that Christians like you in Canada are ready and willing to send help. It's not the amount of aid that comes but the hope it brings. Things are bad but not desperate yet, but it goes on and on until people give up trying. On the other hand the jollies are great. The people are wonderful, and the Gospel here is still clearly Good News. In fact that is my chief delight. I (as a comfortable Canadian) never really understood the Good News concept before. It seemed a poor offer that what the poor were given was 'good news' preached to them. But here THAT is exactly what they want.

Funerals loomed large in the life of every Ghanaian and the obligation to attend services stretching over two days extended to cousins, in-laws, clients, customers unto the furthest margins of the person's connections. It was the established custom in times past that the corpse was brought home from the government refrigerator on Thursday night to be laid in state for the all-night wake. There was a procession to the Cathedral on Friday morning where it was common to see five or six coffins lined up at the chancel step. The full choir was in attendance, every pew was jammed with friends, and a High Requiem Mass was sung. These elaborate rituals were partly an expression of grief for the departed, but they were also a measure of the value that that departed life had had in society, and perhaps most of all the ceremonies indicated the status of the family, their position and accomplishments. If you did not attend other people's funerals, no one would be present at yours, except maybe an illiterate catechist to read the service, and that would be a shame and a disgrace to you and your family which you would never get over, no not until the end of eternity. Therefore even if you felt no great love for the departed, family pride compelled you to put on the best possible funeral.

When Mass is finished the congregation stands in silence while the organist plays the Dead March from Saul. Once the organist had only played the first two pages when suddenly the power failed, the lights went out and the organ died. Without missing a single beat the one thousand strong congregation picked up the melody and harmonies and hummed the rest of the music through to the end, and not a bar was omitted. They then process out, usually singing the Christian's Goodnight which starts 'Sleep on beloved/ Sleep and take thy rest/ Lay down thy head upon the Saviour's breast/ We loved thee well/ But Jesus loves thee best/ Goodnight, goodnight, goodnight' and goes on for another seven similar verses. They then disperse to various cemeteries, and return to the family home for the feast; no sandwiches and biscuits this, but a big beef stew with four or five vegetables, rice and potatoes, and a big pudding. This goes on until it is time for weary folks to go home for supper. Funerals are thus an all day, even a two day affair.

———•———

We drove in the OHC pick-up today from Cape Coast to Bolgatanga, right from the coast up to within a few miles of the northern border with Burkina Faso. We left at 4.30 a. m. as soon as the curfew was finished and we could get through the police barrier on the edge of town. There is a direct road from Cape Coast to Kumasi but that has been unusable for some years so we had to drive up to Accra and take the Kumasi road from there, like driving round two sides of a triangle to get to your destination. The road is crowded but paved and not too bad up to Kumasi, but from there it is unpaved and ground into fine red dust by the enormous transport lorries passing up and down from the coast to the north. I saw one with the sign 'Give Peace a Chance' in lurid letters and another said 'Fear Woman'. These lorries have pounded the dust into undulating shapes like the waves of the ocean, and after an hour you are coated in fine red dust. Boniface was the driver and we took Br Charles OHC and Mavis a university student who wants to join the Sisters at Bolga. There were frequent road blocks all along the way and we were met on each occasion by young, good looking and broadly smiling policemen in tattered uniforms and rattling their collection boxes while pointing out the big sign they had erected 'Merry Xmas'. If we told them we had already used up all our spare change, they asked us if we had any rosaries for them. It is said, and I partly believe it, that you can measure how long anyone has been in Ghana by measuring how far they move from the car when we stop for a pit stop across the desert. The newcomers are the shyest and try to get far from the car and behind a shrub, while the old timers and the locals just step over the ditch. 'What's the problem? A back is as good as a mountain!' they say. I was still one of the shy ones.

As there is almost no petrol or diesel north of Kumasi we had to carry a big drum of diesel on the back for which we had to get a Police Permit, and stop from time to time to top up our tank. The road from Tamale to Bolga (another 100 miles) was at one time paved but is now so potholed and broken up that it is dangerous to drive especially after dark as it was by the time we got there. Then to add to the risk many vehicles were minus one or two headlights, and most were dangerously overloaded. We finally arrived at about 9.30 p. m. exhausted and dirty. Here three Order of the Holy Paraclete nuns from Whitby in Yorkshire, Dorothy

Stella, Moira, and Patricia, teach in a Vocational Technical School and have developed a Women's Centre where they try to do for women on a residential basis what we try to do for students' wives on a weekend. We received a great welcome and nice food. It is a completely different country from down at the coast, flat savannah with few shrubs, round huts of mud bricks with thatched roof, the crying of guinea fowl and the bleating goats. The temperature is between 40-45C all day with no air conditioning. The purpose of our trip was for me to lead a retreat for the Sisters and take part in a refresher course for lay clergy. Mavis was to spend some time with the sisters and this is also home to both Boniface and Charles.

Because they have lived with drought for about ten years the Akosombo Dam which is the main source of electricity in Ghana is now so low that they can't always produce the necessary power any more. We have electricity from 9.00-12.00 each morning and 6.00-9.00 each evening. This is not such a hardship for us as we cook on wood, but it also means that the pumps which pump water through the town can't keep up the pressure, so most days our water taps give us nothing but a low throaty gurgle. This reduced me last week to going to the Water & Sewerage Board and pleading for a tanker of water. This they kindly sent us and prompted by the students I was careful to slip into the driver's open hand a hefty dash so he would want to come back. Later on I had to slip a dash to the carpenters who are finishing the flat for which the family now living in the ground floor of our premises are waiting. The carpenters promised to finish their work forthwith and let us know, so that we will be able to move the family out and have the whole place to ourselves.

———•·•———

I now feel I have made advances in that most essential of Ghanaian arts – how to pass a bribe (dash). It has to be done completely unselfconsciously and as discreetly as possible. It is merely the exchange of a small token of goodwill between equal friends, so there must be no trace of condescension on the one part or of subservience on the other. It is done with confident smiles, and sealed with a casual farewell handshake. Goodness knows they all need a few extras to feed their families on their starvation wages.

However, though life here is endless hassle, I still enjoy the people enormously. The students for example have a completely different attitude to authority from what prevailed at Kelham where it was almost a coming of age rite for a student to stage a little rebellion and take a round out of the tutor in class, or at least indicate he was not impressed with your performance. Here the prevailing mood is to demonstrate your loyalty to the one in charge. They just seem to cohere more naturally as a band of brothers.

At first when I came I always swept and cleaned my own room, but this they found very upsetting and disturbing and insisted that this was their job – my job was a different one. Similarly I started washing my own clothes, until one of the senior students came and told me 'You are the father here, you have a house full of children, it is not right for you to wash your clothes' and he went on to finish my washing himself. But they are also very serious students, they are eager to learn, and feel they are privileged to be here, and every lesson is peppered with questions. The perfect spot for anyone who loves to teach.

These nights have been without electricity since the town transformer was struck by lightning three weeks ago so we tend to go to bed early, but last night not long after I had blown out my lantern and laid down, I felt an ant walking up my neck towards my face. I wiped him out, but immediately there was another then two or three. By this time I was somewhat alarmed and lit the lantern to see what looked like a sheet of black velvet slipping under the bottom panes of the window and down the wall towards my bed, 10, 000 x 10, 000 of them with a single mind and all moving as one. In a panic I rushed upstairs to wake up Fred and Solomon who came back with me. Solomon said "What these boys don't like is kerosene" and they proceeded to tip up my lantern and theirs and sprinkle it all over the floor. This did indeed seem to paralyse them, and when a broom had been fetched, they were soon swept out of the door. I spent the rest of the night sleeping in the library!

———•·•———

Dealing with Ghana Post is always problematical and requires a lot of patience and wit. At long last, after a delay of about six months, a series of so-called puffy envelopes began to trickle in, sent by Bill and Marian Blott and their friends and containing such things as plant fertiliser, lengths of plaid polyester, needles, pens, writing paper and envelopes, and all very much needed and unobtainable here. Then came the big controversy with the Post Office in town who claimed that 270 cedis were due for each packet as customs duty. The cedi is more a notional than an actual value. The official rate of exchange is 35 to the US dollar, but if you go to the so-called 'second window' you can get 135 to the US dollar. An average days wage is about 15 cedis and an egg sells for 12 cedis My salary which is top of the range is 1000 cedis per month, but all vary widely from day to day. Nevertheless 270 cedis is a sizeable sum and there were going to be a series of these packets, so I began a long controversy with the Post Office, using students as my intermediaries to avoid any confrontation. My opening salvo was to say I wouldn't take them. They could keep them. But by this time the students were very involved, eager for the contents of the parcels, and absorbed in the contest of haggling the price. They trailed back and forth between innumerable postal officials and the college at least five times, and finally grudgingly agreed to accept the parcels if they (the P. O. officials) would beat down the price. This they were willing to do and said we could have them for 70 cedis. All were happy and they brought home the parcels.

This was a happier experience on the whole than that of an Englishman we heard of who went to the Cape Coast P. O. hoping to send a telegram to the U. K. After filling out all the forms and paying the fee he asked when he could expect the telegram to be delivered. 'That is very difficult to say, sir' said the girl behind the counter 'you see, it all depends on when we can find a car going up to Accra to take it to our Head Office'.

———•◦•———

Living in an African culture is so very different from anything I have known up to now in Canada, England, or Japan, and I must say in spite of political instability, desperate food shortages, and the frequent collapse of social services, already I find it very attractive. After growing up in western society, it is heartening to live in a place where belief in God is axiomatic, taken for granted, not at all exceptional, where every lorry, taxi and trotro (as they call the little lorries that go to and fro around the town), bears some motto such as 'Glory, by his grace, Jesus never fails', where you pass on the street the 'Come Unto Me All You Who Are Heavy-laden' barber shop. You can be a Christian, a Muslim, a traditional worshipper, but words like atheist and agnostic are not known. Here people are warm-hearted and open and full of life, here the person matters more than any rule or regulation. 'Are you really a friend of my neighbour's uncle?' says the policeman at the road barrier, 'Pass on, sir, pass on.' Here taxis and buses often carry the motto 'God's Time is Best' because they operate on a timetable not devised by bureaucrats or accessible to mortals but known to God alone. They start when they are full, stop when anyone wants to alight, and arrive when everyone's demands have been met. They seem to have reverse notions of authority and authority figures, maybe not universally, but certainly here at St. Nicholas the authority figure is seen as paternal and usually benevolent, he is to be cared for and not revolted against, loved not defied. And as a result the attitude of the students is very different from what I experienced at Kelham. This place for these men is their only chance of receiving any theological training and preparation for the priesthood, so they come here filled with enthusiasm and gratitude, expecting to soak up all the information they can and all they will need to run a parish. All of which makes them a joy to be with. 'Akwaba Akwaba' *welcome* is the word you hear most often if you are a foreigner.

———•◦•———

The father of one of the students, a fisherman from a village not far up the coast, has been drowned and the student has asked me to take the funeral, so today found me with a large crowd of students in a bare and poorly lit chapel not far from the sea-shore with the students singing a requiem mass crowded around the coffin. All the families there were fisher-folk and their poverty was outstanding and moving to behold. After mass we carried the coffin about a mile further along the shore to where they had a cemetery. At one point on the way, we stopped to pour libation and one of the elders held forth at great length and with great passion. When I asked the student next to me what he was saying, he said that this was apparently the third death from drowning from this village in the last twelve months. The elder as he poured out the libation was pleading with the ancestors, 'Please tell us what we are doing which so displeases you, what is our sin? If you show us what it is, we will correct it and will live according to your wishes.' Nothing here happens by chance or without reason, and the most common cause of disaster is malevolence – the hatred or jealousy, usually of some neighbour or family member who put the evil eye on you but, failing all else, it can be attributable to the anger of the ancestors somehow provoked against this small band of vulnerable struggling people. This was the case here. It is all very sad.

Since September we have had three classes underway, thirty-two students in all, so up to full strength. We have been greatly blessed with rain this year so that there is much more food available in the market than last year, though it remains very expensive. Still, feeding the students has not been as troublesome this year as I had feared it would be, just the usual and traditional daily crises: 'We have run out of firewood. There is no fish. The beans are full of mites and unusable'. A friend once told me that there were two words for which no equivalent existed in any known African language. One was 'forward planning' and the other was 'maintenance'!

We are now hoping that the owner of this house might be willing to sell it to us if we pay in hard currency, which we would be able to do. When that happens the next step would be to build a couple of extra classrooms plus a couple of staff bungalows which would make this a viable unit. Meanwhile we have bought some benches for chapel and a dining table from our friend the carpenter and have set up a permanent chapel. We also got the carpenter to make some lockers for the students and one man is busy making additional mattresses for us out of grass stuffed into some corn sacks I bought in the market.

The chapel is just a plaster hut with a tin roof, no glass in the windows, but everything inside is done with great enthusiasm and earnestness. These days we always get a number of people from the neighbourhood drawn in by the sound of drums and singing. There are usually ten or so small children under ten, unaccompanied, partially clothed, hand-in-hand, leading one another on, who struggle in at odd times, genuflect in wobbly fashion, sketch out a rough sign of the cross, and hoist themselves up onto a bench where they sit solemn and silent, dusty legs swinging throughout. Nor do the students find anything to remark on in all this – that's Africa!

One lady came up to me after Mass a couple of days ago with an eighteen-month old baby strapped on her back, and asked if I would bless it. When I enquired whether the baby was sick, she said 'Well, she drank some kerosene a couple of days ago and has been weakly and fretful ever since' So I fell to and sprinkled and blessed with vigour, since when the baby has looked fine. This woman like most, I suspect, has no money for medicines and not much trust in doctors, but holy water – that is something she knows and usually gets good results from its consumption or application. I think it takes the place of most of the aspirin, tranquilisers, revitalisers, sold over the counter in our drug stores.

Brother Emmanuel is one of the young brothers at Holy Cross. He has been a stable novice there for a year or two and is due to take his temporary vows this year some time. He is also a nice person and a valuable part of the Holy Cross team that goes around visiting schools in the Central Region. However an unexpected surprise came Christian's way this week when a nice-looking young woman from Accra with two small children showed up in his office and introduced herself: 'I am Emanuel's wife and I want to know when you are going to send him home to help me raise these kids of his.' So – another monastic vocation bites the dust!

What interests me is that Emmanuel all this year never appeared to be aware of any trace of incongruity or discrepancy, let alone sinfulness in his double life-style. He has thrown himself into the life and work of the monastery with enthusiasm. I imagine that if he was questioned on this subject he would in justification cite a good number of his elders and betters who live in a not dissimilar fashion without any public outcry. After all it is not so different from polygamy where a man is part of two or more separate households and as long as the different segments of his life don't meet, or at least don't clash, all goes along harmoniously enough. Then too, while polygamy is deeply embedded in nearly all African cultures, life-long celibacy is pretty well unknown.

I sometime wonder if the requirement for Christians either to live in celibacy or in life-long faithfulness to one partner does not seem as strange, as unnatural, as perplexing to these people as if we were to tell them that a person was not allowed to urinate as long as they wished to be a Christian. I wonder if that is a bit like what they feel, but I will never know what they feel as there is a very strong taboo against discussing all such matters with anyone except with your own age group and never, ever across the generations; which I think is a pity. Fortunately all our students here are either married or engaged to be married and so celibacy is not so much an issue.

———————

Last Sunday I went with the OHC brothers to a village not far from here where they are conducting a mission. When we arrived at the village the first thing we had to do was pay a courtesy call on the chief and be introduced to him by the priest of the parish. We found him sitting in his quite humble compound flanked by all the big men of the tribe, with his feet on a stool, for they must never touch the ground. We were introduced one by one and went forward to shake his hand, and then there was a speech made for the chief by the linguist, for the chief himself never speaks directly to the people, and thus they avoid all disgruntlement or resistance to what has been said. At least should any anger or blame arise it is directed towards the linguist who has said the words, while the chief looks on like our own dear Queen. The chief is a man of great natural dignity, and very much in charge of the situation. When this mutual greeting was over we adjourned to the church and began Mass. When we had been at it about an hour (i.e. after the sermon!) the chief's throne appeared, carried down the aisle on the head of a henchman, followed by his entourage who took their places on the front row. Then came the chief himself under an umbrella, and loaded down with gold rings, armbands, a golden crown, and wearing a magnificent cloth. What a spectacle! He sat in state on his throne until we came to the dancing-up-for-the-collection hymns, and then after everyone else, he himself went to the back of the church and danced up the aisle without the slightest loss of dignity or poise. When he got as far as the brass band he tossed down a couple of large notes which drove them on to fresh and greater frenzies, and then on to the church's collection basket where an even larger donation was tossed down, amidst much singing and ululating. After that, the Consecration was a bit of an anti-climax. The congregation are so grateful to have the support of the chief that everything else becomes less significant.

We are just in the process of building a new kitchen, or rather improving the old one, by walling in that corner of the courtyard where the kitchen fire is. The students have made a good supply of mud bricks and baked them in the sun until they are hard enough for the wall, and then they smear the completed wall with mud and dung mixed together which gives a hard plaster finish. We are hoping to get some thatching straw to make a waterproof roof. That should please Auntie Ekuwa. It's called self-help!

Here western style pills and visits to the doctor tend to be beyond the price range of most people so for the most basic aches and pains they depend a lot on holy water in which they have great faith and from which they get good results either by swallowing it, rubbing it on, or sprinkling it over themselves or the house. In more serious cases they will search in the bush for a herbalist or someone good with charms and spells, though even such a person is not free. They will always ask for at least a cock, maybe even a goat, for sacrifice. If you should have to go to the hospital, you will need to take with you whatever sheets and food you want, and some member of the family to prepare food and to purchase beforehand whatever medication the doctor has suggested. The result is that whenever you visit the hospital you see cluttered around most beds little groups of family members chatting, with an assortment of pots and pans used or half-used all over the floor. Apart from the need for nursing care most people would probably feel that the worst thing that could ever happen to you was to be left alone, especially if you are not well. 'Everyone needs company.'

One of the students cut his chin open last week playing football on cinder grounds. He had to go to hospital to get it closed, but I had to provide the sticking plaster before the nurses could dress it for him.

September 1985

Today Br Boniface took me in the van down to the market in Mankesim to see if we could buy some large sacks of corn, beans and rice in readiness for the return of the students next week. That way we could have some food in store and not have to live from hand to mouth as we did last year. Mankesim market is quite large, very busy, and noisy and dusty, and always swarming with buyers and sellers, a real hub of life! As soon as we drew up Boniface said to me 'Now you stay in the van. That white face of yours will double the price of anything we want to buy'. So I slunk back in the seat and watched him from afar. He was soon engaged with two enormous and very black market women of traditional build each one with an old bit of sacking for an apron, and both much bigger than Boniface. There appeared to be much shouting and shaking of heads, waving of arms and bursts of shrill laughter. Once, if not twice Boniface made as if to walk away in disgust at their exorbitant demands, only to be waved back into the fray when he had gone a few steps. It was a lengthy process but eventually a deal was struck and Boniface tipped a couple of market boys to carry three enormous bulging sacks and dump them in the back of the van. When he got back inside I asked him 'What were those women saying in all that palaver?' He replied, 'They kept saying, "You are trying to bully us just because you are a man and we are poor weak women"'. I couldn't help but laugh, as Boniface did; it was like trying to bully a pair of elephants.

----·-----

09.11.85.

The main news today is that thanks in part to Bishop John Ackon's intercessions with the owner we have managed to buy this property. We paid £65,000 which is what made it so attractive to the present owner. We are able to do this by means of a grant of £35,000 which SSM donated to us at their last Provincial Chapter, and a grant from Anglicans in Mission – the mission board of the Anglican Church of Canada, presided over by John Rye who worked for 15 years up at Bolgatanga and was a contemporary of Christian and me at Trinity College in Toronto. The location of this house is ideal – not in town but within walking distance, a nice piece of land around, a building in good condition already on it. We can now plan ahead to put up some bungalows for staff and maybe a new chapel, administrative block and library. Wonderful!

We still have the host of kids turning up for Evensong and Mass, sitting perfectly still and well behaved, apparently mesmerised by Anglican Chant and Cranmer's incomparable liturgy. One of the students at the start of term wanted to organise them into a Sunday school, and since then they have been meeting every day for an hour after Evensong. This student has a great gift with children. He never raises his voice and they never misbehave, a rare combination! As far as I can see so far the lessons consist entirely in how to make the sign of the cross, how to genuflect to the altar, which they now do, even three-year olds, with professional precision. They haven't as yet got beyond these basics to the more rarefied strata of God and existence.

----·----

01.01.86

I had a good Christmas this year. On Christmas Eve I went with a couple of students still here to Mankesim where a new bunch of Anglicans have formed themselves into a congregation and are meeting in a derelict (and I use the word advisedly) Methodist church. The Methodists have built themselves a large new church down the street. We were small in number but they were so happy that I had come, and so keen to build a new congregation that it all went with a swing, on the edge of that market where the stalls were still open, the traders still haggling, and the lanterns still flickering amidst the heat of midnight.

In the morning I went with one of the Holy Cross brothers to the prison where they have erected a small chapel in the courtyard, just four posts and a thatched roof, dedicated to St Paul because he was also a prisoner. The chapel was packed this morning. They had a small crèche set, around which they all crowded, even the prison officers, and sang very heartily and in harmony. Of course very few are confirmed so after the communion we sprinkled them all with holy water and gave each one a blessing so none will feel left out. That bit was very popular, with all these thugs in rags throwing themselves on their knees, pushing and shoving and jostling for a blessing. We went back to Holy Cross for Christmas Dinner which took the form of a goat stew – very tasty.

----·----

24.01.86

Inflation here rages on out of control. Last week the government devalued the cedi by half, and this has the effect of making all the money in your pocket worth exactly half as much as you paid for it. This produced much screaming, yelling, protest and discussion, but in the end what can any of us do? Just get on with it as best as you can. Last night one of the students came to see me for a serious discussion. As he comes to the end of his course here he feels it is time for him to marry, so when he was home (he comes from the north near Bolgatanga) he went and discussed the matter with the Holy Paraclete Sisters he had worked with. The Sisters suggested two or three available names with a helpful commentary on each. After much thought and prayer he had made his selection. The next step was to ask his mother and father to summon a family meeting of senior uncles and aunts, to meet with the girl's family and agree the date of the wedding and the bride-price, because here a marriage is a contract between two families, not a whirlwind romance between two young people. All this he explained to me very carefully to show that he was acting seriously and responsibly and not driven by wild passion and emotion. He also wanted to obtain my approval as his Rector. All that remains now is to raise the money to buy three cows to give to the girl's parents because this was the bride-price agreed. Without these cows no marriage can take place, though they are refundable if the woman does not produce children or is unsatisfactory in other ways. There you are – not a word about 'being in love', just a general consensus that she is sensible hard-working woman and suitable for a priest's wife; he never even mentioned proposing to the girl, though I am sure she could exercise her veto if she was unhappy.

10.02.86
'The Shepherds' is the name of a guild for Anglican women which is unique to Ghana. Rumour has it that it was founded by one of the early missionaries to accommodate those church women whose marital arrangements might not stand up to strict scrutiny by the Mothers Union executive. Whatever the truth of that is I don't know, but I do know that it is very popular in all the parishes here. They have an eye-catching uniform of bright blue or bright scarlet cloth printed over with large bland and blameless white sheep, all stretched tightly across the traditional proportions of these stately women. In addition each member carries a six-foot long shepherd's crook, which they link one to another to form a canopy of honour at the church door on big occasions such as

funerals of important members. Well, I looked out of the door one day last week to see a long solid phalanx of these massive Shepherds advancing down the main road in our direction and then turning in at our driveway, with a timid little man in red velvet walking at their head – their chaplain, so I was told. Every woman was carrying on her head a large basin or bucket filled with rice, corn, cassava, mangoes, and even a few trussed up live hens. This was the Shepherds notion of support for the college and all the priests in training, and a very heart-warming notion it was to us. They came to chapel for Evensong which was sung in Fante that night with great gusto, the chapel full to overflowing, but when they came to sing The Shepherds own hymn (A&M 258) they made the roof rattle.

> I was a wandering sheep
> > I did not love the fold
> > I didn't heed my Master's voice
> > I would not be controlled.

How we all enjoyed it, and our store cupboard has been filled for weeks ahead.

09.03.86

One of our students who graduated last June is now in a small bush parish about 50 miles from here beyond Mankesim. The parish is dirt poor, they have no electricity, but it is a great palm growing area. The kernels from these palms are like small nuts, and when they are cracked open and ground they produce palm oil much used in these parts for cooking. Our students always insist on having palm oil soup (rather thick and greasy) with fish added for Palm Sunday although the connection between one and the other is rather hard to see. Our former student has great plans to buy a small palm kernel cracking machine for the parish which will benefit the local farmers by saving them a trip to a grinder in Mankesim, and will produce financial independence and financial blessings for the parish. He turned up on my doorstep looking for a 'loan' so that they could buy the machine. As I still had some personal Christmas gift money left over I was able to help him and off we went to buy this machine in town. It is a small grinding mill about 4' 6" high. He will take it back to the village on Monday – so that gives you an investment in Third World small technology!

They have done a lot in that village to rehabilitate the church since the arrival of their new priest as they had been without one for a long time. The church is built of mud bricks with a tin roof and apse or alcove at the end. They have got a local sign painter to paint on the interior wall of the apse in lurid colours a larger than life picture of Jesus from the waist up facing over the altar and down the church. Rather unusually, the picture retains and incorporates the crucifix that was already hanging on the wall there. This now becomes pectoral cross on Jesus' breast. So in this picture he raises his right hand in blessing while with his left hand he points to the crucifix hanging around his neck and on his face is a look of silent, sad, reproach. Very effective.

11.05.86

A very amusing morning. We were all in chapel at 6.00 to start Morning Prayer and the Eucharist but hardly had we opened our mouths when ten massive great footballers came through the door and humbly took their places in any empty seats left. They were a bit disadvantaged as so much of the service was in English, but it didn't seem to bother them and we sang a couple of Fante choruses which they joined in with gusto. They were the members of the Kumasi Corner-stones football club in town to challenge the Cape Coast Vipers on the pitch next door to us this very afternoon. As we are neighbours to the stadium they came to our Mass this morning seeking a blessing before the match. After the service they all came and knelt in front of the altar while the students sang with feeling and I prayed (voice over!), sprinkled the holy water and blessed them and they departed with thanks. Anyway they won the match!

02.06.86.

Heard today from one of our old students whose wife has just delivered – in this case a little girl, and I am invited to the Outdooring. This is one of the customs here, the first time the new-born is taken out of the house after its birth. The baby is carried by its father who lifts it high above his head towards the east and shows it the sun and the sky and says 'This is the sun, this is the sky' then he faces east south and north, and shows it the trees and the people attending and says 'These are the trees, these are your people'. Then he lays the child on the ground and says 'This is the earth' and lets a little water trickle from the thatch onto the child and says 'This is the rain', and then he says 'This is now your home, this is where you are going to live these next few years, so pay heed to all these. Respect them'. Then a libation is poured while the ancestors are addressed and included in the circle and the child added to the family circle, and it all finishes with a party. I think priests in some places combine all this with a Baptism.

———•·•———

Here in Ghana people ignite very quickly and are soon 'over the top' as in the following letter I received recently from the fiancée of one of our students after she had been to Cape Coast for a visit. 'To be frank with you, Father, when I saw Fred's good-looking appearance and the nice character he has shown to me of late, I was full of joy and thanks to all at St. Nicholas, so that whenever I think of you I thank God. In fact if I live to be a hundred I will never keep silence over your praises all the days of my life. I always say to Freddy that you are a God-given priest brought to Ghana as the great elephant walking before all the priests in order to keep them from the morning dew. May you live to be 100'. 'Over the top' maybe, but hypocritical never, every word was sincerely meant.

———•·•———

03.01.87.

I went to the watch-night service this year at St. Thomas' Annomabu, a small fishing village just up the coast with its own derelict castle from the days of the slave-trade. The small but eager congregation meet in a ramshackle classroom half-roofed with corrugated iron. They have a nice pair of double drums presided over by a 12-year old boy who is a virtuoso; he can make 'Abide with Me' sound like rock 'n' roll. The guiding genius there is Mrs Diana Ampiah who keeps the whole show on the road and whom our students refer to as the Pope of Annomabu, a shortish woman, middle-aged with a quiet manner who sees to it that things happen when and how they should happen. We started off at 9.00pm. with a torch-lit procession through the town, torches being provided by small condensed milk tins full of sand which had been soaked with kerosene and nailed to sticks. So we marched under billowing clouds of black smoke reminiscent of the old transcontinental on the Canadian Pacific Railway. As we went we sang 'O God our help in ages past' at top throttle, or at least the first verse thereof repeated *ad infinitum*, stepping as we went over open sewers, and dead fish, in between drying fishing nets, and the stalls of the market women, all our women dancing as they went, the babies on their backs jiggling to the tune. Our lungs were deeply filled with a combination of kerosene smoke, fish, sewage, sea air, and frying plantain. On we went, past the Methodist Church, singing yet louder still to let them know that the Anglicans were NOT dead! The only untoward event was when the procession was going past one of the many bars on our route and the other churchwarden staggered out looking decidedly the worse for wear. No problem, Mrs Ampiah went into action, I saw from the corner of my eye as I marched on a small and earnest conversation going on between her and her partner-warden, after which he disappeared down a dark alley, only to reappear back in church clothed in his best and in his right mind when we were half way through Mass. I love that woman. No fuss, no recriminations, just a quiet effective solution to a potential problem. When we got back to church we launched into a full sung Eucharist with instructions for a long sermon which would carry us over the midnight hour. Because if God caught sight of us in church at that first hour of the New Year he would bless us in full all the year through. Meanwhile all the babies and under 10's, about forty of them, exhausted by their route march, curled up on the floor and were soon sound asleep, while we sang on and on.

———•·•———

16.01.87.

Now that the two new classrooms and library are in operation it leaves us with a spare room in the house, one which had served as a classroom. I have decided to turn it into a common room, though whether a common room is really part of the African scene may be a bit uncertain. Most of what goes on in the common room at Kelham goes on here around an open fire or in the shade of a fig tree on a hot day. However, I went up to see our Muslim carpenter friend who works under a mango tree up the road who had already made quite a bit of furniture for us, and asked him to make five easy chairs, chairs that will hold foam rubber cushions. He was quite willing and able, but in return he came in yesterday and asked (through an interpreter as his English is a little hesitant) for a blessing for 1987. So I gathered a handful of students and we went into the chapel where they sang gently some Fante choruses, while the carpenter knelt humbly in front of the altar and I splashed him with holy water, laid my hands on his head and prayed heartily that God would bless him, his family and his business in this year ahead. The man only wants to turn his new contact with us to maximum benefit, but what strikes me is this. This man is a typical Muslim and probably illiterate. I doubt he has ever heard the words 'inter-faith issues' or 'inter-faith dialogue'. He only sees that this is a holy place and therefore God must be here; these people are dedicated to God and therefore they must be his agents. If God is here then blessings will be here, and these blessings will overflow for him. You don't ask who owns the ocean before you swim in it. How simple it all is in his eyes. It reminds me of that tag 'What a tangled web we weave when first we practice to deceive'.

———•·•———

31.01.87

Nick Hammersley has taken Sister Joyce and Auntie Ekuwa up to Elmina to buy some fish for us. Elmina is about three miles up the coast and still dominated by a huge stone castle put up on the shore by the Portuguese in 1480, and then owned by the Dutch for a century or two. It was an important place in slave trade days and you can still go round it and see the dungeons where the slaves were kept in shackles until a ship arrived to take them off. Then there is the Gate of No Return which marked the point at which they said farewell to Africa for the last time. They also show you the chapel where those good Dutchmen sang their metrical psalms, and take delight in showing you the gallery from which the governor looked down on the latest batch of slaves to arrive in the castle and selected the woman he chose to share his bed for a month or so. If she should become pregnant she was not shipped out. Although fully convinced that slavery was sanctioned by the scriptures and in line with the will of God, they apparently had a few qualms about selling their own children into slavery. But today Elmina is mainly a fishing port. The fishermen go out in large dugouts carved out of one log, and paddled by a crew of a dozen men or so. They are highly decorated in the brightest colours with patterns and mottos and each evening are pulled up along the shore. The fish are brought up on the beach and auctioned off by the basketful by the trading women. Hence the terrific noise of the bidding, the shouts of the auctioneers, the smell of the fish, the swarms of flies, and the pressures of the crowd jockeying for a better spot, all make for a heady experience. It is another authentic bit of Ghana. Fish is our standby here as we cannot afford meat at all, and chicken is for festivals.

07.03.87.

Yesterday was Ghana's Independence Day, the 30th since they first became an independent country under Kwame Nkrumah. We had a special Eucharist this morning at which the student who preached gave us several long quotes from the writings of Nkrumah who now seems to have been completely rehabilitated after the dubious days at the end of his time when he proclaimed himself Asageyfo (Messiah), and people were encouraged to pray to him, or so Boniface tells me who was a young boy in the Pioneers at the time. When, during prayer time at their meetings they held up their hands and begged and pleaded with Jesus to send them some sweeties, nothing happened, the sky was empty, but if they held up their hands and begged Asageyfo to send them sweeties, clouds of sweeties came raining down on their heads thick and fast. In the afternoon there was a big march-past of all the Cape Coast school children in the football stadium, KK & Acheampong were practicing for this all yesterday with much stamping of feet, swinging of arms, about turns, and salutes. Today this drill was multiplied by about 700 kids, all – since the temperature was about 95F – sweating seriously amidst clouds of dust. Meanwhile inaudible loudspeakers gave unintelligible garbled instructions, a brass band played on, and a spirit of good natured confusion hung over the whole assembly. I did partly hear the parody of 'Grandfather's Clock' but couldn't pick it up accurately. It was a bit like this:

Grandfather's Clock

The white imperialists came to exploit our land for 133
    years,
They came at a time when equality prevailed to enslave our
    dear forbears;
The masses awoke when Asageyfo came,
    to lead us to our goal
And they ran, shattered, never to be seen again
    when Asageyfo came.

Hooray Ghana Young Pioneers!, Cheer Up! Cheer Up!
Our shackles are broken down, Cheer Up! Cheer Up!
And they ran, shattered, never to be seen again
    when Asageyfo came.

Of course the stands were crowded with mums and dads, brothers and sisters come to watch the march-past, and a good time was had by all.

Ash Wednesday 1987

We kept a day of retreat today with a couple of sermons in addition to the regular services and had silence all day. Of course at the Eucharist this morning everyone received ashes on their foreheads, a ceremony that is exceedingly popular here, more so than I realised and for reasons which I cannot really fathom. Everyone from babes at the breast to the seniors hobbling up on canes and crutches must be 'ashed'. It can by no means be omitted. Finally, just as we were sitting down to our silent supper, a policeman appeared at the gate – not a welcome sight. He said he had come from the prison and the prisoners had been waiting all day for someone to come and 'ash' them, and they had sent him to us to enquire 'Was no one coming?' Of course I jumped into the van with the policeman and a few students. The prison is situated in a corner of the old Cape Coast Castle. It was where slaves were kept in chains until they could be shipped off to America and I would say no improvements or up-dates have been made in it since those days. The Holy Cross brothers with some students visit there and had even set up a chapel – a couple of corrugated iron sheets over one corner of the yard. I wish you could have seen the sight that night, a bunch of men in rags and tatters, looking hungry and malnourished and anxious in the dim and patchy light of a couple of 60w bulbs, with the sound of the Atlantic breakers beating against the other side of that wall. All were waiting patiently along with the guards and the officers. I gave a homily on Jonah and the good results of repenting. Led by their own choir they sang beautifully some Fante choruses, and I placed a cross of ashes on each man's forehead, as he knelt on the stones, prisoner and officer alike. It was all very moving, an unforgettable Ash Wednesday.

10.05.87

This morning as I was working in my office I heard a loud burst of screams, instructions and hysteria erupt from the kitchen next door. I rushed out to see what disaster had struck. It seems that Auntie Ekuwa, our cook, had tipped over our large water butt, preparatory to scrubbing it out and there underneath was an enormous rat, as big as a cat. She had trapped it in a corner near the wood pile. By now the students were gathering and one man from the north, Jacob, went into action. He grabbed a log of wood from the pile which he brandished like a spear while stealthily advancing barefooted on the rat, almost mesmerising it with his eyes like a true hunter. In the second when the rat was about to break cover and run for the wood pile, Jacob downed him with one lightning blow of his log and a cry of triumph. In the next instant Jacob had the rat in the kitchen sink cutting its throat with a dull kitchen knife, whilst there were general shouts of victory around the courtyard. Auntie Ekuwa cooked the rat up in a soup with a big ball of fufu for Jacob's lunch. I was invited to partake but declined even though 'Father it is very sweet'. Murray Belway looked shocked when he saw Jacob licking his lips over the rat at lunchtime, but not as shocked as Jacob looked when Murray told him some people in Canada kept rats as pets. To him that was the equivalent of letting your pigs sleep in your bed.

Fufu is the Ghanaian equivalent of British roast beef and Yorkshire pudding. This is the recipe. Take equal portions of cassava and yam and boil them up. When cooked place them in a wooden mortar and then take a long wooden pestle and pound, one person turning it over and the other (woman –according to custom!) wielding the pestle. This will take some time, until the whole mass is smooth and like a ball of uncooked dough. Place this in a large soup bowl and pour around it some clear, hot peppery soup. Across the top of Fufu island lay a few small pieces of fish. Eat it with your hand. Delicious! With three or four together around a common bowl – even better!

09.09.87.

To get from here to Accra by public transport, if you have no car, is not altogether a straightforward matter. In the first place you must be up well before daybreak and hike yourself down to the lorry park where all the Mammie Lorries are waiting to sally forth to manifold destinations. You need to inquire which ones are going to Accra (there are no destination signs) and of these you should select one that looks in reasonable repair, and the one that is almost full, for you know that the driver will never consent to crank up the engine until every seat is full to over-flowing with a few extras on top of that. You climb aboard, and any heavy luggage you have such as would go in the hold of an aeroplane, is hoisted up on the roof and tied down along with any hens, goats, or even lambs that will be travelling with us.

When the driver feels that not another person could be shoe-horned in, we set off but still there are many impediments waiting for us on the way. Between here and Accra there are at least three police barriers, and if the police see market women on the lorry they insist that everyone comes down and presents their luggage for inspection, not, I hasten to add, because they suspect there are terrorists on board our lorry but because they anticipate squeezing every market woman for an extra dash.

Then since these lorries are driven to the edge of collapse and beyond, there is good reason to expect some break down, large or small, on the way. If it is only a burst tyre we can all get out and sit under some shady tree while the driver takes the tyre off to the nearest garage for repair (spares are an unknown phenomenon). If it is something major we have a choice of either waiting an hour or two or three until a mechanic comes, or we can try flagging down another lorry, though this may be expensive as refunds are not a popular concept with our driver.

Then in the midst of the heat and the dust and the sweat we may encourage the driver to stop where a man by the roadside is selling fresh coconut so we can have a cool refreshing drink of coconut milk, or he may be persuaded (another dash!) to stop where a man is holding up a freshly barbecued grass-cutter splayed on a grid, and smelling delicious so we can have some fresh hot meat, after all we have been on the road for some hours. And then of course there are always people wanting to alight and people wanting to join us.

But eventually we reach the lorry park in Accra and alight ourselves, and as we get down we can read and fully comprehend the motto spelled out in bold letters along the side of the lorry 'God's time is best'. You see we haven't arrived late, we haven't arrived early, we have arrived at the time God wished us to arrive, and behind this motto lies a whole philosophy of life. Don't sweat and fret to impose your own rigid inflexible time-table on the variegated pattern of the day. No. Instead, relax, adjust yourself to the time-table God is suggesting for this day, and you will see in the end everything will fit in. This is the way to eliminate stress and tension from your life and enjoy your journey whatever it brings.

09.06.87.

Down at the bottom of our drive at the main road an old woman has a small stand where she sells food to the passers-by – perhaps plantain chips, or balls of bankoom (boiled maize) or palm oil soup. She has with her two small boys about 8 and 9 years old, she may be grandmother to one of them. The two boys, KK and Acheampong, by name come to our Sunday School and also to morning prayer and Eucharist every morning and evensong each evening. Now the old lady has been finding it more and more difficult, as food becomes ever scarcer, to make enough to keep her let alone the boys. So she has packed up and gone back to her village leaving the boys with a teen-age half-sister, but no food. The next news to come to me was that the landlord had turned them out of their room for non-payment of rent, they had been turned out of school for non-payment of fees, and Auntie Ekuwa who had been quietly feeding them from our table was closing down the kitchen with the start of the Christmas vacation. So these two very young boys were to be set adrift in a stormy world to fend for themselves. Fortunately they have friends. Auntie Ekuwa encouraged them to sleep on the floor of one of our new classrooms, it was dry and certainly warm – even hot – and I doubt whether either of them had ever slept in a bed in their young lives. Then the congregation at Philip Quaque church up the road, where they go to school, sent some money for food and the head teacher, a large, slightly formidable lady, called to discuss the problem with me. She encouraged me to take them on: 'they will have a safe place to live and you will have two good house servants, and then they can become priests.' After that my brother and his wife promised to support them. Everyone here seemed to assume that these two young homeless boys would never give me any trouble, and indeed they never did – instead, a lot of happiness. That's how they became a permanent part of St Nicholas and I never washed my habit or any of my dirty clothes or swept another floor as long as they were there. This is the way you acquire family and dependents here.

09.12.87.
A big day this Sunday as two of the students were married at the morning Eucharist, and then in the evening the Sunday School announced they were going to put on a play. This is their method of production. Joseph Amoh who does the Sunday School, tells them the story very carefully, then assigns the parts to the would-be actors, and then unleashes them and lets them go and to make up their own dialogue, so there is quite a bit of improvisation and enrichment. The story they had chosen was the Book of Ruth, which slightly surprised me, a story centred on the loyalty and faithfulness of women was not the one I thought they would have chosen, but I was not looking with African eyes. It opened with the father Mahlon in a rage shouting and yelling at his two sons and waving his belt about in a very threatening manner. He was going to beat them proper if they continued chasing after girls. The young men meanwhile appeared suitably cowed. Then when the boys were safely married and after the famine had set in the two daughters-in-law came on, seen in the market place in Moab, doing some hard haggling with the farm woman who was asking a hundred cedis a stick for her cassava. Unbelievable – these people! Then followed a sad series of events thick and fast. Old Mahlon is bitten by a snake and dies, so there is much wailing and grieving

and a wake and funeral follow. Hardly had that finished when the elder son who was given to drink gets into a fight at a drunken party and he is stabbed and dies at once. More wailing, another wake, another funeral, and then the younger son falls down in the field and dies of sunstroke and we have the third wake and the third funeral. This was clearly to those kids the climax of the Book of Ruth – those three funerals. The rest, Ruth's accompanying Naomi back to Bethlehem, her marriage to Boaz that was quickly dealt with, an anti-climax really. But it was all done with great enthusiasm, these actors needed no prompting; getting them to give the other actors a chance was the problem, and they lived their characters and developed and enjoyed them. I wish you could have seen the faces in the audience – they were on the edge of their chairs with excitement. How I wished I could have understood Fante and got the full flavour of their performance.

Another young lad has surfaced in chapel every day and at Sunday School, Kofi by name; he may even be another grandson of Auntie Ekuwa, but I'm not sure about that. His mother is very poor. She 'head loads' fish from the beach to the market and they give her a few fish to sell on her own. She has to provide for a family of which Kofi at fourteen is the eldest. The father, a fisherman, is living with a new wife further down the coast and he is willing to take him but the new wife doesn't want him and he doesn't want to be a fisherman. He wants to be a car mechanic. So we have been enquiring for a mechanic who will take him on as an apprentice. There is one reputedly good mechanic who has an auto-repair yard almost next door to us, so I have sent one of the students to make enquiries. The answer came back that they would take him on these conditions: we must provide a bottle of schnapps, one bottle of appeteshi (local spirits), three packets of cigarettes (must be Dunbar or Embassy 555) and sixteen bottles of pop. It will all come to 2, 000 cedis or about £5.50p. The apprenticing takes place on Saturday morning at the mechanic's yard. Kofi's grandmother and grandfather have to be in attendance, terms are discussed, an agreement is reached, a little appeteshi is poured on the ground in libation so that the ancestors will be involved and summoned to witness the event. Then forms are signed or thumb printed and the party begins. This apprenticeship last for three and a half years after which he will have to pay more money and offer the mechanic three ducks and a goat for another feast. What a pleasure to see the young guy get a chance to get a grip on life instead of just drifting aimlessly as so many do here for the lack of means or opportunity.

Our young mechanic is doing well. He is at matins every morning at 6.00am. leaving early to change into his work clothes and then off to work where his first job is to sweep out the whole yard. He comes back for breakfast and dinner and returns in the evening for the last part of evensong and for Sunday School which is 6.30-7.30 each evening. I wonder how many motor mechanic apprentices there are around the world that follow a routine like that. He sleeps with KK and Acheampong on the classroom floor but none of them had sleeping cloths so I bought some old flour sacks (as is the custom here) and Auntie Ekuwa has made up three sleeping cloths for them.

———•◦•———

We had a nice service this morning for Mother's Day. There is a woman baker down the road with a large clay oven in her yard, an Anglican and fairly frequent attender at our Mass. Flowers here for Mother's Day are hopeless as they wilt as soon as they are picked, so I asked her to bake about sixty small bread rolls which the children brought up in a basket at the offertory to be blessed and we later gave them back to them to be taken home to their mothers. How many rolls actually made it home into maternal hands, I wouldn't like to speculate. We must have had about fifty kids in addition to the students. We also had three baptisms, two of them grandchildren of the baker, so no charge for the rolls! Then we sang the South African blacks' national anthem Nkosi Sikelele Africa to pray for them and show solidarity with them. Everyone here feels very strongly about apartheid and so the singing was terrific.

———•◦•———

On Good Friday morning we had Stations of the Cross which is a very traditional part of Lent and Passiontide in Ghana. This year

Joseph Amoh had trained the Sunday School children to lead us and very effective they were too. At each station one person read the appropriate Bible text and then the children mimed the action, without a word spoken, without an action or a murmur. After holding the pose for a minute someone read a collect, and we went on to the next station singing a verse of 'At the cross her station keeping, stood the mournful mother weeping' or when that ran out, 'Man of sorrows, what a name'. What was so moving about it was the seriousness, the dignity of the children taking part, not a whisper, not a push, shove or giggle. This was not a children's service but a service for and by adults, in which the children played the adult parts. It brought tears to my eyes.

We have just completed the Easter services for another year and as usual they were performed with much enthusiasm and zeal. Murray Belway who is here says it is like attending a High Church Service put on by a bunch of world cup fanatics! We started Thursday night with the Mass of the Last Supper, including the foot washing, which is very popular here especially with the children. As few people wear socks of any kind and all kick off their sandals at the chapel door, everyone is ready for action and surge forward when the water is poured into the basin and soon the floor is inches deep in water while the singing is unbroken. After Mass we carry the sacrament to Gethsemane which has been prepared in a classroom with enough branches, palm boughs, and greenery to make a temporary jungle. In the procession to Gethsemane a chief's umbrella, procured from I know not where, is carried over my head as I carry the sacrament and all the students are in native cloths with drums, bells and horns as if for the Asantahene. We then, on a rota, kept an all-night vigil in Gethsemane with much recourse to vocal prayer, hymns and choruses. Friday liturgy when we come to the reading of the Passion, the students mime all the actions, and then the altar crucifix was carried in and laid before the altar and we all went up and kissed it from the youngest to the oldest. The next big service was for the Vigil on Saturday night which was more crowded than any, and in the course of it we had 31 baptisms, mostly of children who have joined the Sunday School. The Vigil was in the dining hall area and then we danced through the courtyard into the chapel which was all alight with candles and ribbons and decorations for the First Mass of Easter. How we all danced at the Mass. People here have such a zest for life, such a capacity to enjoy that it all goes with a wham and a pow! We had another Mass at 6.30am. after which one of our neighbours who regularly attends chapel sent in for the students' breakfast a big kettle of sweetened rice, about half a loaf of bread each and a big tin of margarine. What feasting! It leaves you exhausted but inspired and on Monday they go on their Easter break.

We are in the midst of the Wives Conference and it is, as usual, proving a great success. We started it to give some help and support to the wives of all the students who found themselves suddenly and surprisingly on the verge of being the priest's wife in a parish. This is a position of some importance and prestige in our parishes. The priest's wife is always addressed as Mother, and the bishop's wife as Mother Superior, and they usually exert quite a bit of influence. We hold the conference during the Easter vacation when the men will be home to look after the children, and we will have some space to put them up here. It is also a good thing to have when Sister Joyce is around. She is much loved by the wives. The programme is very low key. Some cooking classes – how to work with portable ovens, sewing classes, patterns for making a set of vestments, Bible study and talks on prayer, a session with the people from the family planning clinic – this is very popular and always asked for, though I notice that most still return next year with a fresh baby. Then Matilda Ackon the bishop's wife gives tips on catering for guests, or how to entertain white folks, as most of the village women find this an alarming prospect. Matilda told them that white folks prefer light food such as sandwiches, soups and salads, and she demonstrated how to make a closed sandwich, then an open sandwich before a fascinated audience. We were expecting fifteen to come and 51 turned up. I often forget that for these women words like holiday, time off, away days, are seldom if ever heard. They are working 24 hours a day 7 days a week, so a chance for a few days away free from responsibilities and with the girls is highly attractive, because as with most conferences the most valuable part and the most enjoyable is meeting other women with comparable problems, chatting, even gossiping, and advising one another. It is one of the best things we do.

The Sunday school put on another play tonight, this time the Prodigal Son. It is one of the many occasions when I wish I knew Fante but as far as I can tell they focused mainly on that part of the story when the Prodigal Son was in a far country and going to the dogs. Kofi had the role of bar keeper selling appeteshi (local spirits) to the lad and engaging in dialogue with him. Here they were frequently interrupted by loud bursts of laughter and shrieks of delight from the audience, not a feature I recall from the biblical version of the story but it certainly held the crowd spellbound.

I have been trying to persuade the students that chasubles and copes and other church vestments don't need to be made from silk brocade or embroidered by holy nuns in England. I talked it over with Sister Moira when I was at Bolgatanga and gave her some money with which she bought some local cloth in appropriate colours, and then taught the girls in her sewing class in the Vocational Trade School to sew it up into vestments. She then sent them to me and I have sold them to students about to be ordained at less than half the price. So they will go out fully equipped with vestments and looking like part of the African scene – not imports. I'm not sure how far this idea will catch on. They are still a bit dubious.

An interesting business this morning. A woman came to see me who introduced herself as Sister Barbara Linen. She is one of the Sisters of the Holy Child Jesus, and has been teaching in the Holy Child Girls High School here and also at St. Peter's Seminary up the road. She was clearly a modern nun with a perm, ear rings and a handbag, and she struck me as an eminently sensible woman and an American as well. It seems that the R. C. Archbishop has recently sacked her from her post at the seminary because he felt that her views on the church were far too radical for Ghana. At a recent seminar we held during the Wives Conference on the place of women in the church, she had stood up quietly and said that in the R. C. church women were definitely second class citizens and then sat down again, this in reply to an impassioned paper just read by a local Catholic priest showing how much all Catholics loved the B. V. M. and therefore all women. So I had some inkling of her stance. I think she also feels that lay people should have a larger part in the selection and training of clergy and in the governance of the church. Unemployed now she wondered if she could be of any help here, so she is now one of our part-time lecturers. I am glad of the chance to expose the students to an intelligent woman – it will break down some of their stereotypes of women as exclusively wives and mothers. It will also show that at some pretty basic levels we, the churches, are not divided. Unity has already begun. She will begin with two seminars on feminism. I plan to attend.

It's good to have some good news to record. At last the first of the new bungalows has been completed this afternoon. What a thrill after living for five years in one of the servants' rooms amidst stores, tea-chests and cupboards, and in the middle of college life. How nice to have a separate house full of rooms with terrazzo floors, where you can unpack and make a home. Of course, I said a few prayers and sprinkled a bit of holy water about to get it off to a good start, but that wasn't enough for the students all of whom, naturally, were on hand. We had to pour libation. This you do with a glass of schnapps, standing outside the house, all gathered around. You slowly pour the schnapps on the ground in little portions and in between each you involve the ancestors, those who had any connection with the college or this piece of land, or who had been somehow related to any of the students or to me, and you explain to them that it is now our new house, this is where we live now and they are welcome there at any time and invited to share our life there. Then we asked them for their cooperation and help to make all things go well in that house. The ancestors are a big part of the scene here, and should you neglect or displease them it would not speak well of you nor would things go well for you. So I hope that all is now settled and satisfactory.

There is always a problem with weddings here. When a young man feels inclined to marry, whether the young woman has been suggested to him by his family or he has chosen himself or a combination of both, he will likely seek the advice of his mates and family elders for such a serious step cannot be undertaken in isolation from the family and society, and if he then wants to proceed there is a meeting between his family elders and her family elders in which the number of cows to be paid to the bride's family is agreed, and maybe the place where they will live. The cows will be refunded if the marriage breaks down. All give their consent, libation is poured to bring in the previous generations, and a party is held. This is called marriage by local custom, and it is perfectly legal and what everyone does. The church says that they must then come to church and have a wedding service and their vows blessed before the altar to be not only legal but blessed. However, this they are extremely reluctant to do because a wedding in church means an expensive white dress and a new suit, it means bridesmaids and ushers, a reception for hundreds with food and drink. That is why many of the students have been married by local custom but have not been married yet in church, which the bishop will insist on before he ordains them. It can bankrupt a young couple so they postpone and postpone, and most parishes which average two or three funerals a week, average two or three weddings a year, if that. To try to make a difference we have been saying here 'Weddings can be cheap' and so this morning at Mass one of the students, Kingsley, brought his wife and two children, and they took their wedding vows, he in his cassock and she in a nice cloth, and afterwards there was a celebratory breakfast of boiled egg, a half a loaf, peanut butter and coffee. Much enjoyed by all. See! What could be simpler?

At the end of term I travelled with a couple of our men, Alfred
Asante Ageyaman and Frank Amoah back to their home in Sefwi
Awiaso in the Western Region next to the Ivory Coast. It was the
first time I had been in the thick forest and found it very beautiful.
Richard Barnor also came along as driver so it was a real holiday
for me. Dotted about in the forest are lots of small villages where
people are hard at work carving farms out of the bush, growing
cocoa, plantain and yams. Many villages contain a small Anglican
chapel of mud brick with a tin roof, and we attended one at 6.00am.
on Monday morning to find a good crowd in attendance, all there
before going off to their farms at sunrise. After Mass they made a
presentation to me of a hen, some eggs, some plantain, and a small
donation for diesel. I didn't like to take it for surely they could
ill afford it, but their dignity required such a gesture. They farm
without machinery of any kind except for a cutlass and a mattock
and work every hour of daylight between 6.00am – 6.00pm, when
they return home to cook their supper, at least the women do, on
a wood fire and, with no light but a kerosene lamp, they are soon
in bed. We stayed one night with a priest who had lost his wife.
How kind and courteous he was. After supper he brought me a
bucket of water and indicated I could take my bath out on the
front lawn, but so thick was the darkness that no one's modesty
need be offended. What respect and affection you have to feel
for these people, forgotten, in a hidden corner of the world; just
meeting them fills you with respect and affection.

On the way up to Sefwi Awiaso I asked Frank what subjects he
had covered in his course at the Teacher Training College and he
gave me a list of standard subjects, but the one he had found the
most interesting and most helpful was psychology. I said that I
could well see how this subject would be most useful to any priest,
and he went on to explain further: 'My father at home has an old
flint-lock rifle that has been in the family for generations, but when
I was home last Easter it had disappeared, someone had stolen
it. We strongly suspected that my young brother had taken it to

sell for money for drink, but when we questioned him he knew nothing about it. We pleaded, we threatened, we begged him to tell us where he had hidden it, but he just protested his innocence even more strongly even with tears. We called in the police and they took him to their cabin and questioned him for hours, and he said we were persecuting him. So I said to myself that this was a case that called for some psychology. So I went to the police cabin and gave both the officers there twenty cedis, whereupon they took my brother down to the cells and beat him proper. When he was broken, bruised and battered lying on the floor and the officers, hardly winded, were having a beer preparatory for the next session, he made no further delay and told them where he had hidden my father's rifle.' 'Frank,' I said, 'I have never heard of a case where psychology was applied in a more practical way or with speedier results.'

After the trip around Sefwi Awiaso I drove on to the Kumasi to preach at the ordination. The Ashanti are the largest and most war-like of all the tribes in Ghana and their king, the Asantahene, comes next in order of precedence after the President, or some would say the President comes next after him. But however that may be, he is very definitely an Anglican much to the delight of every fellow Anglican. They have recently built a new cathedral which, while of no particular architectural style, is vast and high and can be seen dominating the horizon from all sides of the city. Some irreverent folks say it looks like a cocoa drying shed. For the ordination it was packed tight and we got under way by 9.00 or soon after. I preached on the text Jer. 45.5: 'Seekest thou great things for thyself? Seek them NOT.' After the sermon and creed there were great sounds of horns and bugles from without and the Asantahene's throne came up the aisle on the head of a servant naked to the waist accompanied by a file of courtiers. Twenty minutes later when the Asantahene's limousine drew up, the Mass came to a complete halt as all the priests forsook the sanctuary and hurried to the west door to greet with all due respect the Asantahene in his regal regalia, and accompany him to his seat. He stayed there for an hour or so and at his exit the whole process was reversed. Mass halted while the Bishop and his priests followed the Asantahene to the west door. After that we went on to do the ordination and finish the Mass and we were allowed to depart at 2.30, rather damp and exhausted and ready for the big feast that had been prepared for us. Definitely what you need most to cope with the spiritual life in Ghana is stamina!

———•———

There was a bent-double old lady who used to come to the Eucharist four or five mornings a week accompanied by a dirty flea-bitten old dog who looked in worse shape than her. She was a solid life-long Anglican but also a great pain in the neck to her daughter with whom she lived. She always had a tale about how her daughter often refused to feed her, or pushed her out of the house, much to the mortification and indignation of the daughter, another solid Anglican, when these tales got back to her as inevitably they did. Anyway, the old lady has now in the words of the Salvation Army been promoted to glory, the funeral is tomorrow, and the wake is this evening. Because she was a big churchwoman and had a large family the funeral will be huge, but also because she was such a regular worshipper in our chapel the students feel they ought to go – but that's not quite right – they want to go, are eager to go – it would be a Big Do. So off we went be-cassocked and ready, to find a large crowd milling around outside the house, while piped music played old gospel hymns, and people chatted until it was time to go upstairs where the body was laid in state. The stairs were narrow and the clergy were many and the faithful past counting as we ascended to find when we arrived at the top that the cathedral choir plus the Cathedral Servers Guild were already in place leading hymn after hymn. There on a brass four-poster bed with fairy lights flickering around lay our old friend transfigured, in a white bridal dress with bracelets and necklaces and long white gloves. We were packed in tight, the bed girded with young servers in scarlet, while sweat rolled down every face, and then they lit up the thurible with a bed of white hot charcoal and proceeded to fill the room with incense. The clergy led prayers, sprinkled holy water, and one or two eulogies were given. It would go on throughout the night but we were excused after an hour or so as we had the next wake to attend.

————•••————

The Anglican Church of Ghana appears to be irrevocably wedded to Hymns Ancient and Modern standard edition plus the two supplements (779 hymns in all) and these are the hymns almost invariably chosen for church services. They, like the rest of the service, are always sung in English. There are included amongst them some good standard classical hymns and there are a lot of over-the-top sentimental Victorian hymns and melodies that have entwined themselves around the hearts of the worshippers. But there also exists alongside the hymn book a whole musical tradition of vernacular songs and choruses. I don't know where this tradition originated, though some say it was an early Methodist missionary that taught them the first ones. They are always short, consisting of one or two scripture verses, repeated over and over. They exist in all the local languages and are set to local melodies by unknown composers that are always lively, lilting, and with a strong beat. These so-called local hymns are much loved and have several distinct advantages. Everyone has a huge repertoire of these hymns by heart so no books are needed when they are sung, a great advantage where many are still illiterate. All that was necessary was to strike up the first line and everyone anywhere would join in harmony. They are in vernacular and have one or two lines of text only and that from the Bible so you can learn them on the spot if need be and remember them easily. They are completely ecumenical, they are neither Anglican, Methodist, Catholic nor Pentecostal and at funerals which are themselves always ecumenical occasions, once begun all can join in. The music actually incites people to dance or at least to clap and take part. They are seldom written down in any official form and have never been codified in an authorised collection; it is an entirely oral tradition to which people continue adding and from which old numbers fade. How a congregation comes alive and begins to enjoy when they lay down their *Ancient & Modern* and begin the sing 'the locals'! I've seen it happen over and over again. One of my favourites is one they often sing first in English, then in Fante, then in Twi. It goes:

I have another world in view, in view
   I have another world in view
   My Saviour has gone to prepare me a place
   I have another world in view
   My Saviour has gone to prepare me a place
   I have another world in view.

———•———

In June 1989 my time at St Nicholas came to a close after six and a half completely absorbing years amongst many wonderful people. I was at that point transferred to Middlesbrough, Teesside in the UK and in particular to All Saints parish where Fr Edmund, our Provincial, was the vicar. Two years later in the summer of 1991 the Society had a request from Bishop John Brown of the diocese of Cyprus and the Gulf, and himself an old student of Kelham. He asked if the SSM could send someone to Kuwait where he had an ex-pat congregation trying to get themselves together again after the traumas of invasion and occupation by the Iraqis. I agreed go, but asked for a one term break before I went. This break consisted of one further term at St Nicholas with Peter Stannard who had followed me as the Rector there. Thus from October 1991 – Feb 1992 I was back in Ghana and so I can add a few concluding entries to the College Log.

It is great to be back after two years away and find everything in the college going so well under Peter Stannard's efficient care, and life generally in the country still improving slowly. There has been lots of rain, and Akosombo Dam, so they say, is full for the first time in fifteen years with the result that we suffer from no more electricity cuts. Another result is that there is an abundance of food for sale at the roadsides. A telephone has been installed, putting the college in instant communication with the UK and the world outside as well as inside Africa. KK and Acheampong are several inches taller,

and, wonder of wonders, now able to communicate with me after a
year at Adisadel College and some study of English. Auntie Ekuwa
still presides in the kitchen and there are 29 students enrolled who
provided me with a great welcome.

Unfortunately Peter has had a recurrence of the eczema on
his feet from which he has suffered each year he has been here
and which none of the doctors he has so far consulted seems able
to control. Then, even more unfortunately in my opinion, Peter
began listening to the lady who cooks for him and who maintained
that that this was an African disease and that it could therefore be
cured only by African remedies, i.e. herbs. So he consented to a
course of treatment with her, she herself being under the direction
of a herbalist in town. The treatment consisted of covering his
legs with a brown herbal mixture, washing it off with sea water
and then smearing them with mud. Such is the measure of Peter's
desperation. He is faced with the likelihood of having to give up
his job here where he is so much loved and needed by men in the
college, and returning empty to England for good unless a cure
can be found. So far this shows no sign of appearing.

Peter has asked me to take a class on Dogmatic Theology this
term but I decided to approach it from a slightly different angle.
Instead of dishing out all the standard material on Sin, Redemption,
the Church, the Sacraments, I would assign one or two questions
such as: Why do you believe in God? Is the God of the Muslims the
same as our God? Why so many different churches? Are they all
the same? Then at the next class they would read out their answers,
and some very interesting answers many of them were, showing
signs of thought and reflection. After everyone had been heard,
discussion ensued and there was seldom any need for me to ignite
it with any questions of mine. Their mates were willing and eager
to assess their theories and to point out their snags and each day
the discussion waxed hot and furious. Today I almost had a riot on
my hands over which came first in time, your reconciliation with
God leading you to repentance for past deeds or your repentance
for the past leading you to reconciliation with God. There is no
greater joy for me than teaching those who are eager to learn and
who appreciate the seriousness of the questions under discussion.

1. Ralph, Mom, Bill, Gerry, Dad and Albert, Canada, 1937.

2. The SSM at Kelham.

3. Ralph on his profession day, 1960.

4. Fr Malcolm Broadhead SSM and Fr Francis Horner SSM on Ralph's profession day.

5. Christmas Day football match at Kelham, 1962. Professed v. Novices.

6. Israel Qwelane from South Africa, John Ackon from Ghana and Ito Maitin from South Africa as students at Kelham in 1961.

7. Ralph in Japan with Fr Edmund Wheat SSM and Fr Moses Kimata SSM (right).

8. Percussion centre of chapel at St Nicholas. KK
and Acheampong.

9. Graduation Class at St Nicholas, 1988,
with Sister Joyce at centre.

10. Auntie Ekuwah in the college kitchen.

11. Fr Tanki Mofama
    SSM blessing
    Ralph after Tanki's
    ordination to the
    priesthood.

12. Fr Tanki Mofama SSM (standing left), Bishop John Lewis
SSM, Ralph, Fr Michael Lapsley SSM and
Fr Christopher Myers SSM.

13. Ralph with Ralph Martin
Allen in 1996; one of the
many children Ralph
baptized who were named
in his honour.

14. Ralph's departure from
Ghana; pictured with
Robert Okine, a former
Kelham student, then
Bishop of Koforidua.

15. At the launch of Ralph's book on John Moschus at All Saints Convent, Oxford, 2012. From left to right: Fr Colin Griffiths SSM; Bishop Christopher Morgan, former student; Ralph; Canon Vincent Strudwick; the Revd Barry Collins, also a former student.

By Christmas Peter's eczema had pretty well crippled him and confined him to bed. This meant that we had to cancel the trip we had planned to the north which in turn meant that I was free on Christmas Eve to take the midnight mass at Mankessim. I took Mrs Stannard (Peter's mother), Auntie Ekuwa and the two boys, Frank and KK along with me. This was obviously a 'big occasion' for Auntie Ekuwa who turned up at the pick-up, ready to go, in her new Christmas outfit. It was some bright white material covered with large scarlet and purple flowers against a background of greenery. The outfit consisted of a wrap-around ankle-length skirt, a tightly fitted bodice with a length of 'carrying cloth' over one shoulder (women in Ghana are never allowed to forget that motherhood is their first vocation) and a kerchief on her head, all of the same material. She is a relatively small woman, not traditionally built, and she looked very smart. The boys admired her greatly. 'Father Ralph,' said KK, 'look at Auntie Ekuwa!' in case I missed the point. Before the mass at Makessim we had a procession through the market singing some Ghanaian carol over and over again as long as required with Frank in scarlet cassock and cotta leading us on with a home-made cross while KK half way down the column was briskly beating out the tune on his drum. There must have been about fifty of us. No matter the hour, the market was still in full swing, the streets were crowded and lined with busy market stalls, each illuminated with its oil lantern. At times we were drowned out with transistors, at times we had to detour around people partying and singing, but with unwavering step and with heads held high our church ladies sang on, marched on until at the end of what felt like three miles we got back to our tumble-down church and began the sung Eucharist with plenty of extra carols, all of us as fresh as daisies. After the service, Joe Allen (the church warden) and his wife invited us back to their place for rice and hot peppery stew, with cold beer and watermelon to follow, all the more delicious in that heat. We didn't get home until 2.00am. but what a fun time we had all had.

By mid-January Peter was confined to his bed and growing ever more discouraged but the treatment still continued with the lady slapping on seaweed and bursting blisters. We then appealed to the Roman Catholic health clinic at Elmina but the sisters there refused to come to us as long as Peter was being treated by a herbalist. In the end however, Peter bit the bullet and decided to suspend the cook's ministrations in order to call in the R. C. nursing sisters in the hopes that they would restore his mobility so that he would then be able to return briefly to the UK and visit the School of Tropical medicine to see what they could do for him. Then with health restored he could return and complete his time here. Meanwhile Murray Belway and Sister Joyce, who were both there at the time, and myself would hold the fort until he got back.

However after accepting this programme Peter said he would like one of us to visit the unknown herbalist in town under whom the cook had been working and inquire from him what course he had been following. So, after lunch with our cook lady and a student to act as interpreter, we caught a taxi into town to do some research. We left the taxi on the edge of the market and the lady led us thorough a real rabbit warren of mud houses, narrow alleys and open sewers until she suddenly turned aside into a small room where a half-naked little old man was sitting on a cow hide on the floor, surrounded by pots and pans of all sizes and with swarms of flies buzzing and hovering above us in the heat. So confident was this man of his methods that as soon as he saw me bending through the door, he assumed that I was Peter completely restored to health and his face lit up in welcome. When I asked for his diagnosis of Peter's condition, he began to scramble about underneath the old bed behind him and pulled out from there a small piece of pumice stone, the size of an egg, with a red ribbon tied around it. 'This', he said, 'is the true cause of that eczema. It is a juju which some person ill-disposed to Peter buried in the path leading from Peter's house to the chapel. Peter naturally and inadvertently stepped on it and that was the point at which the eczema had begun. You see there is an explanation for everything, nothing happens without a cause. To cure it, I went by night and in the spirit, found where the juju was hidden, dug it up, and brought it back here where it would have no power. That is the end, of the story. The man is healed.' The medicine he had been prescribing was made up of various herbs mixed with sea weed and the drink he gave him was from the bark of various trees, mixed with schnapps. The holy water he had given him to wash with was sea water in which certain texts from the Koran on small scraps of paper had been soaking.

Meanwhile back at the college, the two nursing sisters were now on hand, without questions, without reproach, without explicit judgement of any kind, calmly and efficiently cleaning and washing his legs and filling him full of antibiotics. The happy ending is that Peter was well enough to fly by the end of January and returned at the beginning of April to begin the third term, but even so, the experts at the School of Tropical Medicine were not able to pinpoint the source of his eczema with any confidence.

This also meant that I was free by mid-February to return to the UK and prepare for my trip to Kuwait.

Postscript: Over Christmas 2013 I had a telephone call from Ghana asking for a way of contacting Ralph. During his visit to Ghana in 1964 he had been asked to preach to a group of half a dozen people in Accra who wished to establish their own church. He so inspired them that fifty years later a very large congregation was set to celebrate their growth and ministry. They asked for a message from Ralph. He dictated the following to me. (VS)

Epistle of Ralph

Dear Nee, and all at St Francis of Assisi Church in Accra,

What a joy it was to receive your letter telling me all that has happened at St Francis.

'As the Father sent me, so sent I you' and you went forth and multiplied. You obeyed the Gospel command, and your little congregation became the very proof of Christ's Resurrection, for the Risen Christ stands present in you and through you, so it is He who is bringing so many people into the Kingdom.

I am very grateful to be in touch again after all these many years; for I have preached many sermons in my life, but have never before had a message after 50 years, telling me of such an outcome! You will have heard from Fr Vincent that I have not been very well lately, but now I can use the words of Mary Magdalene who said 'I have seen the Lord'; for I am seeing Him in you all at St Francis. My heart is overflowing with joy.

So I thank you all for this blessing, and may you all continue to be blessed.

Yours friend and pastor,

Ralph

6

On Teesside

In 1989 Edmund who was now the SSM's Director was appointed the vicar of All Saints church at the heart of Middlesbrough; this big job came in addition to all the duties and responsibilities that were his in virtue of his being CEO of SSM, and so he quite rightly felt that he needed a brother who could work alongside him and even replace him in the parish on those occasions when he had to travel far and wide caring for the scattered members of the Society. For this reason he asked me to return from Ghana in June 1989 after nearly seven very fulfilling years with the Ghanaians, and I moved into the vicarage in Middlesbrough in July of that year.

Nothing could be greater than the contrast between my previous situation and my present one. From a largely rural society of subsistence farmers, I moved into a parish which did not have a single tree and hardly a blade of grass within it. From an undeveloped world where there was almost nothing in the way of industry I came to an exhausted world where industry had both come and gone with the mines, factories and industries all closed down and people unemployed. From a place where Christian belief was the norm and was practiced with verve and enthusiasm to a land where Christian belief was abnormal and was practiced only by the minority and they mostly elderly, and, of course, from a country where I was often the only white face in a sea of black ones, to a town where a black face was a rarity. As I went to bed each night now, it was no longer the breakers of the South Atlantic beating on the shore that lulled me to sleep; it was rather the shouts of cheer and farewell from the drinkers turning out from the Wig and Pen down the road at closing time.

Middlesbrough had been for nearly a century a thriving industrial town with steel works, coalmines, the centre of the enormous plant of the Imperial Chemical Industry (ICI) employing thousands of men and women, and in addition it was a busy working port at the mouth of the River Tees. However for the last twenty-five years it had been in terminal decline. The mines and the steel works had been closed down, the ICI was preparing to close and the fishing quotas removed much of the fishing fleet. This meant that large numbers of skilled workers were thrown out of work and either moved off looking for work or, if they remained, were on the dole. At the same time the town was being rebuilt. Large areas of working men's house were bulldozed down and replaced with small, neat homes with all the modern conveniences.

The whole area of town known as St Hilda's including St Hilda's church and two schools, one Church of England and one Roman Catholic, was all demolished and replaced. The new centre of town was now a large already slightly dingy shopping mall containing all manner of shops, and beside the mall, where the main road detoured around it, stood All Saints church, untouched by the wrecker's hand, although no family, no parishioner apart from the clergy, remained living within the parish boundaries. It was a large Victorian church, once equipped with a parish hall and vicarage next door, but these too had now been swept away and replaced with a nine story office block in which the first and part of the second floors were now the new parish rooms and vicarage. The church thus stood like a lone post-cyclonic survivor of a previous age, and beside it hung, in a steel frame, the whole peal of eight bells taken from the demolished St Hilda's church. This was appropriate enough since the congregation from that church had been amalgamated with All Saints.

As for the congregation that remained within that church – they were wonderful! There was a considerable group at the core of men and women who had been born in Middlesbrough and had lived all their lives there. They had had good jobs with ICI or the steel mills and so had considerable abilities, they had been in the forces during the war, and they were now part of that vast pool of skilled labour, still in their 50's and 60's left behind by the retreating tide of industry. They had names like May and Ada, Lily and Lilas and Dolly; Jim and Harry, Fred and Ted and they were the quiet unshakeable members of the parish. They supported All Saints, not because they were drawn particularly by its high church services, not because they were disciples of this priest or that priest, they supported this church like they supported Middlesbrough Football club, because they had been born there and they were still a part of old Middlesbrough even if they were now scattered throughout the suburbs and therefore they felt a responsibility for this church at its heart. They belonged to this church and this church belonged to them and through it all ran that slightly sharp sense of humour typical of the north-east. They took a little time while they weighed Edmund and me up, but, once accepted, they were your most loyal friends for the rest of your life. Such is the background of this typical parish on Teesside amidst those years of constant and radical change in UK.

Ralph's Log

The vicarage on the first and second floors of the office block is quite roomy. We have a large sitting and dining room with Edmund's office at one end and the kitchen at the other. Upstairs there are five bedrooms and a shower. The view from my window, as I have mentioned, is a little different from the view at Cape Coast. Instead of a lagoon with a distant fringe of palms at the ocean's shore, I look out on a parking lot, a pub called the Wig and Pen, no doubt in deference to the County Law Courts on the next block, and assorted office blocks, shops and terraced houses. There are five fish and chip shops and six pubs all within a few steps of the vicarage! However, in the distance, over the rooftops, beyond the boundaries of Middlesbrough, I can see the low green Cleveland hills in the distance – a reminder of nature! Edmund and I are here plus a student doing a gap year before he does ordination training, and Br Gordon lives about a mile away in the old St Hilda's district in the curate's house that goes with this parish. Edmund, as vicar, is very easy-going with a good sense of humour while Gordon is ever amiable so that should guarantee a tension-free life for the most part.

The diocese of York has planned to start a lay training course, based at All Saints and meeting here once a week for a lecture and some discussion. There are seventeen people enrolled so far, from young to middle-aged, several are unemployed looking to fill their days with courses, one is a Methodist minister's wife, a couple of house wives and mothers, a couple running a small business of their own and a doctor. Mostly they are just interested in theology and questions of faith or they see it as a preparation to becoming a Lay Reader. I will give one lecture a term and find guests to cover other topics as required; also I will assist them in writing their essays and discussing any problems.

———•◦•———

Yesterday was the feast of St Michael and All Angels and the patronal feast of the Society. These heavenly patrons are a bit like having a friend who grew up in your town and is now a cabinet minister in the government. They are both an example for you to follow and they can nudge a few fringe benefits in your direction from time to time. So, today we all drove up to the priory in Durham where Robert Stretton, who had been a student at Kelham, ordained and now an experienced priest, was making his profession. It was a perfect autumn day for the drive, brilliant sunshine with a cool but not cold breeze. They had the service in the garden as their chapel is a smallish room. This gave us a magnificent view across the valley, over the roofs of the town to the grey stone cathedral rising up on the opposite hillside with its three solid four-square towers like some mighty prehistoric beast. Kojo, a student from St Nicholas who has come here to try his vocation to the Society, was one of the servers. He was keen to hoist up his pant legs to show me he was already in long-johns, but I told him, 'You have seen nothing yet!'

When we got back to All Saints there was an evening service and our flat was declared to be an SSM Priory. We had lots of good wishes and lots of good food brought in from the members of the congregation who all came in for the coffee session afterwards. Among them was Malcolm Broadhead, a former member of SSM and Muriel his wife. They are now in the parish of Stainton (where James Cooke was baptised!) about ten miles away from here, so a nice place for me to retreat to from time to time – a real bonus.

―――――

Last night Edmund and I drove to Hartlepool for the installation as rector of the parish of a former Kelham student. The first person I met when I arrived was Gerald Martin who had been a novice at Kelham for a while. He is a short, shiny, stout and bubbling sort of person who now has his own funeral business in Hartlepool and bills himself as 'every priest's friend'. He told me that, 'at 5.00 this afternoon I was out at sea in a small boat scattering some Hindu ashes over the North Sea while the widow and family sang Hindu chants with many bows while bobbing about on the waves. From there I came straight here for the installation'. What an eventful life he has these days!

―――――

Because the church is situated right on the main street at the point where it takes a sharp turn to detour around the shopping mall, there is an unbroken parade of shoppers and viewers going past our front door most of Friday and all day Saturday. A group of men in the parish have discovered how to exploit this situation. They go around town and collect people's used paperbacks and then sell them from a stall at the front door of the church on Fridays and Saturdays week in week out all through the year. They raise a surprising amount of money this way but the interesting thing is that they don't feed it into the church coffers, instead they give it all away to various charities such as Cancer Relief, Oxfam, Save the Children or whatever else catches their eye. Last year they gave over £8000 in this way, including £200 for Fr Solomon Mensah-Commey, a priest in Ghana and a former student of St Nicholas who visited me here recently and preached at Evensong a sermon for which, had he still been a student, I might have given him two out of ten but more likely one out of ten, or even – 1. All of which goes to prove my theory that congregations are not much affected one way or the other by sermons, either the very good, or the very bad. Those folks in the pew over the years develop a very shrewd eye and a very sharp ear. They are well able to assess the man who is doing the preaching, distinguishing at times (such as in this case) a good man behind a bad sermon or a bad man behind a clever sermon or even a threadbare man behind a threadbare sermon.

I am off tomorrow to take the morning service at St John's, our neighbouring parish. It is a large Victorian red brick building of cathedral proportions seating around 500 and lucky to have a congregation of thirty on a good Sunday. All Saints is about a mile off in one direction and less than a mile from All Saints in the other direction is another massive, though more beautiful church, St Columba's, and this is after they have pulled down three churches in the same area. Of course all these are monuments to the Middlesbrough of the past when the whole central area of the town was wall to wall terraced homes for working men and women. I don't know what the population would have been then but it would have been at least three of four times the number it is today. But even now after all those homes have been bulldozed away and when all three congregations could easily fit into one church, such is the way that an old Victorian church (even a not very beautiful one) can worm its way into the affections, can entangle itself in the heart strings of plain men and women, especially of the older generation; if the demolition of any of these churches was suggested it would ignite such an enormous row, so many demonstrations, such anti-Council agitation that no one dare raise the issue. Apparently these old churches, just by standing there, bring some sort of comfort, like the smell of frying bacon on a Sunday morning, to the lives of many people who live around them even if these people are not so keen on actually attending them.

We had a visit this week from Nick Hammersley who worked with me for a year at St Nicholas as driver and general factotum. He is also an excellent photographer and I only wish I had kept a few of the pictures he took while he was with us. After he left us he did a year at an abandoned children's home in Morocco. Then after much internal debate and with much diffidence he applied for training as a Church of England ordinand and was, for reasons unknown to me and totally incomprehensible, turned down. He came to see me shortly after he got the news and was completely adrift not knowing what he might do next. It happened that while he was with us Malcolm Broadhead came to speak to the parish about the week he had just spent with the Columbanus Community of Reconciliation in Belfast. This community is made up of two Roman Catholic Jesuit priests, an Anglican nun from the Order of the Holy Paraclete at Whitby, a retired Presbyterian lady missionary and a couple of other shorter term members. They live right in the centre of Belfast and their purpose is to demonstrate that Christians of all these churches can and do live together peacefully and can work side by side to meet the needs of the people around them.

Each one has a full time job out in the city although they are living at the heart of a war zone and are meeting heavily armed soldiers wherever they go on the streets. Malcolm is a man of great enthusiasm and so none of this lost anything in the telling. We were all enthralled. Nick was present and is himself looking for something different and something in the way of a challenge, so I suggested he apply for membership in that community. He is a very good-natured guy and a co-operative one who is able to live with contradictions all around him and is able to laugh at himself. I thought he could be a part of the solution and not a part of the problem in that troubled city.

After he left us he kept in touch and he did apply to spend a year with the community. He told us there were lots of horrible sights to be seen there but also a lot of little signs of mutual cooperation and mutual respect as people are doing their best to create a new and trusting atmosphere in which all can live in peace. One of the things the community does is to organise weekend conferences with 50 per cent Roman Catholic and 50 per cent Protestant participation, the objective being to meet one another socially and perhaps even strike up a few friendships. It usually runs smoothly but half way through one weekend a while ago they heard an enormous explosion not very far off. It was a Roman Catholic man, blown to pieces by the Protestant forces. Nick very much believes that it is still not hopeless and that there are lots of ordinary men and women there patiently and privately chipping away at the boundaries.

Most of the country is in turmoil here at present as all the details of the new Poll Tax which Margaret Thatcher is introducing become more and more clear. In fact this afternoon we had a large and noisy procession of protest, waving banners and holding up placards, blowing horns and beating drums going down the street in front of the church shouting unkind slogans to 'Maggie'. What infuriates most people is their perception that those in the low income range will emerge with greatly increased taxes, while those who used to pay the highest property taxes will gain great relief when they only have to pay on the basis of the number of wage-earners in the house. This is a solidly Labour corner of the country and all are hoping that this will be the beginning of Maggie's last days. How they hate her!

That part of the parish known as St Hilda's, where the old St Hilda's church used to be, was completely demolished and replaced with modern two and three bedroom houses complete with up-to-date plumbing and heating. However when all the natives of the area who had been temporarily rehoused while the rebuilding was going on returned to their old pastures, they wanted, naturally enough, to reconstruct the familiar, the homely, the neighbourhood they had grown up in with its pub-centred life, its tribal loyalties and tribal feuds, its violence and its scant regard for property. As a result the new and modern houses soon came to feel very much like those streets that had been torn down. In the midst of the area stands the new St Christopher's school, an ecumenical primary school put together from the old Sacred Heart and St Hilda's schools; so at least we had succeeded in not burdening these children with all of the old prejudices and antagonisms. The children from these homes, at least the pre-puberty ones, showed all the usual enthusiasm of little kids for listening to stories, cutting and pasting and singing songs out of tune though the occasional stream of profanity that issued from these innocent little mouths might knock you backwards. Judith, the Head, is a first rate teacher and person and she has a good staff so that St Christopher's is one of the brightest spots of the parish, and pretty well the only effective impact that either of the two sponsoring churches has on the St Hilda's district. But, while the children enjoyed their school, the parents were often a problem. A while ago one of the fathers turned up in a very truculent mood accusing the staff of some alleged injustice shown to his little girl. He threatened Judith that he 'would get her' if his child did not receive better treatment, and although they managed to get rid of him on that day, he took to stalking Judith in his car until the police were brought in. Hardly had this died down when two parents turned up at school decidedly drunk at 3.00 in the afternoon and proceeded to shout at and swear at their child's teacher because their little girl had not been put at the head of her class although she was clearly better than anyone else. When Judith intervened to protect the teacher whom they were trying to choke to death, they knocked her to the floor. Again the police were sent for and took the couple away but the repercussions on the teaching staff are not small. Judith turned up at the vicarage a few days later saying she just could not face going in to work, so we took her out for lunch and walk across the moors. The case came up some months later and the man was given a prison sentence.

———

Since I came here I have been put on a full salary by the Church of England with the result that I am now being swamped with forms and questionnaires about Income Tax. The problem is that I (like any member of SSM) don't fit easily into any of their categories. They find it hard to comprehend how a man could have no dependents, no property, no bank account, no insurance and be paying income tax for the first time at the age of 59. I will get round most of this by signing over my whole salary to SSM, but the forms must still be filled out and returned!

————•·•————

One of the problems of living in the city centre beside the church is that you become a prime target for all the petty thieves that inhabit these streets. The vicarage has been broken into twice in the last six months, fortunately both times when we were absent. They took about £500 in cash which was on hand to cover our running expenses. It is nearly always young people on drugs and desperate for their next 'fix'. A much more serious crime overtook our brother Michael Lapsley last Saturday. He is a New Zealander, a brother of SSM who has been working in South Africa for nearly twenty years. He has been a great battler in 'the struggle' against apartheid and is a loyal member of the African National Congress. At present he is in charge of a parish in Harare in Zimbabwe. His book *Redeeming the Past: My journey from freedom fighter to healer* was published in 2013 with a foreword by Archbishop Desmond Tutu. He came to visit me twice while I was at St Nicholas and made a great impression on our students. He had just returned from a trip and was opening up the mail awaiting him when one magazine, containing a powerful bomb, exploded in his hands. It was strong enough to blow a hole in the roof of the house and he himself has lost both hands, one eye, most of the sight in the other eye and much of his hearing. These letter bombs are so skilfully prepared that you can drop them, dent them, rip them and nothing will happen until you turn the cover and open the first pages of the book inside which the bomb is hidden. No one knows who sent the bomb but it is most likely the Security Forces of SA or some right wing party members who are enraged and doing their best to de-rail the negotiations that are going on right now between de Klerk and the ANC. De Klerk claims to have little or no control over the extremists, doesn't even know what they are up to. Who knows?

—————

Apart from St Christopher's school, the only other contact we have with the inhabitants of St Hilda's is through baptisms and funerals. Edmund usually designates one Sunday a month as the baptism Sunday at the parish Eucharist and it is surprising how many who have little or no other contact with the church, except the school, still bring their babies to be baptised. This Sunday I had seven, two with single mothers, one Indian lady by the name of Hussein, two gypsy families (who are well represented in St Hilda's) and two problem families but they all wanted their babies baptised. Why? I'm afraid to ask! When I was filling out the forms in the register, I asked the young gypsy mother what name she wanted for her little girl. 'Britannia' she replied. I could not restrain my inhibited soul any longer and said, 'Why not give her a nice Bible name? Mary is a nice name from the Bible.' She was most compliant, and gently nodded her head in agreement. So I will baptise her as Britannia Mary. I feel I have not lived in vain! On these baptism Sundays we always get a larger congregation as all the family members turn up in loyal support, the men in formal dress, that is, white shirts, black pants, no ties, no jackets, whatever the weather, and the women, heavily made up, coiffed and in the most exiguous of skirts.

Again, being in the centre, a lot of funerals of those with no church membership come our way, the assumption still being that everyone, unless they have clearly stated otherwise, must be members of the Church of England. These usually involve a home visit beforehand, a service in church, or at home, and then a trip to the crematorium for the committal. Last week was the funeral of a certain Fred who, as far as I could tell, never darkened the church door but was a faithful attender at the Wig and Pen. As we were riding in the undertaker's limousine out to the crematorium, the chief mourner turned around from the front seat and said to me, 'Well Father, I suppose Fred has now joined the big domino game in the sky.' 'Yes,' I said, in my cowardly way, not being able at that point in time to think of a snappy summary of the doctrine of eternal life or of the teaching on the bliss of the redeemed. 'Yes, I suppose he has.'

Funerals are also occasions, if the deceased is from St Hilda's, when all the men turn out in their white shirts even if it is mid-winter, so it seems that the church still has some hold on some corner in the hearts of these turbulent people. Once when I was in a taxi going to or from the crematorium, the driver wanted to know what church I was from and when I said All Saints he replied, 'Oh yes, I know that church, it's a canny wee church.' Canny is a local word and a complimentary one. I think what he meant was that this church met all his expectations of what a church should look like: flickering candles, stained glass, a scattering of statues all warmly smiling and one of a mother and baby, and the pervasive smell of incense; and the services in that church were all done with the appropriate spit and polish as is befitting when you want to show your respect.

On a less solemn note, I was woken up last night just after I had gone to sleep by the sound of shattering glass as someone fell or was pushed through one of the windows of the pub. This was accompanied by a lot of shouting, cursing and swearing, but above them all rose the piercing voice of the publican's wife who is a member of our congregation though not an excessively devout one. Her cry was 'If you set foot in this pub again, I will break both your legs.' It is not often that we are disturbed by the noise, and being on the third floor insulates us from most of it.

We have Peter, our local Roman Catholic priest, coming to talk to the Lay Training class on Tuesday night on 'What the Bible says about justice and peace'. He is a very nice guy and this is his main subject. He has already done time in Durham jail for daubing a Ministry of Defence building with ashes in an anti-nuclear drive five or six years ago. I think they were concentrating more on the justice than the peace aspect that night! However in daily life he is very non-aggressive with a nice sense of humour. The Roman Catholics are no better off than we are in this neck of the woods. They have a large red brick Victorian cathedral down in St Hilda's but the congregation deserted it a few years ago to build a large building with all the modern conveniences plus a safe parking lot out in the suburbs. Peter is left behind to tend those of his flock still in St Hilda's and he uses one of the side chapels in the derelict building as his mass centre.

We have a meeting from time to time for the religious communities living and working in the North-East. About fifteen came to this one and for lunch I gave them potage au feu Quebecois which is one of the recipes I got from Marj, my sister-in-law, when I was home. I started it off by throwing in a bunch of beef ribs to give it some guts, then some barley, haricot beans and every kind of root vegetable. As some of them had driven quite a distance and as the usual custom at these do's is to hand out a cup of powdered soup and peanut butter sandwiches, this potage, which I touted up as a bit of pure Canadiana, went down a treat. They all had seconds, relaxed and enjoyed. After lunch I gave a paper on 'Religious vows in community life. Are they necessary? Need they be lifelong?' This got a noticeably less enthusiastic reception than the potage Quebecois!

I had a full Saturday. I wrote some letters first and then went down and did the 10.00am Eucharist in the church; this usually draws in a few extras who are in town for the shopping. I then had to be out at the crematorium by 10.45 for a funeral. The crem time-table divides the day into thirty minute slots, so you pull up at the front gate just as the ones ahead of you are pulling out and you finish while the next group is gathering at the front door. This one this morning, like most, was just a handful of mourners, but, like everyone else, they wanted to have two hymns, usually selected from 'The Lord's my Shepherd' or 'Abide with Me' or 'On a hill far away stood an old rugged cross'. With so few present and too shy to sing aloud I ended up singing pretty well solo. Not a pretty sound I can assure you, hearty maybe, raucous definitely! I then came home and did some shopping for tomorrow's dinner and then drove out to see Malcolm and Muriel. Meanwhile it had turned into a lovely autumn afternoon and so we drove out to

North Allerton, a nice old-fashioned country town with a popular Saturday afternoon market in the town square. As Christmas is drawing near the place was jam packed with people buying pork pies, honey, fresh bread and lots of nick-knacks and Christmas tree ornaments such as Muriel loves. We drove back through the rolling Cleveland hills just now covered with heather in full purple blossom. Malcolm's stepson Simon who is in the police force was at home and cooked us a magnificent Indian dinner with lots of rice and curry and crisp bread – delicious. A great day.

***

We are big into money raising this week. It is part of a nationwide campaign to raise money for Children in Need; it has been publicised in the papers and on TV. Our stalwart band of bookstall men turned up with a set of plastic buckets appropriately labelled and sent us out into the streets to rattle and shake them. Not my favourite way of passing a Saturday but there I was wrapped in scarves, mittens and thickest coat (it was bitter cold) propped against the church wall as the shoppers stampeded by. Our group collected £550 mostly in small change but nationwide they have collected millions. But, generally speaking, the favourite way to raise money in and for a church in these parts is to have a Pie and Pea supper. This is a nice hot pie of minced beef sitting like an island in plateful of mushy peas with lots of salt and vinegar. It makes a good meal on a cold night, bolstered up with a few slices of bread and endless cups of tea. After the clearing up there will be a quiz and few songs so, as well as producing some money it binds us all together with food and entertainment.

***

One topic which agitates a good many these days is whether the church should ordain women priests. The subject is due to be decided at the General Synod which meets early next year so there is some urgency about it. The question affects us here as quite a few members of the congregation are, to say the least, uncomfortable with the idea, but more particularly Malcolm Broadhead, one of my closest friends, is absolutely convinced that it is wrong and is threatening to resign as a priest in protest if it goes through. Why? That is one of life's mysteries. Here's a man who is happily married, a good father to his children, a devoted parish priest; he was for some time a faithful member of SSM. He worked for a year in Lesotho, and was totally opposed to apartheid and zealous for the advancement of Africans. He went to Belfast in support of the ecumenical community that stands against violence and prejudice there; he is in favour of ecumenism and of liturgical renewal in the church but when it comes to this one subject, the ordination of women, all reason, all rational argument, all working towards the truth flies out the window and we are in a different ball game. I've only ever heard one rational argument against women's ordination and that is 'It's never been done before' but you could just as well say that modern technology, modern medicine, our global society, has never been done before and we survive precisely by learning to do what we have never done before. Or there is the biblical argument that if Jesus had wanted to have women priests some of the twelve apostles he chose would have been women but that's on the same level as saying that if Jesus had wanted us to use decimal coinage he would have appointed ten apostles, not twelve and if he had wanted racial harmony he would have included a couple of Africans. But in fact no such argument or any argument at all carries any weight in this discussion. As soon as the subject comes up, Malcolm's blood pressure shoots up, his face becomes flushed, his breathing short, his eyes flash panic, and his talk becomes a series of short sharp slogans which show clearly the pain he is feeling but are not directly connected with his thinking and which do not lead anywhere in the direction of a solution to the problem. Why he should feel so deeply, so strongly about this one issue, I have no idea, and I don't think he has either, and yet this baffling mystery seems to be tearing the Anglican Communion apart these days. Malcolm and I deal with it by pretending it is not there and never mentioning it; as for our congregation at All Saints, once they were assured that no woman priest would ever come near them until the day they invited her, they were content to simmer away with a few grumbles, but the fires of rebellion died out.

All this month the war clouds have been building up bigger and blacker with young people being called up and sent off to the Gulf. When the invasion of Kuwait began preceded by the bombing raids on Baghdad, the evening newscast became a daily horror session. One of the older most traditionalist members of the congregation complained a few weeks ago that present day clergy (presumably Edmund and I!) didn't believe in the fires of hell anymore and never preached about them. I said who could watch the news each night and see the horrible suffering we ourselves were inflicting on the helpless women and children of Baghdad and not believe in hell. This was a hell we were creating with our own technology and by our own choices. Coverage of the bombing raids alternated with round table discussions composed of men and women in suits weighing up the probabilities and possibilities of the day's events, giving their opinions with much nodding of grey heads and coming to much the conclusions they had reached the night before.

I have been inquiring into flights to Toronto from Teesside airport which would be much the most convenient for me, but now I discover that Teesside airport is going to be used entirely for the reception of the wounded from Kuwait. From there they will be distributed around the hospitals of UK. They say they are preparing for about 1000 a week, but let's hope that that is just the over-the-top enthusiasm of those who are looking forward to a 'lovely war'.

Here on the home front we have organised an inter-faith vigil of prayer for peace in the church on Saturday 4.00 – 6.00pm. The Muslims, Sikhs, Baha'is and Jews have all agreed to come and make their contribution as will we. Some of our members are not enthusiastic, to put it mildly, for such inter-faith projects. They rather feel (though don't actually say) that allowing all these folks into our sanctuary is rather like, on a bitter cold and stormy night, allowing Mr Fox to shelter in your hen house if he promises to be a good boy.

Just a block down the street from us is the Teesside Polytechnic. It has a good reputation and now with the European Economic Union. gathering momentum every year, it attracts students from all over Europe. Some of them turn up in church on a Sunday and we have had couple of French lads who have been regular worshippers here. I suppose they feel that trying the English church is a part of trying English culture and besides the old distinctions between churches are not so important these days with the lowering of temperatures in all things religious.

This Lent the Bishop of Whitby has been coming and doing a Lent Course here for the whole deanery on the Christian Faith. The bishop, Gordon Bates, is well known to Edmund and me. He was in his final year at Kelham when I arrived in 1957 and he directed the pantomime that first Christmas when I had a lowly part in the chorus line. Perhaps his pantomime skills stand him in good stead here for he presents his material in a lively and attractive manner with a complete absence of any theological jargon. He also has a fist full of illustrations drawn from Teesside life that keeps people interested and often laughing. The topics are basic: the Bible, Jesus, the Church, a moral code. What has surprised me most has been the numbers attending. There have been about 250 each week and each talk has been followed by a good question and answer session. We are so brain-washed by the media into thinking that religion is a left over from the age of the cave man and believing Christians are an extinct species that when we are confronted with evidence that there are still numbers of people out there interested and committed, it takes us completely by surprise.

Last Sunday afternoon after our dinner and our post-prandial naps, Edmund and I had a drive out to one of our favourite spots. It is down at the mouth of the Tees where it empties into the North Sea. You can walk out along the concrete piers that line the river there, and on the opposite bank you can see Seal Sands, which is just a mud flat, on which a bevy of seals are usually lying, sunning themselves and gazing across the river at us with a curiosity even more languid than what we are turning on them. On our side there is generally a band of devoted fishermen, especially on a sunny, breezy Sunday afternoon like this one. I did not see a lot of action amongst them but still one or two nice mackerel were pulled out and there was also something there for the non-sportsmen like us in the shape of vans sending forth enticing odours of fish and chips. Although industry and mining in and around Middlesbrough has almost completely collapsed, the port is still in business; in fact with the advent of container shipping it is expanding all the time, bringing in all the necessities of life we no longer manufacture for ourselves from China, India, Poland and the like. This afternoon, just as on any day, you could see five or six great liners heaped high with containers waiting off shore for their turn to enter the river and get up to the docks.

We are now into the high wedding season with two this morning and another two next Saturday. It is always the custom here to leave a large collection plate prominently displayed near the back door to encourage those folks who seldom darken our doors to give us a hand. Edmund was slightly disconcerted this morning, mid-ceremony, as he was leading the bride and groom through their vows and every eye in the church was fixed on the happy couple. He saw a scruffy young street kid slip through the back door and gather up all the money from the plate, pocket it and then turn to slip away. Edmund said he had to do a rapid mental arithmetic calculation, weighing up what would be the estimated value of the purloined collection, against what would be the inevitable furore of the wedding party if he broke off the exchange of vows to scream 'Stop! Thief!' The result was he just carried on only praying a blessing on the disappearing young thief at the dawn of his career.

I have heard from Peter Stannard at Cape Coast asking if I could go back and spend the Michaelmas term with them. He now has thirty students and is running courses for lay people. As Brother Garry SSM is due to be ordained in June and marked to do his curacy in this parish, Edmund could well manage without me and so it looks as if my return is secured!

Last Monday was a Bank holiday and Edmund and I, being on our own, decided to take a drive out. In fact we went as far north as Jedburgh in Scotland where there are the ruins of a famous abbey. Although Middlesbrough has little to offer in the way of scenery, once you get out of the city and into the countryside you are soon into beautiful almost empty Northumberland and, further north, in the border country with its enormous rolling green hills. It was a beautiful day in the midst of magnificent country and the break did us both good. On the way back we passed through a small village called Kirk Newton in which we noticed an interesting looking ancient parish church. Edmund is never one to pass an interesting church unvisited so we stopped and looked in. I was very surprised when we passed though the churchyard gate to see a row of twelve regulation grave stones, all looking as good as new, of men of the RCAF who had all died in 1943 or 44, all of them aged 21, 22, or 23. One was from Unionville, others from Toronto, Belleville or Trenton. It gave me a strange jolt to come upon these men lying there so far from home. I can clearly recall those towns where they had grown up and I could even imagine the kind of growing up they must have had since they were only about ten years older than I am. I couldn't help but feel a great sadness that their lives had ended at the point where they were just beginning with so much left undone. It reminded me of that poem we had to do for memory work at school, all of which I have forgotten except the last line, 'There is a corner of a foreign field that is forever England'. Or, in this case, Canada. There was likely a Canadian Air Force base near here during the war.

--- • ---

Barbara and Ken Bott are over here from Canada on holiday staying with her sister Ruth in North Allerton. They are great friends of mine ever since I boarded with Barbara's mother, Mrs Tomlin, on Bleecker Street when I was a curate at St Simon's. Monday was

Spring Bank Holiday and the day of the national pilgrimage to the shrine of Our Lady of Walsingham down in Norfolk. All Saints has always been very keen on this pilgrimage and they have hired a coach which is now filled with members looking for a 'trip out' and so I thought that as we would be passing through North Allerton we could pick up Barbara and Ken and take them along with us, which we did. There was a crowded Eucharist held out of doors in the ruins of the ancient abbey next door to the shrine with people from all over England in attendance. The preacher was the Archbishop of Canterbury, Robert Runcie, and after a picnic lunch we joined in a large procession through the town, all carrying candles and singing about five thousand times, Ave Ave Maria – words easy to remember! Ken, Barbara and I walked side by side. The bus left for home soon afterwards. The trip takes about three to four hours but I valued it because it gave Barbara and me a chance for some private conversation about all that has happened in their family and in the SSM since last we met. In fact that chat was more precious than I realised at the time. She did not tell me that she had advanced cancer, and she died soon after her return to Canada.

Later in the week I took them up to Lindisfarne or Holy Island to the north of us. The island only becomes an island at high tide and at other times you can walk or drive your car across the natural causeway to it. It was the home of St Cuthbert and the centre of all his missionary activities, and, resting there just a stone's throw from the Northumberland coast it gives the impression of being a small boat afloat on the waves.

We visited the lovely old parish church, the ruins of the abbey and walked along the shore skipping stones as we went to the admiration of curious seals. Cuthbert, like many of the Celtic saints, seemed to have had a close affinity with nature and the life of the wild creatures. It is said that when he used to stand up to his neck (or was it his knees?) in the North Sea and recite the whole of the book of psalms by heart, the seals would come flopping up to him afterwards and lay across his feet to warm and dry them again. I'm not sure I would appreciate that particular kindness myself! He is one of the few saints whose bodies have survived the smashing up of the ancient shrines during the Reformation and he still lies peacefully behind the high altar in Durham Cathedral. It was another lovely day in a beautiful place with dear friends, and it was the last time I saw Barbara.

———•———

It is now settled that I will spend the next term at St Nicholas in Cape Coast and I much look forward to that. But there have been even further developments since. The bishop of Cypress and the Gulf, in whose diocese lies Kuwait, has appealed to the Society to see if we could send a brother to Kuwait to work with the small congregation there. Since the end of the war the American army has been trying to cap the oil wells which the Iraqis set alight as they were departing, and have been clearing the mines laid all around the city. There is a chaplain and small congregation there but as he is a married man with a young family the bishop is reluctant to send them into such a volatile situation and for that reason has appealed to us. He was trained at Kelham and is a great friend of our Francis so we want to help if we can. The upshot of all this is that after I have finished my term at St Nicholas in January, I will proceed to Kuwait to act as a kind of focus for the re-gathering congregation who are now returning after having fled their homes at the invasion. I am to stay for at least a year until a more permanent arrangement can be made for them.

———•———

During my last few months in Middlesbrough I put down on paper various ideas that were buzzing around in my head under the general title of *A Rule For a New Brother*. It summed up all my ideas of how the Society might now develop from this point onwards. I would have to say though that this inspiration was stillborn and at birth sank without a trace, being received by the brothers to whom I sent it with a deathly silence. This perhaps should have been expected since I had consulted no brother in preparing it. It was all out of my own head and it probably started from the wrong questions, such as 'What did we do wrong at Kelham?' Or 'What can we reconstruct from the bits that are still left?' Many years later I approached the same subject with I think more realistic questions and got, I think, slightly more accurate answers. However this early effort did gain some spurious and unexpected fame when it was seen by Alistair Mason who was at the time writing a centennial history of SSM who included a large quotation from it in his final chapter.

———•———

We came to my farewell Eucharist at All Saints. I always find saying goodbye a wretched business and it was with real grief that I said goodbye to all my friends here who have taken me so warmly into their lives and hearts. I will always be grateful to them for all they have given me and will carry the memories of them with me as I go. Edmund with his usual sense of humour, in the light of the burning oil wells in Kuwait thought it would be appropriate for us to sing as our closing hymn:

> 'Give me oil in my lamp, keep me burning
> Give me oil in my lamp I pray
> Give me oil in my lamp keep me burning
> Keep me burning till the break of day.'

7

Kuwait Days

In March 1992 the first Gulf War was only just over and the people of Kuwait were struggling to resume their normal lives after having been occupied for ten months by the Iraqi army. Amongst those trying to readjust was the small congregation at St Paul's Anglican Church, Ahmadi. Ahmadi is a small residential suburb with shady tree-lined streets (all planted, watered and maintained by the Kuwait Oil company) about twenty kilometres out of the city of Kuwait. It had been set up by the British oil companies in the 1950's when they brought out people from England to develop and run the fabulously rich oil deposits which had been recently discovered. The oil had long since been nationalised and taken over by the Kuwaitis but there still remained a sizable number of expats making their living in Kuwait; in fact the rivers of wealth that were flowing from the oil there drew them like flies, and amongst them were some faithful church members. It was to these that the bishop of Cyprus and the Gulf, The Rt Revd John Brown (trained by SSM at Kelham 1951-1954 and author of *Mainly Uphill: A Bishop's Journey*, published in 2012) sent me to be a focus in their efforts to rebuild their congregation as people began to return and resume their lives again. The pre-war priest was a married man with a family of small children and the bishop was reluctant to send them back while the oil wells were still burning and the mine clearing had only just begun. Hence his inquiry to SSM if they had anyone they could spare for a year or so.

The church itself is a conventional 1950's type of church such as you can find in many a housing estate over the length of England. It seated about 150 and was well kitted out with service books, hymn books, a pipe organ, good chairs, and vestments all ready to begin again. It had sustained almost no damage through the occupation except for the one stained glass window of the Good Shepherd behind the altar which the Iraqi soldiers had apparently used for target practice and it has now been boarded up. The Kuwait government has a strict but kind policy towards the Christians in its midst. Only four Christian churches are allowed, this one of ours, two RC (one their cathedral with a bishop) and one American Evangelical Church. Other Christian congregations must be accommodated within these, so our church is allotted on Monday nights to the Indian Pentecostal group, Tuesdays to the Syrian Orthodox, Wednesdays to the American evangelicals, Thursdays to the Mar Thoma congregation, Fridays to the Church of North India, and Saturday to the Brethren's prayer group. I got so that I attended them all whenever I was free – very mind expanding for me and in the process I have become extremely ecumenical. Up until now I have just not had these opportunities, but now I go clapping with the Pentecostals, wailing with the Orthodox, bowing and vigorously crossing myself with the Mar Thoma, breaking the word with the Evangelicals and joining in heart-felt prayer with the Brethren, and gently diffusing a gentle air of restraint and sweet reasonableness throughout, for surely that is the unique Anglican contribution! On the kind side, the government gave us free electricity for our air-conditioning and met most of our general maintenance costs.

I flew from London to Kuwait, receiving my first unexpected surprise even before we landed. We had been flying over the desert sands for some time when I saw on the ground enormous green carpet-like circles each provided with its own huge rotating irrigation arm. I was told later that this water was being piped up from the depths below the sands and as a result Kuwait now had a small farming and dairy industry, a thing I would never have imagined. I was given a warm welcome at the airport by David Dorrington, the churchwarden, and taken back to his home where I was welcomed by his wife, Sue and a few members of the congregation. I had certainly made a huge transition, from one of the poorest countries in the world to one of the richest; from a culture 85 per cent Christian with churches on every corner and church bells often ringing, to a culture 95 per cent Muslim with mosques provided by the government on every corner and the call to prayer sounding from the minarets from 4.30am and continuing at regular intervals all through the day; from the tropical lushness of Ghana to a land which is one enormous sandy desert floating over one of the richest oil deposits in the world. One result of the wealth is that there are two nations living here as 50 per cent of the population or slightly more is made up of immigrant workers from India, Pakistan, and the Philippines. There used to be large numbers of Palestinians in the past, but they made the mistake of siding with the wrong side in the recent war and are now definitely personae non gratae. The workers live in very Spartan barrack-like accommodation, are mostly single men and are paid a minimum wage most of which, apart from what is needed for daily necessities, they post home to pay the school fees of their children. In fact theirs is indeed a life of continuing sacrifice made up of heat, dust, work, and loneliness. By contrast, if you are a native born Kuwaiti, the government gives you a pension, subsidised housing with enormous compensations for any losses you suffered from the occupation, and you will certainly be speedily promoted to the top of your profession, with an immigrant provided at your side to do the work.

Rehabilitation has been going on apace, and the magnificent eight lane highways that encircle the city have all been restored after the damages inflicted by the tracks of the Iraqi tanks. Nearly all the private houses have been reclaimed and restored. Some of them have been thoroughly trashed by the Iraqi troops who were billeted in them. As these men were mostly shepherd-farmers from the mountain regions of Iraq they were not into sophisticated living and often pulled up the hardwood floors, where they found them, to make a fire in the centre of the sitting room to make the place more home-like and where they could roast the sheep they had just confiscated. In fact the Iraqi soldiers spent most of the ten months they were here, burning, looting, and generally destroying whatever they could lay their hands on. Any good furniture they came across they would bundle on to army lorries and ship back to the market place in Bagdad to be sold for private profits for them. However the shops are now all in full swing again and the restaurants, furnishing, and clothing shops compare well with anything you would find in London or Toronto all oozing affluence. The streets are full of big American cars in good shape. Such is the wealth of this country, it did not take long to recover; this is definitely not Third World! Except that the first day after my arrival happened to be the first day of Ramadan, the great Muslim fast and so all eating places were closed up tight like they used to be on a Sunday in the good old days in Toronto, for no coffee or tea may be sold or drunk not a sandwich must cross your lips until the sun goes down, with heavy fines and even imprisonment for offenders, so the streets had a Sabbath-like feel about them.

The house assigned to me at Ahmadi was air-conditioned with four bedrooms, three bathrooms, a big sitting room, kitchen, laundry, and, to finish it off, quarters for the potential maid in the garden. The diocese also provided a big Nissan Patrol jeep for my own use. It must be the mother of all gas-guzzlers. I don't like to think of the little number of miles it must do to the gallon but the bishop tells me that, as petrol is only 41 English pence to the gallon, that is nothing for me to worry about.

A far cry this from the room I started off with in Ghana so no wonder if my head was reeling and, in some respects, continued to reel the whole time I was there.

Ralph's Log

I have now moved into my house in Ahmadi, about three minutes' walk from the church, and we have also had our first service. This was the service for Ash Wednesday which this year coincides with the beginning of Ramadan. There were about twenty in the congregation, almost all Brits, some having just returned, and a few having survived the occupation here. The first thing that strikes me about the group is that everyone comes here or remains here for one reason only – because of the money, and they are nearly all on short term contracts. They have no notion of settling here for any length of time. They could just as well be on an oil rig in the middle of the North Sea for all the connection they feel with the local people or interest in their culture. The other noticeable thing was the jittery atmosphere. They have all been through a very traumatic experience either living in hiding for some time or fleeing for their lives in panic and alarm, which makes for a feeling of joint insecurity and this binds them closely one another. David Dorrington's wife, Sue, had managed to escape to Cypress to be with their children who are at school there, and David had gone into hiding in their house in order to keep an eye on it and where he could be fed and cared for by the Filipino couple who worked for them. This worked well for a time until one day the Iraqi army surrounded the neighbourhood and did a house to house search. David, along with quite few others, was arrested and transported to Baghdad where Saddam Hussein was threatening to chain them to his guns and other key strategic spots to discourage any allied bombers from attacking. David remained there until the end of the war. Ralph Williams, a banker and the church treasurer also remained in hiding in his own house behind curtained windows and fed by his domestic staff. He apparently used to run up and down stairs twenty or so times a day, or so he says, in an effort to keep fit. When the group came together after church or at any subsequent social gathering, everyone had a tale to tell and one tale would provoke another for they had an obsessive need to get it off their chest and to rehearse again and again what they had been through perhaps in an effort to gain closure to a painful experience.

Ash Wednesday, after our service we attended a reception at the British Embassy. Fortunately the present ambassador and his wife are very faithful Anglicans. He was here all through the occupation holed up in the embassy and always gives a lot of support to the chaplaincy. He sponsored my entry visa and regularly attended our

Friday lunchtime service at the American Evangelical church when we got that going. The reception that night was attended mostly by crowds of British businessmen sipping drinks and swapping stories. David and Sue Dorrington and I stayed on for a late supper, served by a couple of waiters. Two years in Middlesbrough, and six in Ghana did not really prepare me for this!

I now have staying with me, Michael Rawson who was with me in Ghana and is now a student at St Stephen's House, Oxford. He will be here for a couple of weeks and is great company; he radiates a wry assurance and good humour. Yesterday David, one of the church wardens, took us both out for a run to show us the Kuwait that is outside the city boundaries. One memorable experience was stopping in the desert when David switched off the engine and said, 'Listen'. Truly I have never 'heard' a silence so complete, so enveloping. It could almost be felt; not a bird, not an insect, not the slightest ghost of a breath was there. We then drove on to one of the most horrible sights I have ever seen. It is only about 10 kilometres from town at the spot where the road to Bagdad climbs up through a narrow pass in the low hills. When the remnants of the Iraqi army were in full flight down this very road, heading for home as fast as they could go, the Allies waited until they got near this spot and then bombed the pass, thus completely blocking the only road out of Kuwait. They then proceeded to massacre what was left of the trapped Iraqi army with bombs and shells and mortars. The site is still littered with tanks, civilian cars of every description, and all sorts of army vehicles, all of them wrecks and skeletons, burnt to a cinder. More pathetic was the sight of soldiers' odd boots, helmets, bits of uniform, and blankets, all partially covered by the drifting sand. David, who works for one of the Bomb Disposal companies, told us that these guys were just sitting like ducks in a trap with no shelter and no escape and our side went on hammering them until the airmen refused to carry on any longer with it. Such are the glorious victories of war.

On the way back we drove through stretches of desert, reaching to the horizon where uncountable numbers of mines had been neatly planted out in careful patterns, each with its own stick or maybe half a ball protruding above the surface, and all guaranteeing an instantaneous trip to glory if you should stumble against it. Here too we saw the deserted trenches dug in the sand by the Iraqi army, and all around, as at the highway ambush, the ground was littered with boots, belts, blankets, helmets, all the sorts of things that men leave behind when they are fleeing for their lives, while the ground is covered over with all kinds of grenades, mortars, shells, unused ammunition, rather like the litter on a fairground at the end of a busy day of fun. David told us that each mortar shell cost £200-£300 and the mines even more than that. What a waste of money in a country (Iraq) where most are living in poverty, not to mention the lives of men, women, and small children maimed, twisted and discarded as things of no value. Getting closer to the city we passed through a large area of oil wells. The fires are now almost all out and there is an army of American oilmen here rehabilitating the wells, working around large lakes of oil that reach up in places to the verges of the road. The only nice thing we saw today was a few scattered herds of camels and flocks of sheep and goats attended by their herd boys, but even they, especially the camels, didn't look happy, far from it; and who could blame them?

Then this evening we decided to go back into town as Michael wanted to see the gold souks. It was a trip well worth the taking as, once the sun goes down the town is switched back on, all the shops and restaurants are opened and the streets are crowded with people. The souks themselves are long narrow passage ways for pedestrians only, lined on both sides with the stalls of the gold-workers and displaying every kind of gold work, bracelets, anklets, necklaces, rings, ear rings, nose rings, chains medallions, every kind of ornament destined to tinkle and glitter unseen and invisible beneath the burkas of these heavily-veiled women, whose beautiful dresses and lovely ornaments are never to be seen by any masculine eye save that of the husband. The whole market place was full of colour and movement and in fact Ramadan is a time for partying, entertaining friends and making a break in your usual routine while also enhancing your spiritual life, but definitely not a time for long faces and solemn postures. I have heard that in the fasting month of Ramadan more meat and food is sold than in any other month of the year, because of the frequent home parties, the biggest one coming right after sunset and followed only a short time later by a hearty and substantial breakfast to see you through the next day. After looking around Michael and I went into one of the restaurants on the first floors above the stalls and had a very nice meal though we were slightly jolted when the waiter approached us as soon as we sat down and said, 'What would you like to drink? Orange? Lime? Mango? Grapefruit?' However I understand that some of the wealthy business men here are not so strictly observant in the privacy of their own homes where, at the press of a button, the library book case slides back and a fully-equipped bar stands revealed furnished with everything you could wish for.

We had a wonderful service last night for Good Friday. All the congregations that use the church through the week came and the church was packed. Each group more or less did its own thing so we had some nice Indian music from the Tamil congregation's orchestra and some great singing from the nearly all male Indian Pentecostal congregation. Afterwards one of the members, an Indian family, invited me back to their place for a meal with lots of saffron rice, curries and poppadoms all supplemented with little bits and pieces. This man is unusual in having his wife and children here, but it was great for me to be in the midst of a family and in a home once again.

In fact we almost had to cancel the service due to a dust storm that sprang up in the late afternoon and swept down out of the desert. It was a fine dust carried in dark black clouds and driven by a high wind. It swallowed up the whole countryside like a thick fog and soon we needed all the lights on while the visibility on the roads was down to a car length. This left everything inside and out coated with a layer of dust. Now I realise why the Arab men keep that square of cloth draped over their heads ready to be pulled across their face at any time – very practical it is.

—————•—•—————

Tonight just before church one of the men came in and said he had found a big bag of live ammunition hidden behind the church hedge, apparently abandoned there by the departing Iraqi army. Luckily the churchwarden works for the Bomb Disposal people so he was able to take it away for us. So the evidence of the war is still all around us and the Americans (they were the ones who got all the contracts!) are working full time gathering up the unused bombs, rockets and grenades and detonating the mines in the minefields as best they can. They seem to gather everything they have found in a day together in a field not far from my house and explode those all most afternoons about 5.00pm with an ear-splitting bang that shakes the house and makes the windows rattle, though at least you can be sure that no one is likely to get hurt. I read in the newspaper yesterday that the army have destroyed 1,113 tons of bombs in this past week alone and a total of 5,157 tons since the Iraqi left over a year ago. The paper warned people to stay on the highways and not to wander into the desert without a guide, advice I shall scrupulously follow! So while people here are recovering fast from the material devastation caused by the occupation, it will take them a lot longer to recover their confidence and in the meantime it makes them feel really good to have as many American and British soldiers as possible about the place.

—————•—•—————

On a different note: when Michael and I were returning from town this morning, we found rattling along in front of us a small, apparently much used, white half-ton pick-up. Enthroned in the back reclining sideways on, was a magnificent white camel, gazing back at us and around on the scene with a disgruntled disdain, not a little put out at the indignities that the modern life was imposing upon him. I don't know where they were going, somewhere beyond Ahmadi where we turned off. It was a lovely sight, so seldom do you see in this city of glass, steel and concrete any traces left of the old pre-oil Arabia and its nomad people.

———•·•———

The best of news is that I now have my own post box. After two months of frustration, obfuscation, and form filling at the Post Office this miraculous solution comes out of the blue through the intervention of a Ugandan doctor who is a member of our congregation. Dr Edward, like many Africans, is a man of great personal charm, and a top-notch wheeler-dealer, and extremely kind and generous with it all. He has already taken me out for several good meals in the large American army camp where there are thousands of men who are working night and day on the rehabilitation of the oil wells and the clearing of the minefields. The food, needless to say, is all up to an American standard, plenty of it and with great variety. I however am slightly nervous sitting there in this cafeteria amongst all those hulking great construction types, since I am rather doubtful that Dr Edward has any right to eat there and I am certain that I have not the vestige of any such right. So I would wolf my food down at top speed while keeping my eye out for any Military Police approaching our table. Apart from his military duties (if any) Edward is now treating the wife of some man high up in Post Office officialdom, and he has spoken to this man about my problem. A single word from the big man was more than sufficient to release the logjam and I now have my own key to my own box, so let the letters flow. How simple it all is!

———•·•———

The Royal Navy is now in Kuwait undertaking some joint manoeuvres in the Persian Gulf with the Kuwait navy. The captain and officers of HMS Beaver had a reception on board on Sunday evening and I, along with some of the British members of our congregation, were all invited. So there you would find me in the heat of that tropical night on the old Poop Deck, clinking our ice cubes and gently circulating while young Jack Tars in their whites moved around with enormous pitchers of gin and tonic topping us up. I had one slightly inebriated old Scot who came up to me with tears in his eyes to tell me he had been a choir boy in the Piskie (Episcopal) Cathedral in Edinburgh. Then two smart young Kuwaitis came up in white dish-dash (that is the white cassock-like gown they wear) and white head dress. The one told me he was a captain in the Kuwaiti navy and had done his training at Dartmouth in the UK with the Royal Navy. He said that on their ship there they had had a padre and they used to have nice talks with him about God and all that kind of thing, and was I this ship's padre? You could not have met a nicer pair of guys. Out of a crew of about 270, about twenty young sailors were women and there were about a dozen or so who were serious Christians and they asked me if I would come back the next day and celebrate a communion service for them, which I will be very glad to do.

The temperature now is between 36C – 40+, so you don't want to spend much time outside or stray very far from the air-conditioner. Here even the churches are air-conditioned and every car and shop. Nevertheless driving along the other day I saw a couple of kids swimming and their mother with them. She with her head swathed in a black veil was sitting quietly in the water looking like nothing so much as a grey seal off our northern coasts. But one thing you will seldom or never see here, whatever the temperature is naked flesh whether of woman, man or child; even the small boys wear the dish-dash to kick a football about. In fact I find it an almost Puritan life style.

A small disaster on my way back from town today as I was driving along the motorway. First the engine began to heat up alarmingly, then to emit great clouds of black smoke and then to die completely and utterly. I pulled over on to the shoulder and wondered what to do next. I could not see another car on the road, the horizon was a long way away both before and behind and with a blazing sun and a temperature of 40C+ walking did not seem an attractive or even a safe option. I was roughly equal distances both from Ahmadi and town and then as I sat there amidst rising tides of panic a second hand car pulled over in front of me and an oldish (probably my age!) Arab man got out in his long dish-dash and head dress. I would guess him to be a farmer of the rough and ready variety. He spoke little English, in fact the only two words he knew were 'welcome!' and 'friend' but those words sounded sweeter in my ear than any I had ever heard. He took me into Ahmadi to the garage and negotiated a tow-in for the car. When he knew I was from Canada he doubled the size of his vocabulary with 'Ottawa', 'Great Lakes', 'Toronto', all from his school geography lessons no doubt. But whatever his language deficiencies, he couldn't have been kinder or of more practical help to me, a traveller in distress. With one more 'welcome friend', he jumped into his car and drove off down the road. How deeply indebted you are at times to some complete stranger whom you will never see again. I will go back to the garage tomorrow to see what the damages are.

We heard today that there had been an accident. One of the bomb disposal crews had loaded up a truck with mines to cart them away for disposal when it all blew up and ten men were blown to pieces – so death continues even after the peace has been concluded! Our church member who works for the disposal company doesn't see how the mines will ever be completely cleared because the sand is constantly drifting and shifting, hiding some mines and uncovering others and edging them all out of pattern. But still Iran and Iraq, UK and USA are busy buying and making more and more bombs. They told me that the ground level temperature in the minefields is often close to 60C and there they are scrambling around in the sand looking for unexploded mines. They make big money, but I would say they earn it.

The temperature now is pretty constant between 48C and 52C. There is in the centre of town a public tower much like any clock tower in European cities, but this one has, in place of a clock, a thermometer. Rumour has it that the thermometer is pegged never to rise above 49.5C since according to the law here, no one can be compelled to work when it rises above 50C.

I had a call from the Canadian Embassy on Monday asking if I would like to attend a Canada Day Jamboree. They will put everyone in buses at 7.00am and travel about 70 miles up to the Iraq border where there are about 200 Canadians with the U. N. Force. They said there would be a march past, games of all kinds, followed by a barbecue with beef, salmon, and beer flown in from Canada, getting back late at night. I would love to have gone but they only gave me twenty-four hours' notice and I had already accepted an invitation from two of our Indian families for supper that night, and they might be hurt if I suddenly pulled out.

Tonight I am attending another party, this one put on by the Christian nurses at the hospital. They are all Filipinos and this is to be a farewell for one who is now returning home. Some of these Filipinos stayed here throughout the occupation but they told me that when the Minister of Health came to make awards to those who had served, only the Kuwaiti nurses were called forward even though some of them had been here for less than a couple of months while they (the Filipinos) were left sitting on the back row. Recently thirteen nurses at the local hospital were sacked and deported when they were reported to have been praying at the bedsides of some of their patients.

I visited an odd pair this week; they are an English couple and have lived in Kuwait for some years, in fact they were here throughout the occupation, living on food smuggled into the house by their Kuwaiti friends. There was even a day when the Iraqi soldiers broke into the house, helping themselves to odds and ends they fancied while the owners cowered with fear and trembling behind a stack of packing cases in the garage. They invited me to a little party they were having so that I could meet their family. The family turned out to be their collection of birds. They started by taking in birds abandoned by their owners but by now the whole house is one big aviary. It began in the front yard when I got out of the car to find about a dozen hens and four roosters clucking and crowing in welcome. The man said he had bought the roosters as chicks thinking they were hens but now they did nothing but crow. When I suggested they might soon end up in the pot, he went pale with alarm and embarrassment at my gauche manners and gasped, 'These are our family; they stay with us until they die of old age.' In the sitting room upstairs they had about 38 parrots of all sizes and colours, all squawking, some in cages, some walking the floor, and some walking up your arm, leaving little souvenirs as they went. The TV was in the large room reserved for the toucan, while 18 – 25 little zebra finches flitted about in the dining room. Not unexpectedly, the place smelt like a pet shop. This family is not short of cash. He is soon to retire and they are building themselves a place in the north of Portugal; right in the country, to which all their birds will be transported. 'We couldn't leave our family behind!" As they say – it takes all sorts.

Not a good day. I went this morning to pick up the lady who cleans the church on a Sunday morning and on my way back, as I was crossing an intersection, some young guy in a big Chevrolet pick-up slammed into the side of me. Fortunately neither the lady passenger, nor the driver of the other vehicle nor me was hurt but I think if I had not been in the big Nissan Patrol we would have been rolled over. As it was, the police were soon on the spot and we were all taken off to the local police station where we spent the next three hours answering questions, filling out forms, summoning church wardens, interpreters, traffic officers and I wondering what was going to happen to me, an alien offender in a strange land. A little ray of sunshine though. As I sat in the cheerless waiting room, feeling extremely anxious and, I am sure, looking more than apprehensive, one of the Kuwaiti police, a young guy in a smart uniform with polished boots, came over to me, touched my shoulder and said, 'Don't worry! Everything will soon be sorted, and you will be able to go home!' I appreciated his kindness, and, true enough, I was back in time to take our usual evening service at which I, a little shaken, celebrated and preached.

———•—•———

We had a second visitation from the Royal Navy, this time the HMS Edinburgh. The home port of this ship is Rosyth in Scotland and a good number of the crew are Scots. I was contacted by one of the crew asking if I would come and do a Eucharist for them which I was glad to do. We had about 15 – 20 men there, one of whom was the captain, so we were well supported. We sang 'For those in peril on the sea' with great gusto, but I came away with the impression of how crowded and confined the crew's quarters were.

The next day a party of volunteers from the ship, about thirty this time, came out to Ahmadi, armed with buckets of paint and rollers on the end of long poles and painted the whole of the interior of the church in about an hour and a half. They all worked cheerfully with a will and it made a really enjoyable occasion. The church badly needed sprucing up after having been through the war, so now it looks dazzling bright and white, and ready for the big memorial service to be held here on November 11 for those British soldiers who lost their lives in the war. A memorial plaque will then be dedicated in the church to these men.

———•—•———

Peter Stannard, the priest who followed me at St Nicholas Cape Coast, has arrived for ten days here on his way back to Ghana for their new term. But what a hassle to get him in! Kuwait is due to have national elections on October 5, and they (the government) are so afraid there are going to be demonstrations and/or rioting that, as a precautionary measure, they have decided to admit no further tourists until after the election. Fortunately we were able to get around this one by asking the British Embassy to invite Peter as their personal guest, which they were quite willing to do for us. However Peter's visa was not processed until Friday morning and he was due to fly out on the Saturday morning. Everything was OK as he had bought his ticket two weeks in advance in an act of blind faith. They haven't had an election here for six years.

In fact the whole democratic process is a bit of nonsense put on to curry favour with the USA. In reality the country is completely controlled by one family – the Sabah family. The last parliament was shut down suddenly, dramatically and without argument when the Emir told them one day he was tired of listening to their squabbling so they could pack their bags and go home. I wonder if the Queen ever wishes she could do the like.

I have had a very good two weeks with Peter Stannard. The churchwarden's wife has loaned me her car and one of the men of the congregation (here on an oil contract) is living in an apartment with a swimming pool so we went and had a couple of good afternoons cooling off in the pool, which was very refreshing.

We got up early one morning, just at sunrise and went down to the fish market, and there you could see every kind of fish and in all sizes, fresh from the waters of the Gulf, each batch presented by the fisherman who had caught them. The big thing at this season is the prawns which are now jumbo size. We bought a kilo of them for £1.75 and brought them home for a delicious fry-up. The next night David Dorrington and his wife had us for supper and they did sweet and sour prawns in a Chinese sauce – even more delicious.

The parish has agreed to sell the Nissan Patrol and get me a new second-hand car. I couldn't do this job without a vehicle but I am glad to say goodbye to the Nissan Patrol. It is just too big, too heavy, and too expensive. The roads here have all been re-surfaced since the Iraqi left so the combination of good, seldom crowded roads, cheap petrol, new cars and young drivers, plus a sprinkling of women drivers, frequently make driving here a hair-raising experience. I hope my last remark does not brand me as a macho, sexist bore, but... Unlike Saudi Arabia where women are not allowed to drive ever or anywhere, here they can drive though still heavily veiled. Rumour has it that these women, having been trained from earliest infancy never to look a man in the eye, when they come to a four-way intersection, instead of looking around to check who has the priority, look down at their toes say a short prayer 'Be it even as Allah wills' and then put their foot on the gas. But that may be a story invented and circulated by the men!

We had the elections here last Wednesday and it all passed off very smoothly without any riots or demonstrations. The main point of the election was to prove to Mr Bush and his propaganda machine that this was a free and democratic country – but democracies vary! There are about a million people in Kuwait and at least half of them are immigrant workers and so without a vote. Of those Kuwaiti citizens, half will be women and so without a vote, and of the 250,000 male Kuwaitis, less than half will have first class citizenship and the remainder will have no vote. Thus the actual number of voters on the day may have been something like a 100,000 or more, probably less, out of a million people. Even then, when the new parliament meets under the chairmanship of the Prime Minister who is also the Crown Prince and heir to the throne, it is only to advise the Emir as to what he might do.

David Dorrington and Sue announced that he was quitting his job in the Gulf Bank and was going to work in Bahrain. The parish will really miss them, as they both have been great workers and very warm and hospitable persons to have around. I have never been in a place where there is such a rapid turn-over of people. Everyone here seems to be on short-term contracts and as a consequence no one puts down any roots, everyone is plotting their next move. Each Sunday when I look down at the gathered congregation there are faces I have never seen before, and a few familiar faces are missing.

One of the Indian congregations held an anniversary service last night followed by a party at which I was the guest of honour, though to be honest, I had no clear idea of what anniversary it was we were celebrating. The music was wonderful with an accordion, three keyboards, two sets of drums, and a church packed with brown faces (not black as in Ghana!)Some of the saris worn by the women were really beautiful works of art.

Some time ago two healthy broad shouldered American guys turned up and said that they belonged to a group called The Navigators. They had come to evangelise amongst the Filipinos, Indians and Pakistani. They called again today and said their course material had now arrived from the States and they wanted to show it to me. It was all very glossy, texts to be memorised printed in little boxes, colourful cartoon type illustrations on every page and all very attractive. I found their personalities positive-plus even to the point of overwhelming. Peter Stannard who was with me when they first came said the one, 'had an ego the size of a house!' The packaged Christianity they bring is basic and simple in the extreme. For them it consists almost entirely of reading through the whole Bible, underlining the best bits, committing so many verses to memory each week, singing lots of gospel choruses and staying clear of booze and scandal. Its great advantage is that it's a simple programme, not hard to grasp, and in fact not so different from what Islam is offering. It may not be my scene but I admire these two guys. They are moving, meeting, and shaking more people than I ever have. They have lined me up with six Pakistani male nurses from the local hospital in a weekly Bible study which meets in the nurse's residence. When there, we go through a chapter in the big glossy book. I really enjoy these sessions for the time spent with them, but I would never have made this contact apart from our two Navigators. I feel a great sympathy for our young Pakistani brothers, they are keen evangelical Christians, who are exploited, underpaid, separated from wives and families and suffer all this in order just to survive economically and put their kids through school. It is a privilege to know them and to help them in any way I can.

Sister Joyce has arrived and has taken over the cooking. We have great conversation with lots of laughs, mostly about Ghana.

Next Monday evening ninety-six people will be flown into Kuwait, courtesy of the Kuwait government. They are the next of kin of the forty-seven British soldiers who died in the war. There will be a welcome for them when they land at the airport, when the children of Kuwaiti soldiers who also died in the war will present them with flowers. On Tuesday they will be given a tour of the city and various sites prominent in the conflict, including the Matloa Ridge where a large part of the Iraqi army was wiped out by the allied air forces. Wednesday they do a tour of HMS London which is in port and in the afternoon there will be the memorial service in church and the dedication of the plaque with all the men's names on it. On Thursday they will come back to the church for a quiet look and a chance for pictures on their own, followed by a luncheon given by the Kuwaitis and an evening reception at the British Embassy. There will be in attendance an Air Vice-Marshal and two bishops, the Anglican bishop of Cyprus and the Gulf, and the R. C. bishop of Kuwait. All has been carefully planned out and they will leave, fairly exhausted I would think, physically and emotionally, on Friday morning.

———

Our big service has come and gone and everything went off smoothly. The whole Kuwaiti establishment really did their best to welcome the next of kin as was only right and fitting considering these men by their deaths helped liberate Kuwait from the Iraqi invaders. We (for I was included in the party) were all invited to the Bayan Palace on the Tuesday where the Prime Minister who is also the Crown Prince welcomed them. The palace is a pretty awe-inspiring sight on its own. It is intended to give you the sensation that you are in a sheikh's grand tent, so the walls are all lined with coloured cloths and silks, the floors covered with heavy carpets, and there are no windows. A little incongruously, I thought, a good number of crystal chandeliers hung from the centre beam where the roof rises into a dome of multi-coloured cloth. After a glass of fruit juice and some welcome speeches we moved on into another room with a tinkling fountain in the centre, where a lavish buffet was spread out and an army of servants helped the guests to food.

Most of the Brits were ordinary folk from Newcastle or Aberdeen and by this time they were feeling tongue-tied and boggle-eyed. They had never seen the like before – nor had I!

The service in the church on the Wednesday was attended by the heads of the Kuwaiti government and army – a new sensation for most of them I would think, for I doubt if any or many of them had ever been in a Christian church before. The service lasted for slightly less than an hour. Our bishop, John Brown gave a few words, a Bible reading and prayers and then we had the Last Post, Reveille, the blessing of the plaque and the laying of wreathes of poppy flowers. Clearly the next of kin found it a very moving ceremony but everyone was very controlled. We then adjourned to the International Hotel for a buffet supper and the next day the families had the chance to come back to the church on their own to take it in better and snap a few pictures to take home. On the last evening there was a reception and farewell at the British Embassy. From the people I chatted with at these various gatherings I got the impression from just about all of them, that they had found the whole trip helpful and comforting. They greatly appreciated the pains that had been taken by the Kuwaitis and by our Embassy here to receive them in a sensitive way. It was also good that I had Sister Joyce with me for the occasion. I saw from time to time quite a few folks chatting with her in an informal and relaxed way which must have been of help to them.

I have another visitor with me this week, Tola Roberts, an Anglican priest, a Nigerian, and a lecturer in Dental Surgery at the University in Riyadh, Saudi Arabia. This is his story. He had been in the post there for about six months, never mentioning to anyone that he was a Christian, let alone a priest, but then some British ex-pats working there, heard he was a priest and contacted him to see if he would be willing to do a Eucharist for them on a Sunday in the compound of the British Embassy. This he agreed to do but fairly soon the Saudi police got wind of it and they sent a letter to the university instructing them to cancel his contract. The Rector of the University called him into his office and with profuse apologies told him he would have to go. Of course, without a job, there was no way he could remain any longer in Saudi. The other thing that Tola directed my attention to was the deafening silence of the British Embassy throughout. Not a whisper of protest came from them although the offence had been committed on their premises, so loud is the voice of money and oil! Fortunately Kuwait is slightly more liberal than Saudi and so he has come here looking for an appointment in the Dental College here. If he can get one, he would be able to take over from me when I leave which would make for a smooth transition. We get on very well together and his wife Lara and their twelve year old son will be coming from Riyadh to spend Christmas with us here. Saudi is the strictest of all the Muslim countries. Tola tells me that if the police there came across any Christmas cards for sale in a shop, they would throw the cards out into the garbage and would close down the shop, nor are they above giving the odd cut with their canes across any bare flesh they see on the arms or legs of American tourists.

--- • ---

Last night we had a lovely carol service. The original idea in my mind was the nine lessons and carols such as they have at home, but then I handed over one lesson and one carol to each of the nine congregations that use the church and we took off from there. Every congregation did their own thing in their own language and it turned out more like a cabaret than a carol service. We had little girls all in white sporting the wings of angels dipping and diving around the altar; a young people's gymnastic team did their gymnastic display, though it was billed as a dance. In four or five languages, no one could understand everything although as the plot was so well known we all knew where we were and what we were doing. The church was packed with a crowd standing outside and one half the seating was a solid block of Indian immigrant workers who really enjoyed the whole thing. We gave out prizes to the kids, applauded all the star turns and finished with refreshments for all, and yes, we even sang a carol or two. Now the Indians tell me that they are sending off a fax to the SSM Director,

Fr Edmund Wheat, asking that I be left here for another year! Such was the enthusiasm of the moment.

We will have another similar carol service tomorrow for the English congregation, but on this occasion the model firmly fixed in everyone's mind will be the nine lessons and carols, as done by Kings College, Cambridge on Christmas Eve, so we will be restricted to traditional carols with no clapping or dancing or performing kids; in fact, a bit dull!

We had a very good Christmas with a midnight Eucharist at Ahmadi and another one at noon in town at the American church. I spent most of the rest of the day at the churchwarden's place in town, a very nice family from Manchester. Boxing Day I spent relaxing at home with Tola and his family. Lara cooked us a magnificent dinner with all sorts of West African dishes and with much laughter. Tola was given an appointment lecturing at the Dental Faculty here in Kuwait and is very happy to take on the oversight of the church here, though, sad to say, I think there are some amongst the British ex-pats who are not so happy to have a black priest.[15]

I left Kuwait for the UK in January in time to prepare for my next posting which would be at the Anglican Centre, Palazzo Doria Pamphilj, Rome.

8

In Rome

I arrived at the Anglican Centre in Rome in March 1993.

This Centre goes back to the heady days of the Second Vatican Council when it truly seemed that the ecumenical movement was about to take a great leap forward and the re-union of the Christian churches was on the horizon. It was founded under the joint patronage of Pope Paul VI and Michael Ramsey the then Archbishop of Canterbury. These two during the Council had become great mates in a stuffed shirt sort of way. It was intended that this Centre would forward the cause of unity by providing in Rome a good library of Anglican theology and history which Roman Catholic students who come here to study could easily consult, and there would also be small group of Anglicans in residence with whom they could communicate.

Since those days in the 60's the Centre has gone through some lean times and financial stresses as many Anglicans around the world looked on it as an expensive and not very useful luxury. A succession of Directors had come and gone until, last of all, perhaps hoping to save some money, the Board of Governors approached a religious community to take it over, That community was the Society of the Sacred Mission and the brother chosen to go to Rome was Fr Douglas Brown, an Aussie who was there at the station to greet me off the train.

We took a bus to the Palazzo Doria Pamphilj on the Via del Corso where the Centre was housed on the fourth floor. This magnificent setting and location was entirely due to the generosity of the Doria Pamphilj family whose head was the Principessa Donna Orietto Pogson-Doria Pamphilj, a wonderful woman with a backbone of steel who had withstood Mussolini and the whole Fascist regime through all their years of power, such is still the power and the influence of this old Roman family. Donna Orietto was also a devout uncomplicated Christian who, at some point during the liberation of Rome from the Germans by the allied forces, met and fell in love with a British sailor from the Royal navy who was stationed there, Frank Pogson by name. No doubt to the surprise of many, the two were married and to their even greater surprise all these years later, they remained a devoted and loving couple. Their family were great and generous supporters of all good causes, ecumenical ventures among them, and when the Centre was first proposed, offered it the fourth floor of their Palazzo as accommodation.

This apartment contained eight or nine rooms, plus a large room for the library, another for the common room, a kitchen, office, and chapel and had access to the roof garden from which we had a sweeping view of the red tiled roof tops of Rome, from the Victor Emmanuel monument looking like an enormous wedding cake, to the church of the Jesu near at hand, to the dome of the Pantheon and on to the dome of St Peter's rising in the distance. From down below we heard the traffic roaring up and down the Via del Corso which in days gone by had provided the straight track down which the Romans loved to race their horses, and above which, beside our roof, was the many-windowed apartment which Napoleon had dutifully built for his mother so she too could watch the races. With Douglas and me in the apartment was Sergei, a young Russian from Kiev who like countless others in Rome was an illegal immigrant without proper papers. After having served part of a term in the Russian army in Afghanistan, he had fled Russia and ended up living rough on the streets of Rome until Douglas took him in as our cook, which he did very efficiently.

One of the main activities of the Centre was to run a series of seminars through the year, inviting people from different parts of the Anglican Communion to join in a five day seminar in Rome.

The programme is quite simple. The mornings are mostly spent in visits and guided tours of famous sites, and then after lunch and siesta there are lectures and an opportunity for discussion on appropriate topics. One of the things on this week's agenda was a Papal audience in the Paul VI Hall in the Vatican. However it was hardly an intimate meeting since there must have been about two thousand people gathered there from all over. When Pope John Paul II came in, down the aisle, he was greeted like a football hero with people standing on their chairs to get a better look, flashing their cameras to cries of 'Viva il pappa' and lots of flag waving and cheering. Once he sat down things grew quiet, even boring as he delivered his message in a monotone leaving the impression that he had said it all a thousand times before, and maybe he had. He gave it first in English, then French, then German, then Spanish, then Polish with a few words of Japanese thrown in at the end for some Japanese who were here from Kobe. It took about one and a half hours in all, but, apart from the content, you couldn't help but be impressed at this great gathering of people from almost every country, all in festive spirit, in harmony with one another and sharing a common faith. I sat beside a very nice couple from Rochester, New York, just ordinary folk and thrilled to death to see the Pope for the first time and to be a part of that cheering throng. Indeed, considering what was going on in the rest of the world while we sat there, it was reassuring to find that peace is, after all, possible.

The next day we went on a tour of the catacombs. This is an enormous network of tunnels and rooms stretching for miles under parts of the city. It has never been completely mapped and you need to take care not to stray from your party while you are down there. The explanation is that the soil under much of the city is made up of tuffa, a kind of volcanic ash which is very soft and easy to dig but which becomes as hard as concrete when exposed to the air. The tunnels were dug out between 100BC and 400AD. The walls are lined with niches where they laid their dead and when the walls of one gallery filled up with grave spaces, they simply dug down through the floor and created a further level, some of them twenty-five meters in depth. Later on when the Christians in Rome were persecuted and simply to be a Christian was to be under a sentence of death, they used the catacombs for places where they could meet in safety and where they could worship. As a result of those days there are many very early Christian wall paintings of Jesus the Good Shepherd, the five loaves and two fish, and others.

To me the whole place had an eerie atmosphere even today with the strings of electric bulbs stretching along the passages, but it must have been much more so when small communities of Christians gathered under flickering oil lamps, finding there in the depths of the earth, in their prayers and hymns, that security and safety which the Good Shepherd provided and that love and strength which rose up from the family of brothers and sisters as they broke bread together while the soldiers and the police up above were seeking them out to destroy them. To go there was a different and an unusual experience.

Ralph's Log

I seem to be getting stuck into things here and am now enrolled in an Italian class which meets four times a week. There are about forty in the class, the largest part of which is from South America, Argentina, Chile and Mexico. The next largest group would be the Japanese, and then the Americans. I quite enjoy trundling off to these classes in the mornings with my exercise book under my arm, all my homework done, no bigger problem to face that day than the past tense of an irregular verb, to a class where all questions have clear right or wrong answers and the teacher will know what is right and what is wrong and where we should head next. How simple! It takes me back to Grade Four, even to my habit then of dodging behind the person in front if I was not sure of the answer.

Douglas has left for the USA on a fund-raising tour. This place has been funded in the past by the Anglican Consultative Council, a sort of inter-Anglican body, but like a lot of others just now, they are running out of money and so Douglas and the Board of

Management are trying to raise an Endowment Fund to provide some income; in fact the future of this place feels a little shaky! In the meantime I have been looking after one of the seminars which is also interesting with priests attending from Australia, and England and the US.

———•———

One day we attended a seminar put on by a Jewish-Christian dialogue body. It took place within the old Jewish ghetto and we began with a tour around the bounds of the ghetto. They showed us where the gates were located which were shut and locked every evening at sunset and the key entrusted to a watchman. There has been a Jewish community in Rome since St Paul's days. At times they were suppressed and driven outside the city, at times they were tolerated, but confined to living within the ghetto as a kind of open prison. In fact their trade, which was money lending and high finance, made them essential to the economy of the city, perhaps especially to a city of clergymen. It was only after the unification of Italy under Garibaldi in the 1860's when Rome was made the capitol of the new Italy and no longer under the Pope's direct rule, that the Jews were given permission to build their own synagogue on the banks of the Tiber. We were also taken to the church where, before those days of liberation, the Jews were compelled to attend each Sunday to listen humbly to a sermon from a fervent Jesuit, explaining to them without any doubt or confusion that they were all without exception marching straight to hell, as was only right for those who were hated by God for having crucified his only son.

An even grimmer memorial was a large plaque on a wall nearby stating that on this spot in 1943 all the Jews resident in Rome were rounded up by the German troops aided by the Italian police. Here men, women, and children were herded together before being marched to the railway yards and locked into box cars for two days without food or water before being sent off to the death camps from which none of them ever returned. Even in those two final days no voices were raised to protest their treatment, or to defend them, let alone rescue them, not even from Pius XII.

The most interesting thing this week has been the trip we had to see the excavations under St Peter's. The point of these excavations is more than archaeological, the point is to discover the grave of Peter and see whether his body is still in it.

We know for a start that St Peter's was built on the site where the Romans had one of their public stadiums where Christians were sometimes put to death along with the gladiators to make an afternoon show. Peter was crucified in this way in about 64AD and after his death the Christians took his body and buried it in the cemetery on the hillside nearby. These early church members believed very strongly that the power and energy that they had found with Peter in his life, still remained in his body after death, so they would take careful note of where they had put him and other people soon began visiting the grave to pray and for healing and wanted to be buried alongside him. Later on when the Emperor Constantine became a Christian, he levelled the whole area of this cemetery and built a great church on top of it, the first St Peter's, and he lined it up in such a way that the high altar would be directly on top of Peter's grave. When the empire collapsed, they took the body away and hid it in secret places until things calmed down and they could bring it back to its original spot. Centuries went past, the old church grew dilapidated and at the time of the Reformation the Pope decided to pull it down and build a new one. His money raising efforts at the time cause much scandal to the newly-born Protestants, but that was when the present St Peter's was erected. More centuries went by, people forgot about those bones underneath, until we come to World War II when the Pius XII was shut up in the Vatican with little to do and so he decided to make a thorough investigation of the site, which took place in the 1940's. It is these excavations that you can now go into. They have cleared away the dirt from much of the original cemetery and so you come to a little street of miniature houses and alleyways until they point you to a house and say that this is the one directly under the high altar up above in the church. They claim that when they dug out this house they found the bones of a man about 70 years old in a box, bones which had at one time been wrapped in a precious cloth. Is it Peter? Is it true? Some say possibly, some say probably, some say no way! But whatever it is the site itself is very moving. It has the same atmosphere as the catacombs and when you are down there you feel you have severed all connection with the modern world of noisy jets and buses and are walking where our ancestors who went before us walked. The man who guided us was a very English type in a smart three piece suit, rimless glasses, and an impeccable accent, and he had no doubts whatsoever that this was Peter's remains. If so, it is a very strong link with our first beginnings and with one of those who walked with Jesus.

A less satisfactory session was our trip to the Vatican to take a party of Anglican priests who were doing a course here on Ecumenical contacts with the Roman church. We went to the Secretariat for Christian Unity and two priests met with us and gave us a talk. The one started by saying how the ecumenical movement was very close to Pope John Paul II's heart, and it was always in his prayers. In the discussion that followed a priest from the USA said that in his experience in a parish in Washington State, they had had good contacts with Roman Catholics in the period after the Vatican Council but that in recent years there had been a great cooling off and we were now almost back to a pre-Vatican II state of affairs. A priest from England spoke up and said their experience in his parish in England was similar to this. They had had frequent exchanges with the local Roman priest in clergy fraternals and socially, but now, with a change of Pope in Rome and priests in the parish the barriers had gone up again. The priest from Australia also bore witness to the same experience in his parish down under, so this seemed to be a world-wide Anglican experience. In response the second Vatican priest said how very close the ecumenical movement was to John Paul II's heart and was always in his prayers. With that our meeting closed – not much had taken place in the way of communication, I would say.

———•◦•———

A tragedy has overtaken us this week. Peter Marchant, the priest at the English church, All Saints, was killed in a street accident. He was bicycling home late at night when he was knocked down by a hit and run driver and left in the road. (After lying in hospital in a coma for a week, he died without reawakening.)He was a youngish guy from Dublin with red hair and full of Irish charm. He was also an identical twin and when his brother showed up for the memorial service, he caused a good deal of consternation. One upshot of this sad event is that I have been asked to take the services at All Saints until a replacement can be found.

I also visited Ostia for the first time. This is a place easy to reach on the train, right on the coast, and at one time a busy commercial centre, in fact the main entranceway to the city of Rome. This was where all the grain, slaves, animals and timber came in. After the empire collapsed, all regular trade withered away, the port filled with sand and people moved out to safer places. The result was that sand continued drifting in from the seashore and the town disappeared for centuries. Excavations began in the 1930's and a good deal of it has now been cleared and is open to visitors. To walk down those stone-cobbled streets today, being careful not to twist your ankle on the ruts left behind by the chariots and carts of our ancestors, is indeed to enter and become part of a true ghost town. In fact as I went I found myself listening for the sound of haggling in the market, cheering in the stadium and laughing and talking in the streets. I half expected to turn a corner and be met by a group of Romans, big men in togas accompanied by their bevy of slaves and hangers-on coming towards me, as I walked past the large apartment blocks, through the market, down streets of shops where you can still read in the pavement in front of the shops the names of those inviting your custom and a sign to indicate what they were selling. Then there are the large public buildings, the temples, the town hall, the public baths, the public toilets in which, unlike us, they seem to have felt no slightest need for privacy. So you enter a large open hall with a tasteful marble bench running all around the walls at convenient height and pierced at convenient intervals, with a water channel running underneath and a smaller channel in front of your feet for hand washing purposes. It must have had the noisy, relaxed atmosphere of an auction room at a county fair. However the site gains a little theological interest for us if you remember that St Paul most probably approached Rome through Ostia and so likely rested his bottom on this very spot. It is these intimate peeks at our long departed ancestors that make life here so intriguing.

———

Last Sunday at church a young couple turned up who had made all the arrangements for a blessing on their marriage with Peter Marchant and had then gone off on pre-nuptial honeymoon. What was their shock when they turned up in church this morning to hear that since their last seeing him, the priest had been buried and they heard the date of his memorial service now announced? I had a chat with them afterwards and they seemed a nice couple. He was from Belfast and a member of the Church of Ireland, and she was from Rome, and a Catholic. They had met in Paris where they were working and they are going to live in Brighton UK – truly international! I agreed to do the blessing which is fixed for the next Saturday. It took place about thirty-five miles north of the city at her parents' summer place on the coast. Once the blessing was complete we adjourned to the local hotel on the beach for a nine course meal, as follows: 1) parmesan cheese, salami and ham and drinks on the terrace, 2) inside, a sea-food risotto, 3) pasta, 4) a nice piece of salmon and potatoes, 5) fresh salad and a sorbet, 6) a piece of steak on toast, 7) strawberries soaked in Grand Marnier, 8) an elaborate wedding cake with a centre of ice cream, 9) coffee and champagne. A little over the top! But the bride was lovely in long white dress and they both seemed very sincere and earnest. A privilege to be a part of it.

———

I often go for a walk in the afternoon and last Wednesday I walked by chance into the church of St Louis of France, not very far from here, and had my first experience of a Caravaggio, who has become my favourite artist. In this rather dim and dingy church, high up on the walls of a chapel, and needing a few lira in the slot to get sufficient light to see them properly, were three larger than life portraits of St Matthew. But of the three, the one that attracted me most was the Call of Matthew. On one side of the picture stood the Lord in profile with one arm outstretched like a searchlight towards Matthew, and on the other side sat Matthew a very comfortable looking fat and prosperous gentleman in the midst of his mates at the table with a few coins and cups scattered about. Matthew's hand and finger is pointing inwards towards his own chest and his whole face says clearly, 'Who? Me? Impossible!' Such a look of total astonishment and baffled wonder. I loved it at once because it portrayed clearly the sensations of my own heart and my first reactions when I first became aware of a call coming to me. To me the picture seemed to depict a genuine and authentic event.

———

This week we are having another of these ten day seminars which I am now enjoying very much. Each time I seem to meet some interesting people. Last time I made friends with a Presbyterian minister and his wife from Chicago, and this week we have a Canadian priest from Toronto who went to Harbord Collegiate and attended All Hallows Church where he knew Ken Bott and his family. The Anglican world is a small world!

This time, after opening the first session, Douglas disappeared on holiday to Romania, leaving me in charge. Doug is a very genial host for these affairs, though some times, as in this case, a little vague as to the details of the time-table. But, since on this occasion his vagueness led to my encounter with an angel, I make no complaints. Our program called for a trip to Viturbo on the Saturday. This is an interesting old town about an hour away on the train, and containing a medieval papal palace plus a host of towers and turrets studded around the town, erected in former days by competitive merchant families. 'This trip will be no problem,' said Doug, 'just take them to the bus stop for the No. 32 and that will get you to the Termini station.' So off we went, about fifteen of us, to the stop indicated and along came the No. 32 and we headed for the centre. However, a little alarmingly, we never seemed to reach the Termini station. We went into the centre, then through it, and on out the other side. It was now about 11.10 and our train left at 11.30 so I began to sweat a little while the rest of the party, perfectly relaxed, chatted and gazed about. At last, in a panic, I stood up and addressing the bus in general I asked, in English, 'Does this bus go to the Termini Station?' People looked around, some looked blank others shook their heads, all except for one teenage lad, rather loutish and unprepossessing in appearance who must have sensed my alarm and raising his hand gently towards me said 'Calma-ti, calma-ti.' i.e. 'Cool it.' He then got off at the next stop and beckoned us all off with him. He took us round the corner and down a stairway into the Underground where he ran on ahead of us and warned the ticket man to issue 15 tickets. We all rushed through the barrier and on to the train, but when I turned around to thank our deliverer, all I saw was his jean clad legs disappearing up the stairs. We made it to the station and on to the Viturbo train with about two minutes to spare and the rest of the day went smoothly without hitches of any kind just as Douglas said it would. Apparently the bus we should have got was the No 35, but I have always counted this unknown young guy as an angel even without wings or halo, sent by the Lord to deliver us in time of need.

While I was on my evening stroll after supper today, I was attracted by the sound of a brass band playing in the distance. I eventually tracked it down to the island in the middle of the Tiber. In fact the church on the island is dedicated to St Bartholomew and they were keeping their patronal festival with some style and enthusiasm. When I walked over the bridge on to the island I saw the small brass band, all in uniform, sounding like there should have been a merry-go-round near at hand. They were marching up the island, followed by a procession of parishioners with candles and at the rear of the procession was the parish priest in cope, flanked by two servers and behind him St Bartholomew himself, or at least a life-sized representation of him in plaster, taken from the church and carried on the shoulders of the faithful. We processed to the end of the road and then back to the church where a crowd of priests celebrated mass for us amidst clouds of incense. When mass was over we lined up for a chance to kiss some unspecified relics of Bartholomew, held out to us in the priest's hands. Then, all duty done, we adjourned to the courtyard in front of the church where water melon and a glass of wine was distributed to everyone free of charge. What a pleasant and for me unexpected way to pass a summer's evening – refreshment for both soul and body.

———•—

This week has been a week for royalty, starting with the state visit to Italy of the Emperor of Japan and his Empress. I was on my way back to the Centre one morning when I saw from the bus a host of soldiers and police milling about in front of the Victor Emmanuel Monument near us. So when I got off the bus I hung about for a bit and sure enough a fleet of limousines soon drew up and out got the President of Italy, a swarm of lesser junta, and lastly the Emperor of Japan. He gave the crowds (and me) a big wave and a smile and plodded all the way to the top of that monument to place a wreath on the tomb of the Unknown Soldier. He is a good looking man and appeared very smart in the very best suit that the Japanese tailors could provide. Years ago when I was still a student at Trinity I had become interested in this man after reading 'Windows for the Crown Prince' by that American Quaker whom MacArthur had appointed to be his tutor during the American occupation. It was a good book, reflecting well on both tutor and pupil, and it was reassuring now after so many years to see this man fulfilling so well his accepted role.

But that wasn't all! I soon after had a phone call from the Church Warden at All Saints to warn me that Princess Margaret was going to be in town at the weekend staying with a friend and would be attending the Eucharist with us. Sure enough, when I came into church on Sunday morning the lady was sitting in the front row with her lady-in-waiting and wearing an ordinary red dress. I preached on a text from the gospel for the day, 'Render unto Caesar the things that are Caesar's and unto God the things that are God's' but I forbore to apply this to any particular present political situation, saying that as each of us bore the image and likeness of God it was precisely ourselves that we owed to God to whom our lives belonged. This had no visible effect on anyone present! After the service, the congregation remained in their places until she came out. She shook hands with me and confirmed that I was indeed a Canadian, and, without speaking to anyone else, drove off in her car with her two security men who had been lurking at the back of the church throughout.

———•·•———

Rather more in my line, I have started this week teaching English at the Refugee Centre that functions in the basement of the American Episcopal Church. Rome is awash with refugees, partly because of the government policy of doing very little to prevent their entry but then totally ignoring their presence. Their education, health and food needs are of no concern to the Italian Government. Most of these poor folk can't speak English and can't hope to get into the USA, Canada or Australia unless they can pass a language test. To them any one of these three places is like heaven and after what they have come from who can fail to understand that? So I am helping them all I can to get another step along the road of life. I have five Ethiopians, two Somali, one Pakistani, one Ivory Coast, and two Romanians, but the makeup of the class varies from session to session. They are mostly young and consequently full of energy and optimism so I enjoy being with them and helping them all I can.

———•·•———

I did a bit more exploring on my own last Saturday and went out to Tivoli, a town about ninety minutes off on the train. It is famous for its villa, the Villa d' Este, built by some cardinal in the 1550's. His estate takes in quite a steep hillside which they turned into an enormous water-feature with an endless variety of fountains, cascades and unexpected little pipes sprouting out all down the hill so that the whole garden is full of vitality and beauty, and the air is full of the gentle sounds of running water. Then if you turn your back on all this you get a magnificent view of the Tuscan hills receding into the distance. It is really a place of beauty.

From the market square in Tivoli you can take a local bus out to Hadrian's villa. Hadrian was one of the most civilised of all the Roman emperors; his time was during the first century AD and he is the one that has most intrigued me since I came to live in Rome. He seems to have been full of original ideas and imagination. He put up Hadrian's Wall stretching across the whole breadth of Britain in Northumbria to keep out the marauding Scots and barbarians in general; he built the Pantheon with its magnificent dome in the centre of Rome. Some say that he did not see the Pantheon as a shrine 'to every god', but rather as a shrine to 'the God of all', the pervading and creating spirit that gives life to the whole world. The structure of the building itself testifies to this interpretation, enclosing as it does the dimensions of a perfect globe with the spherical hole in the roof spilling sunlight into the whole. Then, as a place of recreation from all his labours of running the Roman Empire, he built this villa. It is now in ruins; much of the marble having been carted off to build the Villa d' Este and similar places, but enough is left spread over about twenty acres, to give you a picture of what it must have been. You can make out the baths, the gymnasium, the banqueting halls with the underground passageways down which slaves would have run carrying platters of exotic food, as well as the under floor heating arrangements, and their methods of taking full advantage of solar heating. So with just a little imagination you can recreate for yourself what it must have been like when the emperor and his court arrived for a brief holiday and the place swarmed with men and women, working, playing, competing and filling the place with noise. One spot that particularly fascinated me was a small room, circular, and completely enclosed by water channels and which would doubtless have contained several choice works of art. This was Hadrian's private den, and when he withdrew into this spot, the rule was that no one must interrupt or disturb him until he emerged. I like to think of the emperor of all the Romans, sitting here, oppressed with problems political and personal, trying to relax in the peace of this room and looking for a little ease. I hope he found it, but I doubt if he did.

———•·•———

This week has been a week of strikes but they are a little different from anything we experienced in this line at home. They are all protesting against the unemployment, and against the Minimum Tax, though to tell you the truth I am not sure what that might be. These strikes are all announced publicly beforehand, not only when they will be held, but how long they will last. The airport people had their strike Tuesday, the public transport had Thursday, hospital employees Friday and so on. All strikes last from 10.00am until 4.00pm and those hours are dedicated to marching up and down behind brass bands with banners and posters, and listening to fiery speeches threatening revolution, bloodshed, and the stringing up of the bloody capitalists from the nearest lamp post. Then at 4.00pm everyone goes back to work, clocks off and goes home for supper. Different strokes for different folks!

———•·•———

I was really surprised to hear the results of the Canadian elections. Who could have believed that the Conservatives would be reduced to two seats in Ottawa? Is the country going to break up? I was amused by an article in one of the daily papers here.

'It appears that Canada, distant land of our dreams, with cities like Moose Jaw, White Horse, Thunder Bay, full of forest, polar bears, snow, and ice is also subject to the same forces of disintegration and regionalisation that are going on in so many parts of Europe and all over the world these days.' And that's how they see Canada.

———•·•———

Two tourist trips this week; one extremely pleasant, and one extremely awful. The first was last Saturday when a lady who is a member of St Paul's (the American Anglican church) took me and a friend of hers out to Subiaco in her car. This is a small place in the hills about forty miles south of the city. The name

Subiaco means 'below the lake'. The lake was created when that wicked emperor Nero, who burned all the Christians, threw a dam across a narrow gorge to make himself a trout pond here since he was apparently a keen fisherman – he couldn't have been all bad! He also built a summer palace here similar to Hadrian's but on a smaller scale. Three hundred years later St Benedict came along and found the ruins of the emperor's old fishing lodge and gathered around him there a small group of young guys who said they wanted to be monks, and that's how monasticism got started in Europe. The dam was smashed in about 1300 so there is no lake any more, but the monastery is still there, built on to the steep hillside. It was a rainy day so we had the place mostly to ourselves and a monk showed us around including the old original chapel in a cave down below, with an old icon of Benedict set up there – very impressive. We had a lovely drive back as the weather began to clear and we drove down those steep valleys with the leaves beginning to turn yellow. The grapes have all been gathered in and the olives are almost ready for picking. A peaceful day!

Then within the week I went to the other extreme and visited on my own one of the grimmest memorials of the war, at the Ardeatine Caves. In 1943 the Italian Resistance organised an attack on a German SS column as they marched through one of the narrow streets of the city. They killed fourteen SS soldiers. When this was reported back to Hitler, he went berserk and commanded that ten Italian men should be shot for each German lost, 140 in all. The army went out, and going at random through the streets, beginning at the place where the massacre had taken place, they arrested the first 140 men and teenagers they could find. These were then marched out to the Ardeatine Caves, a disused marble quarry, and were executed by firing squad. The whole thing soon descended into an ever deeper nightmare. 140 men is a big crowd in a confined space, especially as an ever greater percentage of them inevitably joined the heaps of corpses lying on the floor, and as the German soldiers in the execution squad became ever more reluctant to carry on. In the end this pile of bodies, not all of them dead, were walled up within the cave and left. The area was declared off limits. After the liberation of Rome, the blocked entrance was broken down and, as far as possible the bodies were identified and sorted out, and those so brutally murdered were restored to some form of dignity in death.

When you visit the caves now, within the low roof you see 140 graves each one in the form of an altar shaped tomb, about waist high, with the name and age of one of the men inscribed on the top. There is such a solemn stillness engulfing the place. It leaves you speechless, unwilling to accept or digest what it represents, what it says about us humans.

The big news from here is that the Board of Governors all met here in the library last week to mull over the financial crisis the Centre is now facing. All the funding for the place up until now has come from the Anglican Consultative Council, but they have recently announced that due to 'financial constraints' these funds will cease as of this Christmas. One plan under consideration is for the Centre to move out of the Palazzo Doria Pamphilj and into the basement of the All Saints church in the via del Babuino near the Spanish Steps – a great come down that would be. Part of this package is that I will be the priest-in-charge of All Saints for a year or two until the bishop can make a more long term appointment. It will mean my moving up to the priest's flat next to the church, which is now being renovated and should be ready by next Easter.

Apart from all that we are now in the warm-up for Christmas, the temperatures now run in the 15 – 18 degree range and we are having some pleasant days. At this season the shepherds come down from the hills around Abruzzi and play traditional songs on their bagpipes in the street; also there are quite a variety of street performers. I was fascinated by some guys doing mimes when we were out walking last night. One guy with a stark white face and a top hat was standing on a pillar absolutely motionless looking like a mannequin from a shop window. I waited for about five minutes and still he didn't move. In the Piazza Navona we found all sorts of booths selling all kinds of candies and sweets, with food stalls, in one of which a whole pig was roasting on a spit ready for hot pork sandwiches. There was a merry-go-round going full blast in the centre near the big fountain and rifle shooting for prizes. There were lots of Nativity sets for sale, some junk, and others very fine. It was great to be there and see all the Italian families bringing their little kids around to enjoy the festivities while excitement hovered over the whole street.

––•–

Wednesday was the feast of the Immaculate Conception of our Lady and is a big feast here. They have a big pillar near the Spanish Steps set up in the 1850's when this doctrine was first proclaimed to an unsuspecting world. On the morning of the day, the Rome Fire Department with sirens going turned up at the pillar with their high ladder up which one of the firemen ran at top speed to place a large wreath over Mary's outstretched arms at the top. All through the day people laid wreaths at the foot of the pillar. I noticed one Italgas (i.e. consumers' gas), one from Fiat, one from the Mayor and Corporation. In Italy the big public corporations are still expected to be seen supporting religion. Around four o' clock the Pope rolled up accompanied by a few ancient cardinals and a bevy of priests and nuns. I was there in the crowd packed in tight and watched the Mayor greet the Pope and stood through the Pope's long, almost inaudible, excruciatingly boring, and theologically doubtful sermon which made it clear that the Pope does love Mary but shed no light for me on the meaning of the feast. So ends the Immaculate Conception.

––•–

We had a good Christmas here. The weather was very changeable with sunshine, heavy downpours, sleet, thunder and more sunshine all following one another at half hour intervals. On Christmas Eve at lunchtime I had a small party for some of the students I teach at the Refugee Centre; about ten of them. What a nice bunch they are, all in their twenties and nearly all either Muslim or Buddhist. They brought their own food and as most of them were Muslim they stuck to Coca-Cola. They played tapes, had 'My Fair Lady' on the video, talked and laughed loudly all the time, and took lots of pictures. One interesting thing they told me was that the Pope had come to visit them in the CAFOD hostel where most of them live to wish them a Merry Christmas and bring them some small gifts. Considering that these guys are the forgotten group at the bottom of Italian society, the man went up by a large notch in my estimation when I heard that. I went on to preach at the midnight service at All Saints, mostly to visitors on holiday as most of the regular congregation had gone back to families in the UK for their holiday. One feature of Christmas here is the innumerable nativity scenes set up in churches and all public places. The biggest one is in St Peter's Square and that is more than life size. Some of the ones in parish churches are very old, some 18th century with all the figures in 18th century dress.

Sergei, our Russian cook, did us a nice Christmas dinner at midday. We started with a salad made of fennel, cauliflower cooked with egg, and a salad of peas, hard-boiled eggs and sausages and potatoes in a mayonnaise sauce. After that we had young lamb roasted with potatoes and very tender. He had marinated it for two days in rosemary, garlic, and pepper, before cooking it very slowly with garlic. It was very tasty and tender. For dessert we had the Italian Christmas cake, Pantoni. It is more of a bun than a cake, very light and sweet and not as heavy as our plum pudding. Around the table were Douglas and Aussie, myself a Canadian, Sergei, a Russian, Richard, an Anglican student from Belfast studying at the English College, Ovvideo, a Romanian who, I discovered yesterday, was going to be on his own for Christmas. Out for a walk in the streets after dinner, where there were lots of chestnut sellers sitting by their fires and crowds of good natured people strolling about and shopping. So – a good Christmas.

Sister Joyce has come for a visit this week and I took her yesterday to see the miraculous statue of the Infant of Prague in the church on the Ara Caeli. A few days after we were there the statue was kidnapped by some thieves and held for ransom to the great alarm of the faithful and the great delight of the newspapers who gave it all the publicity they would have given to the kidnapping of any child of noble family. We then went to see the big Jesuit Church, the

Jesu, which is next door to us and whose roof is on the street next to our roof garden. This is an enormous baroque church on the scale of the Union Station in Toronto, and in a small flat next door St Ignatius Loyola, the founder of the Jesuits, lived out his last days. If you are a Canadian Anglican and accustomed to worshipping in modest churches on side streets, it takes a little readjustment to get used to these baroque churches of Rome. They come from an age and a church that has almost completely disappeared. They are built for football stadium sized crowds and every seat in them has a clear view of the stage, the high altar, where the early Jesuits often staged dramatic performances. Around the walls are the tombs and statues of famous missionaries, with a more than life-sized Ignatius gazing serenely heavenward while his foot tramples on the neck of Martin Luther, and around the frame vigorous angels are enthusiastically pitching prostate Protestants into a waiting hell. The roof is an enormous optical illusion in itself giving you the feeling that there is no roof there and you are gazing straight through the clouds and into heaven itself with angels and saints bending over the edges to peep down at us, the congregation below, some even relaxing nonchalantly sitting on the edges of the scene dangling their legs down in our direction. Then down the walls at floor level are ranks of dusty confessional boxes because spiritual direction and one to one counselling was the latest tool the Jesuits had discovered and revealed to the world. To visit one of these churches, and there is almost a duplicate of this one only three or four blocks away, is like visiting another planet; not for centuries has any part of the Christian church felt or displayed such overweening confidence, such arrogant triumphalism. You have to imagine them packed with crowds like those at a Billy Graham rally all singing and shouting and being whipped to ever greater heights of fervour by some energetic preacher lighting the fires of hell all around them.

They have mass here in the Jesu every day at noon and I often walk over from the Centre to attend. While there I used to observe a small man with a bald head and dark suit who walked right up to the front pew and knelt there very devoutly all through mass. When the service was over he would walk back down the aisle to the west door where two 'heavies' would emerge from the woodwork and accompany him to his limousine. I was told that this was Mr Andreotti, the Prime Minister of Italy.

———•—

I am beginning to get immersed in the parish. Last Sunday I had a funeral and yesterday I went down to the coast to take communion to an old lady of 98 years, who lives on her own, the oldest Anglican in Rome! She is small and wiry, a bit forgetful, but with all her marbles intact. A couple of friends joined with us so we had a nice service. I think when some English folk retire, or when their children marry an Italian, retirement here must seem like an attractive option, but as families grow and scatter, bodies become feebler and the health service turns out to be poor to non-existent, some of them have a pretty grim time here on their own.

One of the men, an Italian member of All Saints, drove me back to Rome. He was born here and knows the city intimately, so at lunchtime he said 'Leave lunch to me'. He took me to a place off the tourist path where we could get a real Italian lunch, and so we did. We had: a soup of chick peas and pasta, the tubular macaroni in a cheese and tomato sauce mixed with sheep intestines, a plate of oxtail in a rich sauce, a plate of beef marrow fried and sprinkled with lemon, a plate of Parmesan cheese, hard lumps, on its own, a kind of chocolate mousse with brandy in it, a glass of grappa – a kind of fortified wine, coffee and Amarra, a bitter wine to help digestion. I thereafter headed for home and was flat out for the next few hours.

———•—

This week is the Week of Prayer for Christian Unity and the Roman Catholics here are full of enthusiasm for this, with services laid on every day and everyone invited. Their biggest problem however is the extreme scarcity of any active Christians in Rome who are not already RC. Douglas, as the token Anglican, has been rushing up and down like a one-armed paper hanger preaching here, there, and everywhere. My turn comes on Sunday night when I am to preach at a Theological College nearby for about seventy students and staff none of whom have any English. After I had written my sermon out I had our secretary at the Centre translate it for me and I will read it off her version, no doubt butchering the Italian language as I go. I have chosen for my slightly unexpected text Matthew 10: 34 'I have come not to bring peace but a sword.' Saying we have to cut away all our instilled prejudices against one another learned at our mother's knee and with centuries of tradition behind them and be ready for an altogether new relationship before we can reach real unity. We also had a hymn sing at the Methodist church and a Bible study with the Baptists and ended with an evening of fellowship at St Sylvester's, an RC church, all of which were well attended.

————

I wish you could see the azaleas now in full bloom up and down the Spanish Steps in those enormous pots. They seem to have come into full blossom in only a day and now, on these cloudless sunny days, the Steps are awash with scarlet and white and purple, a lovely sight. I had dinner last night with a United Church group from Vancouver; they just wanted someone local to talk to and answer some of the questions that came into their minds as they walked around. So I tried to oblige. Although their church was in Vancouver, they came from all across Canada, their minister was from Nova Scotia and there was a nice Anglican couple from Toronto, out Mississauga way. I enjoyed the time with them.

————

The Piazza del Populo is only five minutes' walk from the All Saints clergy house and so I had a walk there this morning and visited the church of St Mary del Populo where I found another painting of my favourite artist these days, Caravaggio. This was of the conversion of St Paul with Paul lying prostate, flat on his back beside the road, reaching out his arms helplessly, like a blind man would do, begging for help from anyone. His horse, on which he had been galloping down the Damascus road, a big powerful stallion, is being led away by the servants, and on Paul's face a look of bewilderment, hurt, and confusion, the powerful man unseated, the clever man baffled, reduced to utter dependency. I looked at it for a long while. Also in the church is a nice statue by Bernini, showing an angel grabbing the prophet Habakkuk by the hair of his head (as in Daniel, Bel, and the Dragon, in the Apocrypha) preparatory to carrying him off to Babylon to the people in exile. Habakkuk too looks a little baffled, looking back in the opposite direction to which the angel is pointing him, though I see he has a big box of provisions all ready and packed to take with them for the hungry folks over there.

———•·•———

We do most of our shopping at the Standa over in Trastevere. Trastevere is not really a slum, but it is a very old district with a character all of its own. It is definitely working class and anti-establishment and is the centre of the activities of the St Egiddio community, the most vigorous and the most active socially of any of the modern communities. I took the opportunity today to visit the main church of the place, dedicated to Mary and very ancient. I was much struck by the large mosaic high on the wall covering the apse behind the high altar. It depicts Christ sitting enthroned and crowned in heaven with his mother at his side. But what struck me was that for all their glory and glitter this couple are just homely folks, a man and his mother. He has his right arm around her shoulders as if to say, 'Look Mum, this is heaven, you're going to love it here.' And she is pointing with her right hand at him as if to say, 'Look folks, this is the Lord, keep your eyes on him, and listen to him. That's all you need to do.' Lovely! And the colours on this mosaic are just as bright and fresh as the day they were laid there.

———•·•———

I have Malcolm and Muriel Broadhead staying with me this week and the other day we had a trip out to Orvietto. It makes a good day out, only about an hour away on the train, north of Rome in Tuscany. The town itself perches on the top of one of those Tuscan rocky outcroppings but was catapulted into fame, even notoriety, in the Middle Ages when the priest at the cathedral, while saying mass one day, was startled to observe, during the elevation of the host, great drops of blood dripping down from the host on to the corporal cloth beneath. This cloth he wisely preserved and on the strength of this spotted piece of material, now framed behind glass and hanging high up in the roof, Orvietto became one of the most popular centres of pilgrimage and a new cathedral was built on top of the hill there to house the miraculous cloth. When you leave the train station at Orvietto you get at once into a funicular lift that takes you up to the level of the cathedral and the town. It is a town typical of this part of Italy with narrow stone paved streets, towers, and lots of shops selling amongst other things beautiful pottery and plates of all kinds, but what attracted me most was a woman in the market square with a pig on a spit over a charcoal fire selling hot pork sandwiches. Of course we all had one and sat eating it, resting our weary feet and gazing over the ramparts at the sun-soaked Tuscan farmland all around us.

We had a great service last Sunday, June 6, which was the fiftieth anniversary of the allied forces arriving in Rome to liberate it. June 6 was also the fiftieth anniversary of D Day, and also the fiftieth anniversary of the reopening of All Saints after it had been closed for four years because of the war. I looked up the church register for that service and was proud to find there the signature of Father Martin Knight SSM, who was at that time a chaplain to the South African forces and who was still on the back row in Kelham chapel for some time after I got there. When this service was first mooted I was a little nervous lest it become a great patriotic and military occasion to the greater glory of a few generals and their ilk, but Douglas made the excellent suggestion that we should ask the Principessa Orietta, Pogson-Doria-Pamphilj, the head of the Doria clan and our landlord down at the Centre, to preach the sermon for us, After all she was here and had lived through the whole business. Her family had been against Mussolini from the start and remained ardently anti-fascist up to his downfall. She agreed to come. She is the most unpretentious person who arrived at church on her bicycle on Sunday morning and, at the end of the service, talking very simply, she told us what the confusion was like first of all when the Fascists collapsed, then what the terror was like when the Nazi seized control of the city, and finally at long last their relief and jubilation when the Allied troops arrived. She told us what gate they marched in through and all the other intimate details. Because her family were so well known as anti-Fascist, when the Nazis took over they had to flee from their Palazzo on the Via del Corso and go into hiding for the whole time of the German occupation in Transtevere, hiding in the priest's house, never being allowed to go near a window or show their face. She spoke very quietly, humbly, and still came across as a most impressive person. After the service she actually apologised to me for not making her communion with us that morning. She said she was in the habit of communicating in Anglican churches in the UK, but dare not do so in Rome.

———·•·———

I had a nice couple from the congregation in Kuwait drop in on me yesterday. They are Americans and he was at that time working for Foster-Wheeler rehabilitating the oil wells that had been blown up by the retreating Iraqis. When that contract was finished the company told him they had no more work, so here he is now, a man of 50 accustomed to making good money and having a challenging job, wandering from place to place looking for a job like any teenager. Very dispiriting!

———·•·———

21.07.94
A week ago I had a delegation from the South African Embassy, two nice looking young women, one black, one white, who said the embassy would like to have a service at All Saints to celebrate the return of South Africa to the Commonwealth and to dedicate and bless their new national flag. They wanted to have it on the same day that a similar celebration would be held in Westminster Abbey in London which was going to be attended by the Queen. This service was one of the highlights of my time here. Of course, being July, our own choir were all away on holiday but then I had a letter

from out of the blue from some boys' school in England saying that their choir would be in Rome that week on holiday and would like to sing at All Saints on that Sunday. So, unexpectedly, we had this nice choir in surplices, red cassocks and ruffs processing up the aisle ahead of us. The South African Ambassador followed the choir carrying the new South African flag which he then laid upon the altar and I blessed it while the organ played the South African national anthem. I then took it and draped it over the pulpit. The Ambassador read the Old Testament lesson, a young woman from the embassy (black) read the epistle and an RC Franciscan read the gospel and preached. After the service we adjourned to the garden where they (the Africans) had provided us with copious supplies of South African wine. It was such a thrill for all of us, me included, to be part of such a service, all the more so since as little as two years ago no one in South Africa, the UK or anywhere else would have believed such a thing was feasible or even possible. How many prayers and how much spilled blood had made it so for us?

———•·•———

I left Rome on August 29th and returned to Toronto where I lived and worked for a year with the Order of the Holy Cross at their priory on High Park Avenue.

9

With the Basotho

Some vocabulary:

Basotho. The Sotho people
Mosotho. A Sotho person
Lesotho. Their native land
Sesotho. Their mother tongue

In 1996 I was living in Oxford, joining the tutorial staff of the St Albans/Oxford Ministerial Training Course at the invitation of Vincent Strudwick, its Principal. This was a non-residential course preparing people, especially older, experienced applicants, for ordained ministry. Vincent had redesigned the course to reflect Father Kelly's idea of theological education in this very different setting. I much enjoyed that year working with Vincent and was expecting in the following year to move up to Whitby to become chaplain to the Order of the Holy Paraclete, when, one day, our SSM director, Christopher Myers, asked me if I would attend the forthcoming General Chapter of the Society due to meet at Durham Priory in August. I was not one of the delegates, but they needed someone to act as chapter clerk and take down the minutes. As the SSM South African Province had already been closed down some years previously, due to the shrinkage in the number of brothers working there and their advancing years, and as it was now almost ten years since I had left behind my Ghanaian experience, African matters did not appear as even the smallest blip on my radar when I showed up at the first meeting of the chapter, notebook in hand and pencils sharpened. However we were all surprised indeed when the Director announced that he had decided to re-open the work in South Africa, and that there were already two Basotho men living at Maseru Priory who had expressed a strong desire to join the Society and who had been welcomed (though illegally!) into the priory by Fr David Wells SSM. These two were now looking forward to the novitiate and eventually full membership of the Society. The Director went on to say that he hoped to kick-start the old African work into new life by replacing the present remaining three brothers with a completely new group who would, he hoped, build up a new black province for SSM in Africa. He finished dropping these assorted bombshells by saying that in the light of my time in Ghana, I would be, in his opinion, the right person to begin working on this ambitious project. After a minimum of those gestures and words of dissent that modesty demands on such occasions, I couldn't help but admit that my heart leapt for joy at the prospect. It would mean that I would be living again in an SSM priory and working with my brothers again for the first time since I had left Kobe Priory in Japan in 1982.

It would also mean living again in Africa and living alongside African people whom I had so much loved and appreciated in my time in Ghana and then too, it has to be admitted, there flared up in my heart the phantom hope that we might re-found SSM in Africa and watch it grow and expand again on the new foundations of African men inspired by Fr Kelly's ideas as we had been, a dream that had haunted many SSM members since the day Kelham had closed its doors in 1972. High hopes but there were also a few flaws in our thinking which bore their own fruit in the years that lay ahead of us.

Perhaps we, the SSM contingent imported into the priory, had too clear a vision of what we hoped would develop here. Our plans were too fixed. We remembered all too clearly what life had been like at Kelham and that was the plan we worked to. We didn't think enough about letting go, being flexible, and letting the old seed grow on the new soil and develop in its own surprising ways. Then too we were almost completely ignorant of the background of these new recruits. These were not working-class English men from Tyneside or Manchester such as we had known at Kelham. Most of these men had grown up in grinding poverty such as we had never seen, and often in the middle of war and violence and that fixed their approach to life in ways we were slow to recognise.

Lesotho, my destination, was a small land-locked country within the borders of the Republic of South Africa. It was about the size of Wales and like Wales was very mountainous. It was often referred to as 'the Switzerland of South Africa', or 'the Kingdom in the Sky'. They lived in great poverty, eking out a meagre living on the high mountain slopes by subsistence farming. Up until recently the men had been able to supplement their family income by going to work in the gold mines of Johannesburg. The great disadvantage of this was that it split up husband and wife for years at a time with disastrous effects on marriage and the family. The men, once at the mines, were confined to men's hostels where the hours not spent underground or sleeping were passed in boredom, gambling and amidst throngs of prostitutes who came to work there. The result of all this was that the men usually returned to Lesotho infected with HIV Aids which they then passed on to their wives. Today in Lesotho about 40 per cent of women between 15 and 40 are HIV positive or have Aids, all of which is destroying family life and has terrible implications for the future of the country.

Like most men who work in mines the Basotho are hard men accustomed to tough lives, and from the very beginning Lesotho has had to fight for even its small place in the sun. In fact the country owes its whole existence as a nation to one man, their first leader and chief, Moshoeshoe, the national hero. In the early nineteenth century when white farmers from the Cape colony, like their counterparts in Australia and Canada, were pushing further and further into the interior carrying everything they possessed on covered wagons, they gradually dispossessed the indigenous people, the Basotho, from their ancestral lands which included most of the good farm and in what is now the Free State; in fact many Basotho still refer to the Free State as 'the conquered territory'. Thus the Basotho were driven further and further back into the mountains until they lost heart and were in danger of being wiped out completely or retained as slaves for the Boers. Then Moshoeshoe arose, a local chief who set up his camp on Thaba Bosiu (Mountain of Night) and, like Gideon of old, called on all the Basotho who were willing to fight for their land and their freedom, to rally around him. But Moshoeshoe was more than a warrior. He was a wily old bird who knew he had no chance of withstanding the oncoming hordes of whites on his own, and so he looked around for an ally and defender, and his eyes lighted upon that original 'iron lady' Victoria, Queen of an Empire on which the sun never set, and, through the governor of the Cape Colony, he threw himself and his people on the mercy and might of the Great White Mother, asking her to stand between the Basotho and the Boer. He promised in return that Lesotho would be the green blanket thrown over the shoulders of the great queen to keep off all cold winds, and the Basotho people would be the fleas in the queen's blanket. History does not record Queen Victoria's reply to this offer but the result was that Lesotho became a British Protectorate and survived down to 1967 when it became once again an independent nation. Moshoeshoe as well as being a statesman had a sense of humour, at least if some of the stories told about him are to be believed. While he was still encamped at Thaba Bosiu, a tribe of cannibals attacked his home village, captured and killed his father and his attendants and devoured them. Within the year a group of young Basotho, incensed that such a thing should have happened to their chief's family, rounded up the guilty parties and led them as prisoners before Moshoeshoe so that he could exact vengeance and do to them what they had done to his father, but Moshoeshoe answered, 'Why? Why should I eat the graves of my ancestors and my dear father?' And he let the men go free.

Later on when the French Protestant missionaries (Paris Evangelical Missionary Society), appealed to him for permission to begin working in his territory, he welcomed them in and often visited and had meals with Revd Casalis their leader and his family at Morija where they had their headquarters. Then when Roman Catholic missionaries sought permission to come and begin work, he welcomed them in as well. Last of all the Anglicans appealed for permission to come in, with some trepidation, since many people felt that two competing Christian bodies were already more than sufficient provision for one small country. However, Moshoeshoe's reply was, 'No, let the Anglicans come. Then I will be like a man with three cows so that if two run dry, I will still be able to call on the third.'

This sense of humour did not disappear with the death of Moshoeshoe, as Fr Frank Green SSM can witness. During his first week in Lesotho at Teyateyaneng in 1957 he was sent (first time on horseback) to say Mass at a couple of villages in the hills which were part of the parish. He found the villages, said the Masses, but when he turned back towards Teyateyaneng, he got hopelessly lost. Here he was in a strange country, where every hill looked much like every other one, with night drawing on, and rain threatening, and no idea of where that path was that would lead him home. As he wandered and pondered, nearly despairing, he met an old Mosotho standing on the side of the path, wrapped securely in his blanket with his conical hat on his head and leaning on his staff. Desperate, Frank mustered what scraps of Sesotho he knew so far and asked the way to TY, but all he got in response was a puzzled questioning look. Frank vainly trying to remember his last Sesotho lesson and, speaking slowly and more loudly, repeated the question. The old man, squinting, looked up, still more puzzled, but as Frank turned his horse back down the path he had come he was startled to hear the old man say, clearly enough, 'I think, sir, if we used English we would get on better.' At which they both burst into peals of laughter.

And so it was that in January 1997 I came to Maseru Priory, having been met at the airport by Fr David and Br William Nkomo, the only black brother at that time. The priory, in the style of many dwellings in Lesotho, was built of cinder block with a corrugated iron roof. It was just a series of rooms joined together, each room provided with a window or two and an outside door.

At the priory this line of rooms took the shape of a horseshoe with the chapel at the centre, the common room and kitchen at one end of the line, and the office and shower block at the other. This left eight rooms, one for the library and seven for the brothers,

with a very pleasant courtyard in which a bird bath was the centre-
piece. When I arrived, David, Clement, and William were in
residence, all due to leave shortly for distant priories. Tanki, one of
the two candidates had already been sent off to Grahamstown to
begin studying for the priesthood, the other one, Lebohang, was
still with us.

Naturally enough as I settled into my new home, I mentally
compared it with what I had known in Ghana. They were both
African countries but they had completely different histories.
Ghana, although it had been at the centre of the slave trade, was
in modern times almost completely free of racial tensions and
Lesotho, although it was one of the few countries in Africa united
in the use a single language, was a turmoil of conflicting groups,
parties and interests. In Ghana politics was scarcely ever mentioned,
in Lesotho political questions were in your face every day. I went
to Ghana in 1983 just after J. J. Rawlins had seized control of the
country for the second time in another military dictatorship, and
one result of this was that there were no more elections, no more
voting, no parliament, political parties or public speeches. Politics
became a private vice. Whereas in Lesotho in 1997 it was only
three years since Mandela had been released from prison and they
had held their first free election in the Republic of South Africa.
With Mandela at the helm they were labouring to deliver the
country from the tragedies and travesties of the apartheid years.
Lesotho was not a part of South Africa, it had always maintained
its independence, but it was completely enclosed by the Republic.
It had no international airport; all flights abroad had to begin
in Johannesburg. They used to say that if the Republic caught a
cold Lesotho sneezed. On the South African newscast which we
watched every evening we looked on spellbound as crisis after
crisis unfolded in the Cape Town Parliament and in the sessions
of the Truth and Reconciliation Commission, which was meeting,
often under the chairmanship of Archbishop Desmond Tutu, in
various locations around the country.

The other new problem for me in Lesotho was race. In Ghana,
no whites had ever been allowed to own land in the country and
so there was never any colonial settlement or colonial culture.

Whites only came for a job and left when their contracts ran out. Nkrumah, Ghana's first President, used to say that he was going to erect a gigantic bronze mosquito on a pedestal in Accra with the inscription, 'This is who saved Ghana from the white man!'

The consequence was that while I was there I was seldom conscious of being a white man, nor were the others! In Lesotho the question of race was always there just below the surface. While apartheid had never been part of Lesotho's public policy, apartheid attitudes often prevailed amongst the white portion of the population. Whites had their own church (St John's) and lived in their own district in Maseru. Typical was the question put to me by one of the new recruits from Johannesburg within days of his arrival. 'Father, do you like blacks?' I said that I liked some blacks and not others in exactly the same way that I liked some whites and not others. I didn't like/dislike people on the basis of their skin colour, but I' m not sure that he saw the point I was making. Where he had grown up, your relationship with other people was always dictated and controlled by the colour of their skin.

Ralph's Log

The priory is in a good location, about thirty minutes' walk from the centre of town but without any near neighbours as it is cut off by a donga (a ravine) on two sides, with the Maseru High School grounds on the other side and an unpaved dead-end road at the bottom of the property, providing the only access to the place for cars. This makes for quite a quiet and private spot which has been nicely planted out with plenty of large gum trees and a double row of poplars up the front drive.

———•———

The first hint of violence came on Sunday 16 February. I was planning to accompany Clement in to town for the Sunday service at St John's where he is in charge, in fact he had asked me to preach, but while we were getting ready we heard in the distance a number of gun shots followed by the rattle of machine-gun fire.

As we asked ourselves what it was all about, a phone call came from one of Clement's friends warning him not to leave the house today since, in any case there would be no one at church. It seems that few weeks ago a group of junior police officers arrested their senior officers. This led to a strike by the whole police force which ended in a stalemate until today when the army was sent in to arrest the rebel police officers, hence the shooting this morning. Unperturbed, Clement and I spent the morning under our gum trees in the garden playing scrabble. Late in the afternoon we received word that it was all over, but whether there were any fatalities, or how the problems were resolved, no one seemed to know. Peace had returned and that was enough!

————•••————

Meanwhile great upheavals are going on within South African society. I went with David to our bank in Ladybrand in the Free State (only about 25 miles away), to register my name as a signatory on our priory account. I noticed two or three black men serving behind the counter and an equal number of black women. The customary calm orderly atmosphere of a bank prevailed with everyone speaking in hushed tones. Nothing so remarkable in all that, you may think, but up until a few months ago such a sight had never been seen in Ladybrand. The bank would have had white staff only to wait on the white customers and there would have been a separate counter for blacks. Progress from abnormality to normality and all done with impeccable manners. Perhaps the most striking thing was the way these changes were so calmly accepted by the white customers – not a whisper of protest or longing for the old ways.

Steve de Kleer, a novice from Australia, joined us this month, sent here to broaden his experience of SSM. A very kind generous guy and probably the most extroverted person I have ever met. Within weeks, he had met and talked with everyone from the church and most of the people from the neighbourhood. The men who lived in our area had formed themselves into a voluntary vigilante's brigade to patrol the area at night after there had been a series of muggings, break-ins and rapes around us. One night a car full of us were returning to the priory about ten p. m. when we were stopped on the road by a group of armed men who wanted to know who we were and where we were going. 'We're going to the SSM priory down the road.' I said, somewhat cockily, but this drew an absolute blank and total incomprehension until one of the men said, 'Oh, do you mean Steve's place?' 'Yes', I said, 'I mean Steve's place' and they waved us on through as the best of friends. Sadly, only a few weeks later, one of the vigilantes was found murdered and lying in the ditch when the sun came up one day. Still, I sometimes wished that I had a little of Steve's outgoingness and even occasionally that he had a little of my reserve. But to each his own!

April saw my first long trip out of Lesotho, about 750ks down to Kwazulu-Natal for a religious life conference. I went with Steve, Lebohang, and Sister Josephine Mary and another sister from the Precious Blood sisters at Masite. We drove through some awesomely beautiful country, the most beautiful I have seen since I left Canada! At one point we drove through the Drakensburgh mountains which you could see from a long way off, rising up from the farmlands, a solid high rampart of rock like the Great Wall of China. You couldn't help wonder at the determination of the early Boer settlers who were said to have dismantled their wagons, and carried the parts, plus all the contents over the peaks on their shoulders, in addition to leading their wives, children and oxen. As we got down nearer Durban the mountains gave way to gently rolling hills, all covered with sugar cane of a beautiful deep green colour. In fact all along the way I couldn't help but be reminded of that verse in Isaiah, 'Your eyes will see the land of far distances.' The roads are good and seldom crowded. We passed though Ladysmith and several other spots where there had been great battles during the Boer War. All very interesting and enjoyable.

The winter arrived suddenly during the last week in May with temperatures dropping to OC or even – 2C at night, making any midnight trips to the toilet a rather chilling experience. However it would climb as high as 15-20C during the day. The days are usually sunny, with almost no rain and, if you can find a corner out of the wind and in the sun wrapped up in your blanket, you can be very comfortable. This is how I see Lebohang doing his studies most mornings. We have occasional snow flurries here, but up in the mountains villages are often snowed in. Lesotho is the only country in Africa which has a regular snow fall.

———•—•———

During the first week we had the sad news of the death from a stroke of Lebohang's mother at Masite. Funerals here are elaborate affairs that began this time with Robert Stretton SSM and me going with Lebohang to the mortuary where they picked up the body and put it in the back of his brother's half ton pick-up. This we followed down to Masite to the family home, two small rooms of cinder block with a tin roof sitting on a hillside. We took the coffin inside where the parish priest was waiting to say the mass on the kitchen table. The room was packed to suffocation with old church members all wrapped in their winter blankets and singing hymns in Sesotho.

When it came time for communion, I was handed the chalice and as I was administering it to the people I could see, over their heads through the open door, a young steer flat on its back with its feet in the air just to the edge of the courtyard, struggling feebly while a group of men were sawing at its throat with a dull knife in preparation for the feast. When we came out from mass, they were busy skinning and cutting it up for the cooking pot. This mass was the beginning of the all-night vigil but we went back home and returned next morning for the funeral proper. It was due to start at 10.00 but finally got under way at 12.00. This time we had carried on the back of our truck an iron-work frame that was to fence in the grave at the end, and had the mother's name around it in iron letters. By 12.00 there were two to three hundred people there, nearly all locals or members of the family. In Africa mourning is never a private sorrow or individual loss. Mourning is a community loss and a community obligation encompassing contacts and relations to the fourth and fifth remove. All this quite regardless of how you might feel about the deceased or their character. A funeral attended only by a handful of immediate family would be a family disgrace and an insult to the departed; it would be truly scandalous. As they say, 'A person only becomes a person through other people.' (This has been famously expounded by Archbishop Desmond Tutu as 'that African thing *Ubuntu*'). By now the crowd was too big for any room and so the coffin was laid on two kitchen chairs in front of the house and we gathered around it. There were a few prayers from the catechist, maybe a Bible reading and then followed fourteen speeches, beginning with the husband who gave a blow by blow account of her last illness. The men stood on one side of the circle and the women on the other. I noticed that even though these men were farmers, none of them had any problem about standing up in their blankets and gum boots and making a speech of some length and fervour. Public speaking is what every man can do here. Eventually when all this was completed, we all fell in behind the coffin and walked to the cemetery, a rough piece of land on a hillside about half a mile off. By this time the crowd had swollen to about 800, men first and then women, all led by a man carrying a spade high aloft in his hands and as we went we sang hymns in deep harmony, all known by heart. I was deeply moved. I felt tears in my eyes. Why? I had only the lightest connection with the departed but it is always moving to lay aside your individuality for a while and do a very human thing, in a very human way, with fellow humans. We did it as a village and it occurred to me how seldom at home we get a chance to do anything as a village or as a parish, or even as a family. We do most things on our own or with one or two.

After the burial the men, in strict order of precedence, took turns filling in the grave while the women sang yet more hymns, or the same ones over again! And then we went back to the house where, after washing our hands in water in which gum leaves were floating, a meal was served to all present. There was beef, rice, carrots, pumpkin and salad and no one held back, except the family who were running up and down distracted with serving the whole countryside, maybe not 5000 but close to it!

The final ceremony took place on Sunday morning when all the men of the family had to shave their heads, and all the hair was burned. I was not present for that one.

———•·•———

Strangely enough we were at another funeral at the end of the month, this time for one of the priests of the diocese. The bishop decreed that every priest must attend and so we all assembled, an army of priests in their albs, a platoon of Mothers' Union heavies in their blue uniforms, a gaggle of Holy Name nuns, as well as all the parishioners he had ever known. We met at his village, a handful of houses, thatched rondavals and a small stone church in the midst of pretty open land surrounded at no very great distance by purple mountains capped with snow. It was a day of brilliant sunshine and as there was no tarred road for miles not a motor, not an airplane, could be heard, the only sounds to break the silence were the tinkle of cow bells, and the barking of dogs. The Eucharist was celebrated outside the church, after which we all filed past the body and there were the customary fifteen to twenty speeches. Again the head of his family gave an account of his last days, then one of his children, his church warden, the chief of the village, the headmaster of the church school, the head server, an old classmate, the head of the Bernard Mizeki Guild, and various friends relations and acquaintances. What gradually emerges from this battery of speeches is a picture of this one life in all its fullness and that shows us one of the most unexpected aspects of these Basotho funerals. There is certainly grief and a sense of loss that go with all funerals but, in addition to that, you begin to realise that this is really a celebration of life and a proclamation of faith, faith in the resurrection, yes, but even more than that, faith in the goodness of life and in the value of this person. It is a proclamation made in the presence of death by the whole community of the living. After the speeches we carried the coffin to the grave, about three hundred in number across the rough fields for half a mile, singing innumerable hymns as we went. Again, it was a corporate ritual, a social performance held in honour of no great personage, but of a humble village priest and a common village mother. We have lost the knack of this sort of thing in the west.

———•—•———

These days the bulk of the evening newscast from South Africa is taken up with extracts from the daily activities of the Truth and Reconciliation Commission. This is an effort to deal with the enormous residue of hatred and desire for revenge left behind by the apartheid era and now lying just below the surface life of every town, village and community in that country, and waiting like so many time bombs to explode with fatal consequences at the slightest touch. It meets under the motto of, 'The Truth Hurts. Silence Kills.' And it is fascinating to watch. The idea is that those who are guilty of crimes against humanity such as torture, murder, wrongful imprisonment etc., can come forward and make a total confession of their crimes and ask for amnesty. If they can show that they were only carrying out their duties as their part in the great war to save their country from communism, and if they can show some signs of repentance for their deeds, the commission with the assent of those assembled for that meeting, can grant them amnesty. If they don't come forward and confess and receive amnesty they remain liable to persecution in the courts from their victims or the victims' families. On last night's news we saw a group of very prosperous, middle-aged business men (former police and prison officers) sitting and telling the court how they had murdered this group, beaten this prisoner to death, all in the line of duty and in obedience to their orders. These confessions were in the presence of the families of the murdered people who had been notified of who would be on trial. Last week those responsible for the torture and murder of Steve Biko appeared. Another night there was a former police officer who was asked to demonstrate to the court what he had done. He laid a man flat on the floor face downwards, sat on his back, and pulled a wet denim bag over the man's head and face, twisting it tight around his neck and holding it there until the man was on the point of suffocating. 'This', he said, 'was the water-bag treatment.' As the demonstration unfolded, the man he had done this to was sitting there not three feet away in the front row observing every detail for accuracy. Many people are not sure whether all this washing of dirty linen in public will lay the ground for lasting peace or for lasting strife and war but, surprisingly often, the families of victims are willing to give amnesty if only the former policemen will tell them where they buried the bodies when they had finished with them. This means that the family can then reclaim the body of their loved on and give it a Christian burial, and so bring this chapter of their lives to a conclusion which, without the body, they could not do.

Our Michael Lapsley, at the time when he was a parish priest in Harare, Zimbabwe in the immediate post-apartheid era, received a letter bomb which blew off both his hands, destroyed one eye and left him partially deaf. Last week he received a notice from the Truth and Reconciliation Commission that the three men who had sent him the bomb were now applying for amnesty and would appear on the following dates. They worked for the South African Security Forces, which Michael had long suspected but didn't know. In fact he had no certainty about who had sent him the bomb. This latest turn of events places him in a bit of a moral quandary. Does he want to attend the hearing and really meet these men face to face for the first time? Not an easy question. It is sometime easier to forgive people in the abstract rather than particular people face to face.

It is September and at last spring is coming, the peach trees are a mass of pink blossom, the apricots are all in white, with one or two of each around most of the thatched rondevals alongside the road as you drive along. What a lift it gives to the spirits after all that shivering of recent months.

We have a new recruit, one named Guguletto from the Johannesburg conurbation. He is an excellent drummer and has a good voice and encouraged by this we have begun to have a Sesotho hymn every night at Evensong. They have their own Sesotho hymn book here – Lifela tsa Kereke (Church Hymns). Its origins are lost in mystery but it is probably pre-1914 and many of the translations were doubtless done by the early SSM missionaries. It is a book of standard traditional hymns, leaning in a high-church direction. One of the most popular hymns in the book is 'Let all mortal flesh keep silence' sung to the tune of 'What a friend we have in Jesus'. That gives you some idea of what it is like! Every Anglican has been singing from it since infancy and the book is firmly entrenched in the affections of the people as most hymns are connected in the singer's mind with countless past moments of family crisis or celebration. A further advantage is that the collection is small, only about 200 in all, so that all that is necessary at a big funeral or celebration is for someone to strike up the first line, and the whole gathering will join with the leader, vigorously, whole-heartedly, with no need for either a book or an instrument. The other point is that organs are almost unknown in Lesotho so the hymns for the most part are either unaccompanied or, in more recent years, accompanied by drums – and what a difference the drums make.

A hymn like 'Abide with me,' which accompanied by a harmonium can be fairly drearisome, when accompanied with a drum, gains new life and spirit, especially if you have a good drummer like Guguletto whose hands fly across the drums like birds.

He leads with his own beat and his own rhythm and the singers fit in the words and tune as best they can. 'Abide with me' emerges like the latest number from the top of the hit parade. The other memory that I have of Guguletto comes from one afternoon later on when he was helping me clear out some of the battered, unused text books from the library which we carted to big bonfire in a small pit in the garden. As several of us stood around the fire chatting and relaxing Guguletto said, 'This just reminds me of the neck lacing parties we sometime had in our location at home.' These parties were popular in apartheid days (inspired it is said by Winnie Mandela) and at them any informer suspected of passing information to the police was tied to a post while burning tires were tossed over his head to cover his shoulders like a necklace until he died in agony. Such were some of the memories some of these men brought with them hidden in their baggage when they came to try the religious life in SSM.

In October Robert Stretton plus Steve and I began regular Sesotho classes. We were lucky in our tutor who was a young and attractive woman who did her best to jolly us along through all the basic material of grammar, vocabulary and conversation. However I have to admit that I found my old brain was just too stiff, too rusty to be able to accommodate about 3-4000 new words of Sesotho as well as all the intricate by-ways of colloquial speech. Although I learned enough to say mass in Sesotho, I never was able to join in Sesotho conversation or understand what others were saying. This was an enormous drawback and I bitterly regretted that I had not come to the country in my twenties or even forties rather than in my sixties. It meant I could never engage in relaxed conversation with people or penetrate Basotho culture. Those I met had to do all the work painfully trying to turn their ideas into shaky English. I was thus barred from a large and most important part of life here – easy chat. Luckily St John's church had a policy of English only in their service and nearly all the members of the parish were fluent English speakers.

1998

January is a hard time of the year for most Basotho parents. It is the start of a new school year and fees have to be paid before a child is allowed to set foot within a classroom. If you are a woman with four to five children of school age earning a minimum wage as a cleaner, cook or trader in the market, with food and clothes for the children to provide and the school books to be bought in addition to the fees, the total sum is a crippler. I heard all this from Alice who cooks for us in the priory and has two young girls plus a mentally disabled infant son. Then I had another fourteen year old lad coming to us in tears. His two older brothers had already been thrown out of school for non-payment of fees; his father, a drinker, is just one more liability and eviction now awaits him too next week if he doesn't produce the cash. He desperately wants to get some education as even kids of his age realise that education provides their only hope, though a slim one, of getting a better life. Luckily the family had sent me some Christmas money and I was able to use it for this.

A more cheerful aspect of the educational scene is Theological Education by Extension, always referred to here as TEE. This is a scheme supported by all the churches for a theology course by correspondence. It provides a three tier system, beginners, juniors and seniors. It covers all the subjects found in the curriculum of most theological colleges. For each course it issues a booklet in English aimed at people for whom English is a second language, and each chapter of the book is followed by a series of questions which the student sends in for marking and suggestions to the tutor that has been assigned to him/her. The whole scheme in our diocese is under the supervision of Judy Gay, an American priest whose energy and enthusiasm enables the success of the whole venture. The great thing is that TEE opens up the opportunity of studying theology to many scattered and isolated people in Lesotho and elsewhere in Southern Africa, married women, mothers, and fulltime workers supporting a family, who could not possibly take two or three years off to attend college, let alone pay the fees. It also means that people whose primary education has been so patchy or scratchy that they have had no chance of getting the necessary paper qualifications for college entry, now have an opportunity to join the beginners class and if they are able by hard work and zeal to bring their English up to a basic standard, they can, with Judy's enthusiastic encouragement, begin to study theology at a college level.

It is a serious course run by an ecumenical theology board in Johannesburg and leads to a diploma or degree. Bishops are willing to accept it as an academic preparation for ordination. Typical of the TEE students was a farmer Judy and I went to visit one day down near Leribe to give him a hand with the assignment he was preparing to send in. I will never forget that day. This was a straightforward honest farmer making a poor living on very rocky soil with a wife and five children. He was working on the book of Amos in his Old Testament studies, so we sat under the apricot tree blossoming beside his house (it was September) and went over the questions he had prepared and listened to the additional questions he wanted to ask me. It was such a thrill to listen to this guy, an ordinary man who was interested in theology, 'What was Amos' idea of justice? And does that apply still in Lesotho?' In another corner of the garden Judy was helping another student who had come to meet us there with her questions on Church History. After an hour or two the farmer walked us around to see his beasts and his crops and his wife brought out a substantial meal of meat stew, rice, pumpkin, and leeks which we ate together under the trees. Another day we went to the home of a middle aged woman tied completely to her house nursing her dying mother. She too had a sharp mind and soon saw the point of the questions we were raising, a joy to teach. Without TEE her life would never get beyond cooking, cleaning, washing, and nursing. Helping this sort of person who had no other possible access to college-level education was one of the most enjoyable things I was able to help with in Lesotho.

Amongst those seeking help at the gate to pay school fees was JJ Rasethuntsa, an interesting character who had become a part of the priory scene. He came from the mountains and, as a good looking young man, had been a protégée of Fr Clement at St John's. From that time and still he has been a server at the church, for many years the only server. In fact he deeply loved that church and seldom missed a service whatever his drink problems might be. His father had arranged for him and bullied him into a marriage which became a total disaster except for its one issue, Teboho by name, a nice lad who was now about fourteen and whose school books for the year I was glad to provide. After the departure of his wife, JJ had brought the lad up with great devotion in a little shack on the edge of town. JJ came to me last September and offered to make a garden for us out of the untamed wilderness at the back of the house, beginning with a crop of potatoes. He did more than that for he is a skilled gardener, and over the summer has turned the scrub into a model garden with wide beds, and trenches between them, from which garden we are now eating lettuce, tomatoes, radishes, beans, carrots, all fresh and delicious. As time has gone by, he has told me a little about his childhood. Like so many Basotho boys he had been sent at the age of ten or eleven up to the mountains with the family's little flock of sheep and goats and the odd cow to herd them and to safeguard them all through the summer. It was a very tough introduction to life for any boy and woe betide the one who lost a goat or a sheep. It was the equivalent of an English family withdrawing all their money from the bank, cashing in their life insurance and then giving it all in bank notes to their twelve year old son to look after while he was on holidays over the summer. These boys are usually provided with a sack of mealies (corn) to last them until the autumn, and otherwise they live on whatever birds, mice, or rats they managed to kill with their catapults. JJ still never travels without his catapult in his back pocket and remains an excellent shot. I saw him one day bring down a large horned owl from the top of a gum tree in the garden with one shot. When our Robert protested at the destruction of wild life, JJ explained that this was how he had kept alive as a herd boy, and besides, he could get a good price for the dead owl from the sangkoma (herbal doctor) who used parts of the owl to make their spells and potions for the sick and troubled. He had a lively, warm and outgoing personality and he took it upon himself to teach me Sesotho. He greeted each of my attempts at idiot Sesotho 'How are you?' 'It is hot today', with cries of glee as if Confucius had spoken.

———•—

Last week Bill Blott sent me a lovely tape of classical music, mostly Bach and Handel. It had been prepared by the daughter of a friend of his for her Dad, and, in order to get a rise out of the old man she had inserted into the middle of the classical items a piece called, 'Did Jesus have a little sister?' Bill had deleted this one from my tape but it would have been the favourite of these guys here who are all (as they were in Ghana) fans of Bob Marley. We can't go even as far as the shops without the strains of 'Precious Memories',

'Whispering Hope', 'Daddy, my Daddy, teach me how to pray', 'It is no secret what God can do' reverberating around the cab.

———•·•———

We are beginning to gather a few recruits; Eric is from Mozambique whose mother tongue is Portuguese and speaks English but not Sesotho. Michael Maasdorp is an Afrikaner who is a former student and novice at Kelham, a former priest in Johannesburg and now a consultant in his own business. Petrus is from Johannesburg, a former member of the P. A. C. (People's African Congress), the most extreme of the black parties whose racial policy was summed up in their motto, 'One settler – one bullet.' Thebeethata is from one of the Bantustans set up as puppet states by the National Party. He is a loyal, but thankfully non-verbal, supporter of the Bantustan's king and the National party – still.

Rumour has it that he worked for the Secret Service in the apartheid days, turning over the names of local trouble makers to them. He is also an extremely devout and pious young man. It is good to see some additions to the core of local Basotho, but it does mean that the house is now too cramped and so we are building three additional rooms next to but not connected with the main block. They are in the same style; cinder block, one block thick, with a corrugated iron roof, and a shower and toilet at the end.

———•·•———

On the day before Palm Sunday we went off in the van with JJ and some of the lads to collect palms for tomorrow's procession. JJ swore he could take us to the right place to find the correct trees because, in the absence of palms in these parts, the Basotho, instructed no doubt by the early missionaries, insist on having the authentic branches such those Hebrews waved in Jerusalem at that first procession. The problem is that these trees are not all that common, but off we went under JJ's directions down some deeply rutted country roads, winding over rocky outcrops with cliffs all around us. The tree JJ pointed out to us at last turned out to be a withered wild olive with storm-tossed branches growing out of a fissure in the rock face half way down the cliff-side. Undaunted, the young guys, led by JJ, clambered down the cliff face and began clipping off these authentic branches. However, hardly had they begun when an old crone appeared on the brink of the cliff cursing, screaming and ordering us to desist forthwith – at least I gathered that that was the tenor of her cry. But no Mosotho is ever at a loss for words so the verbal confrontation between our party and her waxed sharp and furious while the clipping continued apace and JJ and the old woman disputed the ownership of the tree. The situation grew in complexity but also in safety when a second old crone appeared further along the cliff edge. This one we had taken the precaution of bribing with six rand before descending, and she urged us to pay no attention to 'that old cow' as she was a nobody and knew nothing. Meanwhile the clipping continued and the pile of branches sent up to the van continued to grow when a final and fatal disaster threatened in the shape of a small herd boy who passed by with his little flock of goats who imagined that all this greenery had been especially prepared for them and had to be driven off with wild shouts and alarms. At the first opportunity we fled in the loaded van pursued by the curses of one old girl and the blessings of the other. It is certainly a more lively way of collecting palms for our procession than ordering them to be sent by post from the church shop.

We are having a week or two of warm autumn days, the golden leaves are slowly falling from the poplars along the front drive, we are still eating beetroot, spinach, carrots and lettuce from the garden, and I am feeling remarkably content. Long may it last!

May 23 is election day and people are holding their breath to see if we get through it without violence or rioting, with the party that loses accepting defeat graciously and not calling out the army and the police to keep them in power – as has happened before. Poor Lesotho is in decline. During the apartheid days it achieved a certain notoriety as a refuge to which those wanted by the South African Police could flee, and as a base for the activities of those who resisted the regime. At one time the South African army raided Maseru by night, arrested some and shot other men and women who were part of the struggle for freedom. That's how much respect they had for an international border. Those days are now gone. The British embassy and others are being closed and, in addition, with the fall in the price of gold, the Johannesburg mines no longer need men from here thus increasing the poverty and unemployment on this side of the border. Many say that the best thing for Lesotho in the new situation would be to join the Republic but our local politicians resist this vehemently and patriotically while South Africa is reluctant to tackle yet more education, medical and housing problems. They have enough of those as it is.

———

A sad blow for us was the sudden unexpected death of JJ. He was here working in the garden in the morning, had dinner with us, and then woke up in the middle of the night, according to Teboho his son, coughing up blood. He was 43 years old. They say he died of TB but that is to avoid the stigma that would accompany the truth. He died of Aids. We shall miss him greatly here at the priory. A week later we took the van and collected the body from the hospital morgue and took it back to his place to lie in state all night with his wife sitting at his head. Just as we were driving away from the house I witnessed the last minutes of the steer designated for the funeral feast. They took a long spike and drove or inserted it between the shoulder blades behind the head. The steer knelt down gently and passed on peacefully! Next day, after the requiem mass under a tarpaulin in front of his shack, we put the coffin in the back of the van and prepared to march off to the cemetery behind a man leading the way with a spade held aloft.

But before I could start the engine, there were cries of 'Wait! Wait!' until they had brought the hide of the beast killed the night before and put it in next to the coffin. Then at the cemetery, three men jumped down into the grave and eased the coffin into its place and then draped the cow hide over it to provide him with a warm blanket as he journeyed onwards. They don't want him to appear there in scruffy clothes. Then the grave was filled in by the men in strict order of family precedence while the women urged them on with hymn after hymn.

We had a nice day at the end of this month. Largely through the efforts and initiative of Thebeethata and the young novices, we have started a club called 'The Friends of SSM'. Of course Africans are the greatest 'joiners' in the world and when membership brings a small wooden cross to wear around your neck it is irresistible! As a result our conference day at the priory was swamped. We had a couple of talks on prayer and worship to which they listened attentively, but for me the highlight of the day was the Eucharist at noon. I put some of them in charge of music, some did the intercessions, and three young girls did the sermon. The music was almost non-stop, all in harmony, and all very beautiful. It was accompanied by vigorous drumming, clapping and dancing, just as in Ghana. The intercessions were done in the way they like best with everyone humming in the background while one passionate voice rose above and over the whole thing –very moving! As for the sermon, each of the three girls took a part but it was all in Sesotho so I can say nothing of the content; all I can say is that what they said was what they truly felt and believed. We all enjoyed it and all felt the better for the day. The Friends have begun to contribute to the welfare of the country by going around in groups for week-end visits to the villages giving talks and educating the youth on HIV Aids, its causes, how to avoid it, how to live with it, how to nurse those who are dying from it, and teaching them (oh, shades of our sainted ancestors!) how to use condoms.

Unfortunately we seem to be due for more political upheavals. Although Lesotho is one of the few African countries united by a single language, it is bitterly divided into many factions. There are the wealthy wage-earning English speakers such as those who fill St John's church, and there are the subsistence farmers scratching out a meagre living on these rocky hills. There are those who support the monarchy and want it to have more power, and there are those who want a republic or who want Lesotho to join the Republic of South Africa. There are university graduates and there are illiterates. There is the Roman Catholic Church, the largest religious body, and there are hundreds of Pentecostal congregations as well as the usual denominations.

At the recent elections the ruling party won all the seats in Parliament save one and ever since the three opposition parties have been screaming (perhaps with some reason) that the voting was rigged with bribery and bullying to give that result, and they want a new election. This last week a great mob of people has been camping at the gates of the royal palace demanding that the king dismiss Parliament and call a new election. He, poor man, is a gentle not very decisive character who clings to his role as a constitutional monarch like the British queen and teeters on top of the fence. Yesterday the mob blockaded the Parliament buildings and held the members hostage. Mr Mosesili, the Prime Minister, only escaped by means of a ladder. Apart from that nothing more serious than a little window smashing has happened so far.

Next a pleasant interlude when I was offered a ride to Swaziland to visit the priory of the Order of the Holy Paraclete from Whitby. Their leader, Sr Dorothy Stella, is an old friend of mine from Ghana days and is now principal of a Technical Training College near Manzini where they teach young people a trade such as sewing, cooking, farming, plumbing, jam-making, you name it, so that they can earn a living. It is a big college filled with restless students and unhappy staff so her job is not an easy one. The other sister in the house is running a home for sexually abused and abandoned girls. I was amazed at the difference between Lesotho and Swaziland because Swaziland is a bit further north and so closer to the equator and warmer; nearer the Indian Ocean. The sisters have paw-paws and bananas growing in their garden and we drove through fields of sugar cane and pineapple on our way there. They took me for a day to a nearby game park and we saw lots of crocodiles, hippos, deer, ostriches and giraffes. The topic of conversation there is nothing political at all; it is the approaching Cane Festival when all the young Swazi girls dance out into the fields topless to gather cane to build a new house for the Queen Mother. It sound innocent enough but during the proceedings the king strolls through the dancers and selects the young woman he wants to be his next wife. I think this year's choice will make his sixth wife, one of whom is the daughter of an Anglican priest, so you see there is no disgrace in it. Each wife has her own house and servants and doubtless as the group number increases so the individual burden becomes lighter. The sisters were wonderful to me and it made an enjoyable break.

September 27

Well! Things have fallen apart altogether here after a group of junior army officers arrested their senior officers, locked them up and started to take over the government with another military coup as their objective. However Nelson Mandela decided that he could not afford to have revolution and mayhem going on in the heartland of his republic and so he sent in the South African Defence Force supported by troops from Botswana. The first we knew, or even suspected, of this was when we woke up on Tuesday morning to the sound of a fleet of helicopters hovering over our heads and the sound of intermittent gunfire coming from the centre of town. It is said that the South Africans are so unacquainted with Maseru that they drove their line of tanks up to the entrance of the Sun Hotel which occupies a prominent place on the hillside, thinking that was the royal palace. However they made no mistakes about finding their way to Katse Dam up in the hills and taking charge of that. It is the source of much of Johannesburg's water supply. Meanwhile, with the advent of foreign troops, all social constraints evaporated and mobs of local people were roaming the streets, smashing windows and looting shops. All Tuesday and Wednesday there was a procession of people going past our gate loaded down with new clothes, furniture and food, and we could see pillars of black smoke rising from the town as they set the place alight. Our only bad experience was when a group of about ten yobbos, high on drugs and alcohol, turned up at the gate demanding our car so that they could go and 'defend our country'. There was nothing we could do, no one we could appeal to; the police were probably busy looting for themselves. So we handed over the keys and off they went to collect as much loot as they could lay hands on. The South African forces half expected that they would be received as liberators by the folks here but far from it. The Lesotho armed forces withdrew with their weapons into the hills above the town and began firing on the South Africans in the centre and that is how they went on for the rest of the day volleying shots at one another over the heads of the townspeople. The SSM were very supportive of us and kept phoning regularly throughout the day but there was little they could do. I then had a call from the Canadian Embassy in Pretoria inquiring for my welfare and advising me to get out as soon as I could. When I explained that there was a problem for Michael Maasdorp and I (the only two whites left in the priory) to get down to the border post through the rioting mobs, they said to get myself ready with a small overnight bag and some on would call and pick us up in half an hour. How quickly as I packed that bag, not knowing when or if we would ever get back, did I have to sort out my priorities. What was really essential to me now? My Bible and prayer book, or extra underwear? All my papers or an extra pair of shoes? In half an hour a beat up old car arrived to collect Michael and me and as we drove down the main street of town, it looked like Coventry the morning after the big raid. We were taken to a private school with large grounds where all the residue of whites was gathered. Eventually the South African army formed a procession of one tank five cars, one tank five more cars and so on, and we headed for the border post with, thank goodness, no confusion about directions this time! Over the border, they took us as far as Ladybrand and as we drive up the long hill out of Maseru we looked back to see the heavy pall of black smoke hanging over the town. Fortunately the Community of the Resurrection fathers had been in touch with us and had driven down to Ladybrand to meet us. What welcome faces they seemed to us as they drove up! It was now too late to drive back to Johannesburg that afternoon so we turned aside at Modderpoort, just a few miles out of Ladybrand, to stay the night at what had been SSM's St Augustine's Priory and the headquarters of all our mission work, and was now a luxury tourist lodge where we finished the day with a first class meal on the front porch there. 'Not bad', we said. 'for a bunch of refugees!' What a tragedy that day was for Lesotho. They had nothing to start with and they ended up with that much less, nearly all the damage being self-inflicted.

After five or six days in the C. R. house in Johannesburg we were able to load up the van with groceries and head back to Maseru where the town was in chaos but relatively peaceful.

October

Things continue to quieten down thanks in large part to the troops here from Botswana and South Africa who are still very much in evidence on the streets. The curfew has been relaxed a little. It is now 9.00pm to 4.00am and the government has promised new elections in eighteen months' time. Rumour has it that there are still five hundred Lesotho Defence Force men hiding up in the hills waiting for the foreign armies to go home before exacting revenge but they are not today's problem! Michael Maasdorp has located his car, abandoned and battered in an empty lot on the edge of town.

Stephen returns to Australia and Robert to the UK in the new year and Michael Maasdorp will transfer to the English Province, thus leaving me as the only non-African member of the priory; perhaps a little daunting, but then living with whites hasn't always been pure bliss either!

November

This month the Director called for a General Chapter of the Society to meet in South Africa. It was in a beautiful spot in the heart of the wine growing area near Paarl, so we were surrounded by blossoming vines, high purple mountains and sunshine while being coddled in luxury. One highlight of the chapter for me was a visit to Cape Town where Michael Lapsley had arranged for us to visit some priest friends of his who were working in the midst of those endless acres of what we would mostly call shacks or slums and which are now termed Informal Settlements. Many of the houses are made of cardboard and iron sheeting and without electricity or piped water. We visited a number of clinics, nursery schools, churches and recreation areas and could not help but admire the courage and resilience both staffs and parents display in their efforts to make life a little more human, a bit richer and safer for their children in an environment of poverty and violence. Another aspect of this counter culture was our tour around Robben Island. This was conducted by a man who had himself been a prisoner there for eleven years. He showed us Mandela's cell, the rock quarry where they chipped rocks, and told us about some of the degrading customs of the daily routine. Again we were over-awed that a man could come out of twenty-seven years in a place like that, structured to demean the inhabitants and strip them of any power, and still emerge with his integrity intact and well able to step forward and assume leadership of a country of this size and complexity. And all these things took place within easy view of Cape Town across the channel but completely out of contact with it.

1999

February

I had a chance this month to pay a leisurely visit to Modderoort, SSM's headquarters in Africa from 1902 – 1990 and have a leisurely look around. It was very moving to visit the cave in the cliff-side where the first community that began work here in the 1860's, the Community of St Augustine, made their home for the first years they were here. It is now fixed up as a chapel and regarded as a very holy and powerful place by the Basotho who like to come here to pray. I wonder that that first community did not all die of pneumonia or TB living as they did for several years in a damp cold cave but they were willing to do all that and more to spread the good news. By 1900 they were reduced to two men and they had lost most of their contacts in the UK so that further recruiting was not possible and so they appealed to Fr Kelly of SSM to take over the mission work which he did. There is a lovely Gothic chapel with a bell tower outside still in place though no longer in regular use. When I went into the vestry of the chapel what I saw told me the whole story of their approach to missions in those days, so different from the present times. There in the vestry bookcase were all the books, five or six different sets that we used to sing the high mass at Kelham. So here in the heart of Africa surrounded by native people and Dutch farmers what they wanted to do was to recreate in detail the worship they had known in Kelham chapel at Newark, Nottinghamshire, England.

I thought as I looked around the vestry that these men who worshipped here must have been very homesick; far, far away in a strange land where perhaps they had not even chosen to go but simply went because they had been told to go. The priory became a kind of citadel; when you stepped through the door you stepped out of Africa through all the miles and back into the 'mother house' in England. The brothers with some exceptions never learned the local language; Africans were not allowed on the front porch where most of their socialising with the wealthy Boer farmers took place; in the refectory you never had margarine and marmalade (which you always called 'squish') on the same piece of toast and many other similar Kelham based customs. Yet these same brothers worked hard and sacrificially, they wore the SSM habit wherever they went, said all the daily offices faithfully every day in the chapel and some them now lie at peace in the cemetery around the chapel. They established churches, schools, a Teacher Training College for Africans, and opened a hundred ways ahead for countless village young people who were despised and exploited by the government. What a mixed history they left us, and what a beautiful spot they chose and built up faithfully over a hundred years.

———•———

June

This month came the elections in South Africa, the first ones since the very first one in 1994 when people like Nelson Mandela and Desmond Tutu voted for the first time in their lives. Although not a part of the republic, Lesotho is completely dominated by it and everyone here was greatly relieved when the elections passed off without violence, even more smoothly than in '94. It seems that the people here are still in love with the ANC (African National Congress) and all the opposition parties could ever hope for was to muster a realistic opposition. They didn't manage even that. The last I hear the ANC had 66 seats; the next in line, the Democratic Party had six, and the rest less than that. The old National Party that ruled with a rod of iron all through the apartheid years is crumbling away, no longer credible even to the whites. I was pleased to see that Colonel Viljoen, the leader of the extreme right wing of the Afrikaners who wants to establish a white Bantustan, i.e. an enclosed estate for whites only, got one percent of the votes so it looks as if the crazies are not going anywhere at present.

For three days this month I was part of an attempt by the Anglican church of Lesotho to elect in synod a new bishop. Our speeches lacked neither eloquence nor effort but they were also prolonged and painful, acrimonious and unsuccessful. How I hate church politics! The meetings were chaired by the archbishop, Jongkonkulu Ndungwane by name, and Primate of the Anglican Church in these parts.

He is a man of considerable political skill and eloquence but even he could not stitch together the various factions of the church here. The divisions in the church are a copy of the divisions in the country. Each group fervently invoked the Holy Spirit from time to time to come and 'do things our way' but the Holy Spirit did not oblige and we remained divided. In the end the matter was referred back to the House of Bishops to select a man for us, much to the chagrin of many participants who may have felt that they were the obvious answer to the problem.

At Pentecost sister Julian Mary died. She was one of the Precious Blood sisters at Masite. There were three bishops, about twenty-five priests and large crowds of folks present at the funeral and the singing was full-bodied and robust. Once again I attended a triumphal crowded funeral for a person who was socially almost unknown and of little importance. Sister Julian Mary was one of the handful of sisters who came out from Burnham Abbey in Buckinghamshire in 1957 to establish the new priory of Our Lady, Mother of Mercy at Masite. This is a contemplative community so the sisters don't go out preaching or visiting congregations; their main and only work is to worship God day by day in the chapel and, in addition they would say, that the most important thing they do is to maintain an unbroken watch in front of the sacrament in chapel. Here every day from early morning until last thing at night you will see a sister kneeling there praying for those in need and trouble who have asked for their prayers. There is no publicity connected to this work, it is just what they do and have been doing in good times and in bad times for more than fifty years. People send in names to them from all over Africa and UK and I sometimes wonder how many people and situations have been calmed, reconciled, and renewed by the prayers said in that chapel – but I suppose only God knows the answer to that. Though dedicated to intercession and prayer, this does not separate them from the life going on all around them. In the apartheid days they were great supporters of those men and women engaged in the struggle and provided a refuge to which those fleeing the police often escaped. They are also completely integrated with the village people, their neighbours in Masite, and find fees for youngsters at school, e-pap (Mealies fortified with vitamins), and give financial assistance to men and women trying to make a living on small farms where the land is poor and machinery almost non-existent. The extent of their integration with the village was made clear two months ago when one of their thatched storage sheds burst into flames in the middle of the night. The oldest sister was sent to ring the chapel bell while the rest formed a bucket brigade. They were soon joined by all the men and women of the village, roused by the bell, who fought the fire at their side until the flames were extinguished and the priory saved. But then too at Julian Mary's funeral the feast for 250 – 300 people was prepared and served by the village women, and we' re not talking about ham sandwiches here; it was beef stew, chops, chicken and every kind of vegetable. At Sister Mary Josephine's Golden Jubilee of profession all the village came and had a party in her honour with singing and dancing in front of Mary Josephine draped in a Basotho blanket with a Basotho hat fixed on top of her veil, laughing and enjoying the whole thing. The sisters are now a small group of about eight women mostly elderly, some Basotho, some Afrikaner, some English but I can testify to their warm humanity and to the seriousness of their dedication. While all through these fifty years of upheaval people all around them have been busy making war on one another and killing one another, these women in a far corner of a forgotten kingdom, have quietly got on with making peace and spreading love.

July

A minor mishap on Sunday when it was my turn to do supper. There are now seven of us here plus Tanki who is here having a break from his parish, a visiting priest and two friends, ten in all. A good number, but this group is one of the easiest to cook for. I have yet to see anyone here refuse any form of food on the table, right down to the catsup, the mustard and the honey mustard. Clean plates, empty bowls, no complaints, no slacking are the orders of the day – always. I started a chicken stew bubbling away early. This dish always reminds me of my Dad as it was his favourite and we always had it on his birthday. I went back before Evensong to pop in the dumplings and found all ten of them clustered around a big coal fire in the common room, absolutely glued to the TV watching Bafana, Bafana (the South African soccer team) playing Angola. It was a close run game ending in a tie so there was much shouting, cheering, jumping up and crashing down. All was well until I went back into the kitchen after Evensong to check on the dumplings only to find they had not risen in the slightest. They were floating on the top like miniature cannon balls. However I dished them up without either explanation or apology and not a single crumb was left at the end of dinner. See what I said about how easy they are to cook for? The game had given them such an appetite; everything was grist to their mill.

I had a trip last week to Kimberly where the Precious Blood sisters have a House of Prayer and where I was to give a couple of talks to their people. Kimberly is about 450ks distant nearly on the border with Namibia. The scenery as you drive along reminds me a lot of Saskatchewan, absolutely flat and with few outstanding features. In 300k you pass through only two towns and they too are very Saskatchewan-like and in the same distance you may only meet two or three vehicles. Kimberly was the heart of the diamond trade and in the centre of the town is the Big Hole about a mile wide and a mile deep from which they excavated all those diamonds that made so many people rich – except the miners who dug them out. Nearly all the population here are coloureds i.e. every possible mixture of black and white and they all speak Afrikaans. They have a very good museum, a reconstruction of 'old Kimberly' as it was at its peak, and I found that fascinating. Nowadays it is a much more sedate little town. I had a great welcome from Sister Camila and the talks seemed to satisfy the folks.

About this same time I decided that we would paint out the chapel which has been looking increasingly shoddy. It is not a big space but has a very high ceiling and so scaffolding is necessary. I think you could call the job labour intensive with eight young guys who were willing and eager to get going, but none of whom had had any experience with wielding a roller brush. Once they all got going and I looked around it reminded me of that Walt Disney film, *Snow White and the Seven Dwarfs*, with our young guys swinging from top to bottom and bottom to top of the scaffolding, singing without let up, now in chorus, now in solo, and slapping paint over the walls, over themselves, and over the carpet. As I had already decided to replace the carpet, I let all that pass with equanimity. Four weeks afterwards the chapel looks very bright and new, with a new crimson carpet, new curtains which Sister Camilla picked out for me in Kimberly and shining white walls – perfect!

August

We were sitting in the common room last night around a big coal fire when the talk turned to the subject of ghosts and who believed in them. It turned out that I was the only one present prepared to commit himself to total non-belief though some wanted to qualify and closely define what they believed. Then Ephraim said he could prove that ghosts were with us every day by the case of his uncle who lived in his home village near Leribe. This man worked in the gold mines in Johannesburg while his wife and children remained in the village. Sadly, when he was home for Christmas his small boy died, about seven years old. They arranged a funeral but the father said it would not be necessary to have a feast or kill a cow. This boy was 'no but a lad', he had never worked or married and for him a simple reading of the funeral service would be sufficient, and that's what they did, and the man returned to work. However the next time he came home some six months later he was met by his mother extremely upset and in tears. She said the little boy had been coming to her in the middle of the night and night after night, shivering and weeping and repeating, 'Grannie I'm cold, Grannie I'm cold.' But the miner said that that was only old women's superstition and did nothing before he went back to work. Six weeks later there was an explosion in the mine where he was working and the tunnel he was in collapsed in two places, once in front of him and once behind him. He was caught like a rat in a trap. It took four to five days before his mates managed to dig him out and get him back to the surface. The first thing he did after he had eaten and showered was to go to the manager and ask for leave for a special trip home at once. Leave was given and as soon as he arrived back in his village he arranged a funeral feast, killed a cow and poured libation for his small son. After that the boy never troubled his grannie again. So who was that, if it was not a ghost? We had no answers.

———•·•———

October

The director of SSM, Edmund Wheat, and Fr John Lewis visited us this month and they seemed suitably impressed with what they found. I think that this priory where there are eight young men in residence whose average age would be in the mid-twenties must make a reassuring contrast with the priories they have been to in England and Australia. While they were here we discussed what kind of membership we should offer these guys. Somehow it didn't seem quite right to ask them to take life-long promises of celibacy, poverty and obedience, especially as they had come to us with such vague and ill-defined ideas about what the religious life and SSM was all about and had experienced living under those conditions for such a short period. Then too it seemed too individualistic for them to make these solemn promises one by one as each one's trial period came to a close. After all, as they say in these parts, it is by other people that we all become persons, not just by our own individual choices. Being good Anglicans all, the upshot of our discussions was a compromise. We drew up a service of commitment to be added to the usual Wednesday afternoon Eucharist. During this service the last comers to the priory could make, if they wished, a commitment to the Sacred Mission for one year.

Those who had already been living with us for more than a year could if they wished make a commitment to the Sacred Mission for a further five years, and at the same service Michael Lapsley and I would renew the life-time commitment we had made many years ago. Thus we all committed ourselves to one another and to the Sacred Mission, and felt happy with that. There was a big crowd of High School students and Friends of SSM in attendance, as usual on Wednesdays. We had the service outside in the courtyard and it was followed by a feast – a really good an enjoyable day

2000

April

At Easter this year Tanki was ordained to the priesthood and is back living in the house for the first time since I arrived here. Up until now he had been mostly living in the theological College of the Transfiguration at Grahamstown. He is a man of enormous energy and enthusiasm and his coming to live here has been a great blessing to me. Since his arrival he has got the email working again after a long lapse, the fax machine functioning once more, and he has bullied the builder into completing at last the long delayed extension of two blocks of two rooms each down by the gate. He then went down to the office of the electricity corporation where our application to have the new addition connected had sunk many moons ago without a trace. Fortunately the woman in charge of the office had been a classmate of Tanki's in their childhoods and so all obstacles and barriers disappeared as if by magic and Tanki was allowed to look through an enormous pile of dog-eared and dusty application forms that were overflowing on the lady's desk. There deep in the pile he found our application form and our two new blocks, after only minimal bribes were paid, were connected up within the week. So life goes on!

Tanki comes from a small farming village down near Morija and his family are eager to put on a big feast to mark his ordination. He is after all the classical local boy who has made good and it is something indeed to celebrate. He would have been a herd boy in the hills but for the intervention of an older brother who sent him to a primary school and paid his fees. From there he went on to do the Theological Education by Extension course, and then was ready for the College of the Transfiguration at Grahamstown. He persuaded Fr David to take him on as a novice at a time when the SSM novitiate had been officially closed and there hadn't been a novice for some years. He has thus been professed in SSM and ordained to the priesthood at roughly the same time, not a bad record for a boy from a small village. No wonder his family is proud of him.

May 14

Today we all went down to Tanki's old home, a collection of stone-built straw thatched rondavals where the extended family live. All around you could see in the distance the rolling hills of the Lesotho lowlands which stood out so clearly on this bright and cloudless day. When we arrived we found about 500 people gathered, in fact the whole neighbourhood for miles around, all those who knew Tanki or any of the members of his family. Tanki introduced me to his old teacher in primary school, a tall, traditionally built woman looking splendid and impressive in her Mothers' Union uniform. She has taught and is still teaching at the same school where Tanki met her as a boy. She has been teaching in that village school since 1957 and has had seven children of her own in the intervals. Meeting her, I could not help but feel that there would be no discipline problems in any of her classes.

We started off with the Eucharist in front of the main house and as soon as we started there rode up about fifteen men on horseback who formed themselves into a semi-circle at the back of the congregation. The Basotho are great horsemen and great lovers of horses; they often treat their horses like we would treat the family dog. All these men were Tanki's contemporaries. After the service there followed about twenty-five speeches led by a fiery harangue from Tanki himself dressed in a traditional blanket and fur hat. I gather he was denouncing the crowd for their lukewarm attendance at church, but they all took it in good part. It was what they expected him to say and what they felt he should say on such an occasion. Speeches were followed by an enormous meal, beef stew, every kind of chicken, every kind of vegetable, all cooked in big iron pots over a wood fire. This was followed by trifles and jellies. After we had eaten our fill, the entertainment came on. First the women did traditional women's dancing. This seemed a bit strange at first as they were all sitting/kneeling firmly fixed on the ground moving only their upper bodies and arms to the rhythm as they sang traditional songs. I have heard, though I only partly believe it, that this style of dancing was a result of a compromise worked out with the first missionaries who found the former women's dances were too provocative and suggestive for any Christian assembly. Then the young men did their traditional dances (on their feet!) and then the horsemen displayed the tricks their horses could do.

The most popular number was a young man who explained that his horse was very tired after a hard day's trekking and needed to sleep. So he turned and whispered in its ear and the horse lay down flat on the ground, legs stretched out. Then his master threw a blanket over him, and then curled up himself with his back to the horse's back under the same blanket. They seemed to be sound asleep and even snoring noises came from the man (not, I think, the horse!)

What a memorable day it was borne along as we were on waves of affection, pleasure and pride.

About this time Michael Lapsley came and conducted for the priory one of his Healing of Memories workshops such as he does all over South Africa and in various troubled spots throughout the world. It was my first experience of them and I am now totally convinced of the value of them and of Michael's work. There were three main events in the workshop that stand out.

1. On the first morning we were all given a large sheet of paper and told to draw a picture of our life, including all the events both good and bad that stuck in our memory, no matter how far back they were. This took us most of the morning and in the afternoon we met again and each one displayed and explained his picture. The rest of us were asked not to correct, criticise or even comment, all we had to do was listen carefully. In fact everyone was given permission to open up and bring out all those hidden things that had damaged or destroyed their lives – permission seldom given to us in everyday life. All the rest of us were expected to do was acknowledge and absorb what had happened to this person. I have been

living with these guys for the better part of three years but I learned things about them that day I had never guessed before. We had pictures of herd boys and sheep, of soldiers with guns burying alive innocent people, of women hiding up in the trees while soldiers hunted for them down below. One picture showed a complicated network of tunnels, as in a gold mine, with only one small shaft to the surface because, the man explained, all our real life, our biggest decisions, dangers and wounds, were down below the surface, hidden from view and must never be exposed to the gaze of the public. A little chilling that one, but certainly accurate for that man.

2. Then one morning we were asked to comb through our memories and then write down on paper all the negativities, that is all the things that made us angry, all the harms we couldn't forgive, all the mistakes we had made we could no longer undo, all the tears we had shed. When we had finished we didn't share the contents of our papers. Instead we went to chapel and had a Eucharist in which, after the general confession we processed out into the courtyard walked around the fire burning there and then threw into it our papers. We then returned to the chapel leaving all those negativities being consumed behind us and, freshly forgiven, tasting the freedom and joy of the Christian way, we sang a song of thanksgiving.

3. Before the last session we were all given a lump of potter's clay and asked to fashion a shape that would tell others what in your opinion the priory was all about. Some made a dove of peace, some a Mosotho rider with his horse, some a plain cross. I made a round kraal such as the shepherds often make in the mountains out of the field stones there to be a shelter for the sheep, a place where they can be fed and counted and healed of any wounds. All these we placed on the altar and then had our final Eucharist of thanksgiving.

In short it was a most useful exercise from each one of us drew some benefit.

After it was over Michael took me to call on the king, Letsie III in his palace. They had both been for a while contemporaries at the University of Lesotho and so had had that kind of contact. The palace looks like a block of luxury flats in the centre of town, and the king, who is about thirty-eight, is a most humble relaxed and amiable person dressed on this occasion in a pair of jeans, pullover, trainers and a baseball cap. He and Michael had lots of easy-going conversation and then we left. He is Roman Catholic, educated at Ampleforth in the UK, but he comes to our cathedral and makes his communion on the big occasions.

From June to August I had a long leave in UK and Canada, and when I returned the guys were all at the airport to greet me and again another big welcome at St John's on Sunday morning.

The Director arrived a week after I got back to do an inspection of the troops and feeling very strongly that the time had come to turn the priory over to African leadership. I am very much in favour of that though maybe not sure that this is the best minute to do that. Perhaps all leaders feel something like that when their time comes to move on!

We held an election and the brothers voted overwhelmingly for Tanki to be the next prior and Eric (from Mozambique) to be sub-prior. As for me I will clear out for six months or so to give the new team a chance to find their feet. Colin Griffiths, one of the Australian brothers, is now Rector of Alice Springs and is looking for someone to keep him company there and help with the work. This new venture sounded attractive to me so off I went in November.

I was in Alice Springs from November 2000 until February 2002 when I returned to Lesotho for a further period.

February

Here I am back again as we move into autumn. I arrived back in time for what is a tradition here for the first Friday of Lent. The three religious communities, Community of the Holy Name, Leribe, Society of the Precious Blood, Masite and ourselves meet in a church near town for a day of recollection and prayer. It is a very African affair, the organisation is sketchy, the time-table is spontaneous, the activity non-stop, the singing beautiful and the prayer hearty, prolonged and sincere. There was not a minute of the day left unoccupied by sermons, prayers, offices, litanies and processions until, on the verge of exhaustion, we came to the end and unpacked our lunches and indulged in a bit of chat before we departed.

There is no shortage of work to do here, my post at St John's is still vacant, the TEE has collapsed since Judy Gay went back to the USA, and the sisters at Masite want me to resume as what they used to call their chaplain but now call a priest counsellor who is really a priest-mute who will nod his head in a grave and thoughtful way while the sisters are convincing themselves that what they want to do and what they are going to do is the right thing to do and what God wants them to do. So that the priest will add his blessing to the end of the process. The days have long gone by, thank goodness, when sisters allow themselves to be bossed about by a mere male.

April

This month Tanki went on holiday and left me in charge of his present church, SS Mary & John, Botshabelo. It is an old church, not far from town, and in its early days it was the chapel of a little colony of lepers, a Leprosarium, and is still called by some 'the leper church'. However time marches on and since they can now detect leprosy almost as soon as it appears and overcome the virus with powerful modern drugs, leprosy is almost non-existent in Lesotho. Meanwhile Maseru has expanded greatly and surrounded the church, which is now situated on the borders of a huge mental hospital that has replaced the leprosarium. The congregation is very warming robust and welcoming. They are the other side of the coin you see at St John's. Here they are all farmers, soldiers, police, staff from the hospital and a few patients. Most speak only Sesotho and the services are all in Sesotho. This means I have to say the service in Sesotho butchering the text as I stumble along, but they are very tolerant, even complimentary, and they provide an interpreter for the sermon. The singing is wonderful, led by a good choir supported by drums; in fact it is here that I met for the first time Mosia Sello hammering away on the drum at the front of the choir and he is now an SSM brother and a priest of the Anglican church – and a good one too. I will need to rush out here at 10.30 on Sunday mornings after I have completed the 8.30 at St John's. I enjoy it here though. In many ways it is a much more typical Basotho congregation.

June

Me Alice who used to cook for us came to see me one day, mostly to ask for help to pay school fees for her two girls. She is now working in one of the sweatshops on the other side of town where material is sent in from outside and sewn here into shirts, shorts, nightwear, or whatever you want. The workers are divided into teams and the amount earned by the team is fixed by how many of the finished products the team has turned out. It is a clever arrangement because it means that the management can depend on internal pressures within the team to keep everyone working at top speed with no slacking. There is almost no other employment available for women except this factory work or hotel maids. Alice told me that if all goes well, with no hitches, she can take home about 500 Maloti a month (about £35), that is to feed educate and clothe herself and the two girls and a helpless mentally disabled boy. I had assumed that all of these shops were owned by the Chinese who are a large and increasingly important part of the business world here, but no, I heard from home that Hudson's Bay Company of Canada owns some of the sweat shops and sends their shirts to be sewn up in Lesotho. I guess there is not anywhere in Canada where you can find women like Alice who are so unprotected and so desperate to work for so little because the alternative is starvation.

July

The HIV Aids situation just gets more and more grim. They reckon now that in Lesotho and Botswana about one in three or one in four people are HIV infected. It is like living with a rolling time bomb. An RC nun across the road who works on the Aids programme for the RC church says that in ten years' time many of the villages that cluster around Maseru will be deserted. Even now we see many families decimated. The father brings the infection back from the mines in Johannesburg and then the wife gets it and soon they are both gone and the children are left on their own with the oldest, maybe just eleven or twelve, left to look after their siblings. There are plenty of families like this up in the mountains with no income and little help. Yet the stigma attached to the disease still remains. No one will say at a funeral that he/she died of Aids; they died of TB or asthma or pneumonia, never Aids. One priest told me that this stigma is the fruit of a hundred years of preaching by the missionaries that sexual sins were the worst kind of sins and brought the greatest disgrace and shame on any family. So we taught them how to be ashamed. There are great sign boards all through town 'No condoms – no party', 'People who care use condoms', 'The ABC of safe sex – Abstain before marriage, Be faithful to your partner, Condomise'. The first two of these three are the platform of the Roman Catholic church, but I' m not sure that any of them make much difference to people's behaviour.

This month at the Sisters place in Masite I heard the best talk I have ever listened to on the subject of Basotho culture and African religion. The speaker was the RC bishop of Bloemfontein, a young guy, African, very bright and very humble with it, with a good sense of humour. He pointed out that most Basotho are walking a double track with one foot in the church and one foot in the witch doctor's kraal. If they feel on any occasion that they would get a better result from a traditional healer than they would from the church's holy water, then they will go to the healer, because healing, help and solutions is what religion is all about in a difficult world. He also said that in his opinion, and not everyone would agree with him, in the Basotho tradition there was no Supreme Being ruling over the universe and in charge of the whole show. You had spirits that inhabited certain rocks, pools or trees and above them the next rank was the ancestors and there was no one above them. Thus it was the ancestors that served as the gods of the Basotho, they were the ones that must be placated at all times, and your destiny was largely in their hands. He spoke of many funerals he had conducted where there was a strict Catholic Service conducted with a requiem mass, sprinkling of the coffin with holy water and the censing of the coffin, and then after the coffin had been laid in the ground and people were preparing to go home he would hear family members inviting their friends, 'Are you coming back to the house for a cup of tea?' Here the bishop burst out into laughter 'Tea?, Tea? You would never find a teapot in that house.' Those words were merely the code for inviting people back to pour libation, trickling a few drops of whiskey on the ground to placate the ancestors, and commending the recently departed to their care; but all this was done only after the priest had been safely seen off the premises and they were back in their own yard. He went on to suggest ways we might 'Africanise' our services, burning bowls of rushes and certain grasses and wafting the smoke over the worshippers. I only wish I had a tape of his whole address.

September

We celebrated St. Michael and All Angels, the SSM's patronal feast, with a big conference for the 'Friends of SSM'. There must have been between forty and fifty young people in their teens and twenties here from Friday evening until Sunday lunch time. They slept in the class rooms of a local school but all their meals were cooked and served here, organised by the brothers and friends. I did a quiet morning for them on Saturday and in the afternoon they had a young guy suffering from Aids talking to them on HIV, how to avoid it, how to live with it if you contract it. His advice was mostly to live as healthy as you can, eat healthy food and avoid stress. He really held them spellbound, every eye was fixed on him, and indeed he was an impressive good looking young person. We had a big festal evensong after his talk, and then Sunday morning a big outdoor mass starting with a procession up the front drive led by eighteen servers in scarlet cassocks and surplices, then a bevy of drums, rattles, incense, banners and whatever else was to hand. The former bishop Philip Mokoku, a great friend of SSM, celebrated in the courtyard and that was followed by another big meal. It was wonderful to feel the priory pulsating with the energy of all the young folks, but, as I understand is the case as with grandchildren, it was also wonderful to see them depart and peace and have order return.

2003

March

Tanki is away on holiday so I am again looking after Botshabelo but this week I had to go to one of the outstations of their parish at Ha Makhoati. This place is just a string of tin-roofed huts along a country road, but they have a primary school and are in the process of building a High School. We had the service in the primary school and as it was the first Sunday in Lent we were packed out. Africans have a great devotion to being ashed (placing with ashes the cross on each forehead as a sign of penitence) and that custom is repeated on this Sunday for those who could not make it to church on Ash Wednesday. I wish you could see the church, a long low building filled with battered and ink spattered benches and desks, the sun shining brightly through the many gaps and empty spaces in the roof, and not a whole pane of glass in the place. When we came to the ashing, I looked down the church to see an endless line of humanity stretching down the aisle and out into the yard, many of the women holding their babies in their arms. I ashed them all one by one including those chubby little smiling infants on whose guiltless brows I traced the cross and reminded them, 'Remember you are dust, and to dust you shall return.' Meanwhile non-stop and enthusiastic hymn singing was carried on by the congregation, some executing a few dance steps as they worked up the line. In fact an air of happiness and joy pervaded the whole church rather undercutting the sombre message of the words. This all took place in a temperature of about 38C. After communion all those who had not received communion which included all the babies, again lined up the aisle for a special blessing and sprinkling with holy water. We started at 10.30 and finished about 1.00 but no one complained. This, after all, is the day's entertainment and relaxation and social gathering. When we were taking our sodden vestments off in the classroom next door I noticed on the blackboard the remains of Friday afternoon's lesson. It was a list of all the kings of Israel and Judah from Saul to the bitter end with Herod. Still, I could not help but wonder if that was really the most useful thing that any small boy or girl living in Ha Makhoati in these days could be learning by heart on a hot Friday afternoon. After church the churchwarden invited us back to his house for lunch. He must be the richest man in the parish, and we were ushered into the sitting room of his new brick house where everything seemed shiny new. We were all fairly hungry by this time and I mentally envisaged a little cold chicken and some fresh salads slipping down nicely. However what his wife brought out were big steaming bowls of chopped up sheep's intestines floating in a clear soup with a couple of slices of steam bread lying along the margins. I ate it all with thanks, but refrained, unlike the rest of my crew, from asking for seconds.

It is services and days like this that I have enjoyed most of all during my time in Africa and will always remember them with gratitude.

I left Maseru on June 2 to return to Alice for a couple of weeks with Colin Griffiths and then both of us travelled up to Darwin where the bishop had asked me to conduct the clergy retreat for the diocese. This was followed by a holiday in Canada and the UK and I returned to Maseru in September. However by now I was 73 and Tanki and the young brothers were well able and eager to take over the running of the priory so I looked about for a less strenuous and taxing field of ministry. I returned to Alice in October to re-join Colin there.

10

Land of Oz

I arrived at 11.30am on 'the Ghan', the train that runs from Adelaide
to Alice, at that time the end of the line. I had caught the train at
3.00 pm the day before. It is a gentle way to travel with much less
hassle and fuss than at the airport, though it has to be said that as
you gaze from your window along 1500ks of track there is not a
lot to see except flat scrub land stretching to the horizon before
and behind with the occasional acacia or spinifex. The Anglican
church of the Ascension is in a modern style with a towering
spire almost in the centre of town and with a modern rectory next
door. It was built not long ago to replace an old mission church
which had grown too small. The town itself reminds me of some of
those towns on the Canadian prairies with wide dusty streets and
no near neighbours. The Alice (as they call it) sits on the Stuart
Highway in the dead centre of the country, with Darwin 1500ks to
the north and Adelaide 1500ks to the south. Colin as the Rector
of the parish has responsibility for a 1000k stretch of the highway
with a congregation 500ks north at Tennant Creek, and providing
a service every other month for the tourists at Uluru (Ayers Rock)
500ks south of here, all this with only the odd petrol station or
motel scattered along the highway in between.

When a person first arrives in Australia they may be forgiven
for feeling a certain sense of disorientation – an upside-down feel.
All the plants and beasts they are accustomed to seeing at home
they no longer see, and all the plants and beasts they now see are

unlike anything they have ever seen before. Even the landscape is not what I was expecting. I had been expecting a flat sandy desert similar to the scene in Kuwait, but here we are in the middle of the MacDonnell Range, perhaps the oldest mountain range in the world. At one time they say it reached as high as the Canadian Rockies but it has now been worn down by millions and millions of years of erosion to a more modest height. Instead of mountain peaks what we now see are long ridges of corrugated hillsides which the Aborigines, who know every stone in their land as well as you know the furniture in your front parlour, say are the caterpillars from the Dream Time, now taking their rest. Many other things contribute to this 'upside-down' feel. Christmas comes at midsummer, often in the middle of a heat wave, but we still sing 'In the bleak midwinter – frosty wind made moan' before we adjourn to cold salads, cold beer and cold meats to replace the traditional turkey dinner. Then Easter comes in the autumn with life subsiding and dying all around while we are celebrating the resurrection and rebirth of new life.

Even the rivers here are upside-down with the water seeping out of sight down the sandy river bottoms several feet below the surface, while up above there is nothing but dry sand and gravel. Only the line of graceful river-gums marks the river banks and the course of the river. The Todd River, when it flows, flows through Alice, only coming to the surface at long intervals so they say if you see the Todd flowing three times you are bound to return. The famous regatta 'Henley-on-Todd' has to be run with a crew whose feet protrude through the bottom of their shell which they must hold steady with their hands as they gallop over the dry river bottom towards the winners post. It is a famous sporting event, second only to the camel races and the Melbourne Cup, but the river, so long as it lasts, is always the topic of every conversation on the streets of the town. Unfortunately as soon as it has gone a few miles beyond the city limits it is swallowed up by the ever-thirsty desert sands.

You might even say the original inhabitants of this land, the Aborigines, are the most 'upside-down' feature of the landscape. Because the town is now the centre for the law courts, social and medical services, government agencies and shopping malls, Aborigine people, rather than living in their own independent settlements scattered through the outback, often prefer to be in town in order to enjoy a little litigation, have the assistance of the dialysis machines at the hospital, take advantage of the ready availability of alcohol and to roam about amidst the great display of goods to be seen at the malls, all brought up the Stuart Highway by the Road Trains. In my innocence I had thought that because I had always enjoyed living within African culture amongst African friends, the Aborigines of Australia would be a welcome expansion of both my circle of friends, and my knowledge of another culture. I was completely wrong in this expectation. The Aborigines remained a complete mystery to me from the first day to the last. Perhaps the hardest thing for me to come to terms with was the great difference there is between Africans and Aborigines. While nearly all Africans are exuberant and welcoming to all visitors and remain fascinated by, and, with some discrimination, attracted to most aspects of white culture, the Aborigines are just not interested in white fellas at all. To them we are a rather boring and irrelevant part of the local scene. A favourite resting place of theirs in town was to sit on the sidewalk out of the sun engrossed in their own conversations, but seldom even raising their eyes as you went past them down the street. Another favourite gathering place was to sit in a good-sized circle in the dry bed of the Todd River chatting and drinking the hours away while the whites, always short of time, rushed up and down, making a living and making appointments.

I often wondered what it was they found to discuss though all those days, and I was told that Aborigines have one of the simplest economies of any people in the world, since private ownership of anything is unknown. What is my brother's is mine and what is mine is his. No requests to borrow or keep any item can ever be refused. Thus they don't accumulate clothes or possessions and since the whole territory that belongs to their tribe is 'home' to them, they are free to move off anywhere to any new place for no clearly discernible reasons. All that set up is simplicity itself, a model for any member of a religious community, but they also live under one of the most complicated family networks. Relations are traced back to the twentieth remove and people born in the same year or the same place are also related to you as 'skin brothers and sisters'. Who you can marry, who you can work with, what you can do, and in fact a host of daily issues are all settled by reference to your skin relationships. This becomes a veritable minefield of obligations and sins which it takes a lot of discussion to sort out, if it is ever possible to do so, but it certainly takes much dialogue. Sadly the things about white culture that attract them most are booze, guns and cars. So most of them lived a feckless sort of life and we had frequent calls at the Rectory front door for a hand-out of beans on toast and a cup of tea. They would also come in to church towards the end of the Sunday Eucharist and sit in the two back rows impassively, incuriously, and exuding a pungent and powerful smell, since neither water nor soap were integral to their culture. Then at the end of Mass they would all surge to the front of the queue to get their coffee and cake which they would then proceed to eat in their own circle out on the front lawn. In church on a Sunday morning it was like two separate ships passing in the night with never a signal but whether they were excluding us or we them it would be hard to say. It was not a happy arrangement. We could manage to tolerate but not to befriend one another. But perhaps even that was better than our fathers and grandfathers had done. They organised shooting parties to go into the outback around Alice and shoot them down as cattle-stealers. I am sorry to say, except for one lovely lady (there is always an exception!) I never attained a friendship with any of them. This lady, who later became our church warden, is a remarkable women and she painted me a lovely picture in the Aborigine style as a going away present. I have it with me still.

After I had been only a couple of months in Alice to mark the millennium, the Director, Fr Christopher Myers, called for a big SSM jamboree in January, to be held partly at Maseru in Lesotho, and partly at a retreat house in Assisi in the Free State R. S. A. All SSM members who were willing and able attended. The jamboree was socially very pleasant and there was much laughter; the retreat house out on the veldt was ideal but whether it carried the Society much further forward, I would not be so sure.

———•—•———

I returned to Australia early in February, landing first in Adelaide where the brothers at the priory said they had a spare car which I could use provided I was willing to drive it back to Alice, which I was very willing to do. I set off in a temperature of 35-40C. Once you got on the Stuart Highway there were no turn offs, detours or spaghetti junctions until you reached Alice 1600ks up the road. Of course it was much too far to do at one go, and by afternoon I found myself approaching the town of Coober Pedy which was to be my stopping place for the night – indeed there were no other alternatives.

This town is the centre of the opal mining industry where it appears all you need to do is dig a pit straight down (some go as far as 90 feet), extracting the opal dirt and piling up the spoil in a neat little hill at the top. The result is that as you approach the town it appears to be surrounded by a host of miniature pyramids which present a striking picture, especially in the rays of the setting sun. The biggest problem facing the miners is that they are at the very centre of the Australian desert where temperatures reach 55C every day for weeks and months of the year. The solution the locals have arrived at is to go underground. 70 per cent of the population live in houses dug out below the surface. The advantages are obvious. You don't need an air-conditioner; the temperature remains a steady 25C night and day, winter and summer. If you suffer a little from claustrophobia, you simply paint a large picture window on the wall of your sitting room with grassy fields and flowery meadows beckoning you outwards and a purple mountain range on the distant horizon. What more could you want? If the family grows, dig out an extra room; after all, a four bedroom house can be dug out in a day and, if you are lucky, you may uncover enough opals to pay for the whole enterprise. I wasn't adventurous enough to find the underground motel, so the one I stayed in was very traditional, very seedy, and very hot. I would like to have been there on a Saturday night so I could have worshipped with these modern Anglican troglodytes in their underground church but I was in a rush to be off the next morning early. I made Alice Springs by mid-afternoon where I had a nice welcome from Colin and the folks who were cleaning up the church for Sunday.

Ghost town 04.03.01

Colin likes to take Monday as his day-off so today we set off looking for the Arltunga gold mine, though all the gold has long since gone and the miners have departed. It is now a historical site. We drove along the Ross Highway until just beyond the Ross River Homestead and then turned onto a dirt track where we almost came to grief in the sand that lay deep and soft over the roadway and into which our back tyres sank alarmingly bringing us to a soggy stop However with a few sacks crammed under the wheels we managed to get some grip and get on our way again. The mine site has been well cared for by the Tourist Board with shelters provided for those who wish to picnic and a lot of historical material posted for those who wish to learn more, but nothing can really cover the essential grimness of the place. There in the heat (it was just over 40 C) were the ruins of a few derelict buildings, amongst them, rather ominously, a police cabin and a sturdy jail and the inevitable pubs. We learned that when gold was first discovered at the turn of the century, prospectors appeared from all parts of Australia and from the rest of the world. They could get as far as Alice on the train and then they bought a wheel-barrow in which they deposited all their worldly belongings and pushed it through the waterless desert, past the tropic of Capricorn, nearly 100ks, until they reached Arltunga. When they arrived they found themselves part of a semi-lawless group of drifters, digging in the dirt, on very poor food and too little profit. No one made any big killing at Arltunga. Colin and I ate our picnic at one of the tables provided out of the sun, but soon hurried to get back into the air-conditioned car and away from the clouds of flies that hovered over the whole scene. It was an instructive day; it confirmed me in my suspicion that Australia is a hard land of few comforts and it provided hard life for the hard people who came here looking for a fortune and new life.

Our Outstation 04.04.01

Now my turn rolled around to drive up the Stuart Highway to provide a service for the congregation at Tenant Creek. This group has recently joined forces with the Lutherans to form a more viable group. As a result of this arrangement the Lutheran pastor from Alice goes up one Sunday a month, we do another, and they are on their own for the rest. In fact one of the moving spirits behind the congregation is a Lutheran lady, Anne by name, who runs a big general store in town and at whose table I have had many a tasty meal. I usually leave here about mid-morning on Saturday. The trip takes about five hours and the driving conditions are ideal with a long mostly dead straight road, perhaps meeting two or three vehicles in the course of an hour but with no occasion to overtake anyone. Frequent companions on the trip are the brown wedge-tailed eagles with their 2.5m wingspan, plus a few falcons and kites. They hover over the road with an eye open for the abundant road-kill which gives them their running buffet. The famous Road Trains, four or five coaches long, roar up and down this road all through the night, every night at great speed, stopping for nothing.

They bump off, with careless abandon, the gently grazing kangaroos that happen to be in their way. In fact the eagles are the main traffic menace, as they waddle away from the table after an over-indulgent meal. It is only slowly and gradually with much effort they get themselves aloft again. Nature lovers are urged to stop their cars, get out, and drag the kangaroo carcases off to one side out of the path of the traffic. I'm afraid I failed in this public duty. I usually stop at Tea Tree for petrol and an ice-cream, but I never feel moved to turn in at Barrow Creek which has been the hub of a murder investigation for almost a year now. There was an English couple involved. A man was murdered at the roadside by someone who had flagged him down asking for help. Nor do I turn in at Wycliffe, another seedy motel and petrol station whose link with the 'morning star of the Reformation' I have yet to discover. Tenant Creek began with a gold mine, which, due to the slump in gold prices worldwide, has long been closed down so that most of the population are unemployed or retired or both. There is also an Aborigine Camp there. I arrive mid-afternoon and have a nap in the small room at the back of the church thankfully provided with an air-conditioner, and then go out to eat with whoever of the congregation has volunteered to feed me that week. The Church of the Holy Name is small but lovingly cared for. By the second or third visit faces have become persons and friendships are formed. They have solved the music problem for the small congregation with a tape recorder holding all those surprisingly up-to-date hymns which are so dear to them and which are activated by a half turn and deft flip of the switch on the channel finder by the 'Music Director'. I like going there. They are so friendly and welcoming and we all enjoy the service. Besides it makes a nice break from the pressures and tensions of city life in the Alice!

The Sorry Camp

Colin has lived here for six or seven years and has a real interest in and dedication to Aborigine life and culture. When we were out driving the other day he told me about their Sorry Camps, which are an important part of their common life. Apparently when some disaster overtakes the tribe, a murder, a pestilence, a feud (internal or external) or witchcraft, or unexplained or unexpected deaths, the tribe downs tools (if the phrase has any meaning for those who never take them up!) and set up a new camp in a new place and give themselves over, all together, to being sorry. They howl, they wail, they sit on the ground by the fire and cover themselves with ashes. Attendance at the Sorry Camp is a strict obligation for every member of the tribe from infants in arms to ancient ones. The first work of the camp is, by their cries, to register and make public the 'not rightness' of this situation. The second task is to identify the cause of this disaster because every disaster has some cause behind it; nothing happens in this world by chance. Responsibility for the disaster is usually pinned on one person, though to us the perceived connection between the so-called guilty party and the disaster may seem a little fanciful, as when a young mother is savagely beaten up because she fell asleep in the afternoon and her little girl wandered into the path of a car and was killed instantly. To accomplish the work of a Sorry Camp there has to be a payback of some kind, generally through the acceptance of a pain equivalent to the pain that has been inflicted. It is very much an eye for an eye and a tooth for a tooth arrangement. In the recent film, *Ten Canoes*, made in Australia by an Aborigine company, the man who had unwittingly killed an (unknown to him) hunter in the bush, had to stand or dance in one spot while the kinsfolk of murdered man hurled spears at him until they had fatally wounded him. That was his payback and that was the finish of the business between the two tribes. It is still the custom in Aborigine communities. If you have injured a man you must sit still in a circle of the elders while the one you have wronged or one of his kin runs his spear through your thigh. The police these days do not interfere and a Red Cross ambulance will be standing by to take the injured party to hospital. Payback is always painful and often cruel, but the Aborigines see it as a means of peace-making and bringing hostility to an end, a hostility that could lead to a long-lasting feud that, once launched, could wipe out both tribes. Payback makes unity possible after harm has been done and so ensures the survival of the people for a further generation.

----•----

Uluru 11.03.01

This weekend it is my turn to go down to take the service at Ayers Rock, or Uluru, the Aborigine name by which these days they prefer to call it. The first time I was due to make the trip I asked Colin for instructions on how to get there. He told me, 'Get on the Stuart Highway, which runs within two blocks of the Rectory, and drive south for 300ks, then take a right turn on to the Lassiter Highway and drive for nearly 200ks and you're there. Can't miss it!' And that's exactly how it was. I will never forget my first evening there when after supper I drove over to the rock and got out and walked as close to the base as I could.

I was completely gob-smacked. Partly it is because there are no trees, hills, or outstanding features near at hand. You are standing in a flat and characterless plain and, without warning, this wall of pink rock rises up in your face as if it had just thrust itself up from the depths of the earth. Smooth unpolished rock as high as a skyscraper, stretching to the right hand and the left, occupying all your peripheral vision. It was like nothing I had ever seen before or since. It seemed outside time, from a place without clocks. It is very easy to understand why the Aborigine people feel, when standing here, they are in the presence of something more than human, in the presence of a spirit that is divine. For them Uluru is a holy place and should be treated with all the respect and reverence that we give to our cathedrals and ancient churches. They are not happy when they see the tourists climbing over it, just as we would not be happy if we saw a party of tourists practicing their mountaineering skills on Westminster Abbey. The tourist village, a mile or two off from the rock, is enormous with tour buses driving in and departing every hour of the day and night, plus an airport near at hand. In the village you can find malls, motels, posh hotels, coffee shops a variety of restaurants, paper shops and all the other paraphernalia of a modern town. Apparently all this depends on water pumped up from bore holes and already people are wondering how long it can last. A few years ago the Rock and the land around it was handed back to the Aborigine people after they had successfully appealed the case before a Land Rights Commission. Everyone who enters their territory since that date must pay $15.00 to the local people whose land it now is. It must be a steady little earner. At my Eucharist Sunday morning in a lecture room we had six folks; small in number but an interesting group. One couple were farmers on Jersey who told me they had already booked for a bowling tour in South Africa later in the year, so it looks as if farming on Jersey is reasonably profitable. Oddly enough their parish priest was Barry Giles who had been a novice and a roommate with me at Kelham hundreds of years ago. There were also three from Docker River, about 200 miles deeper into the outback, and also a couple from England. We all had lunch together and had nice conversation; people have who have never met before nor are ever likely to meet again, but have just shared the sacrament together in common fellowship.

Railways expansion 15.07.01
Big doings in town today when John Howard, the PM, appeared to turn the first sod for the new railways line from here to Darwin. This he did with much fanfare, trumpets and speeches plus a lot of enthusiastic flag waving from the kids. The section from Adelaide to Alice was completed in 1929 but it seems to have run out of steam at that point and never got any farther – until today that is! They have been preparing the sleepers for this section in a factory up at Tenant Creek for some time now.

Missionaries 03.08.01
I have met a lovely middle-aged couple who are members of the parish here. When they discovered that Colin was going to be down in Adelaide on my birthday, they invited me for supper so that I would not be on my own. Theirs is a rather sad story. They began as Baptist missionaries, full of faith and love and ready to give their lives for the spread of the gospel amongst the Aborigines. They went off to live and work in an Aborigine village and were eventually defeated by the culture that enveloped them. I may have got this wrong and they said little about it but my impression is that what proved the insurmountable barrier was that these people have no idea of individual ownership of anything, or individual initiative. If I saved up and bought a car, immediately that car became the property of all and thus became the property of no one, and I was re-absorbed back into the community on the same footing as all the others. For us, and particularly for us Christians, individual ownership and individual choices are the key to our personal and community life and development. Whereas with them all choices, all property, all decisions are communal – and you as an individual cannot rise above it, dent it, or change it. This couple toiled on heroically until he had a bad nervous breakdown and had to be hospitalised in Alice for a lengthy spell. Happily

they have now taken control of their lives again. They are holding down good jobs in the hospital laundry and are worshipping with us, and throughout they have remained faithful to each other. They make a quiet but solid contribution to the life of the parish. I look on them as modern heroes and martyrs of the missionary movement. It is a privilege to know them.

----·•·----

Funerals 16.10.01

We had a big Aborigine funeral on Saturday and in this they are very much like the Africans. Funerals are serious business. The church was packed with all the men in black trousers and white shirts. After the service in church and the committal in the cemetery, I was talking with one of the sons of the deceased, an enormous man who, not surprisingly, told me, 'I can't wait to get home and get into some comfortable clothes and then some of us will go hunting.' I asked what they would be hunting and, surprised that I needed to ask, he said 'Kangaroo – that is the best meat that you can eat, especially the heart, the liver and the tail. So we will have a big feast tonight.' The way they cook it is simply to heave the whole carcass, just as they have dragged it in, on top of the fire. They will roll it over from time to time until it is done to their perfection and then haul it out and cut off the bits they fancy, with men having the first cuts! At the last election up here in the Territory one of the candidates was had up on a huge bribery and corruption charge because he had been caught distributing kangaroo tails among the local Aborigines – different strokes for different folks!

----·•·----

Fiji menus 01.11.01

Last Saturday I went to a barbecue out at the children's village (St Mary's) where some of the staff are from Fiji and today did their own style of cooking. They dug a good-sized hole in the ground and lit a big wood fire in it. When this had died down to a good bed of hot ash, they put in a wire basket filled with chunks of meat, lamb shanks, chicken and kangaroo tails for the children, all wrapped in tinfoil. Then came the potatoes, pumpkin and whatever else you fancied, similarly wrapped. They then covered the whole thing with wet hessian (in Fiji this would have been palm leaves) covered this all with earth until no smoke escaped and then went away for three hours of rest and relaxation. When they dug it up everything was delicious, meat falling from the bone. We were surrounded by kids of all sizes busily peeling the skin off those tails as if they were bananas and licking their lips and fingers over the meat. Delicious!

A Correctional Institute

I didn't do prison visiting while I was in Alice but I spent quite a few Saturdays with Enid, a member of the parish, working at the Visitors' Centre set up at the prison gates. The Northern Territory Correctional Institute is about 20ks south of town on the main highway. The Prisoners' Aids who are based in this centre have raised enough money to buy their own bus which they use every Saturday to ferry relations and friends of the prisoners back and forth from town, and providing an air-conditioned space where they can wait their turn to visit. They liaise with the guards to keep the visitors moving smoothly to their appointments. They also listen to their stories and sell them cold coke and crisps to pass the time. About 95 per cent of the inmates here are Aborigine so organising visiting appointments and bus times is no small task as these are not a clock-oriented people. Through this work Enid and I did get to know one of the prisoners. Let's call him Joe.

He was white, born I'm not sure where, but brought to Australia early in life. When he was about 20 years of age he got involved at Darwin in some drunken dispute with an older man whom he murdered with a baseball bat. For this he received a life sentence, which generally in the Territory means about 25 years of which he had served five or six. We got to know him when he had to be taken to Alice Springs hospital for stomach pains and was made to wear steel shackles on his legs when he was taken in. This sight so shocked one of the nurses who is a parishioner of ours that she appealed to us to do something for him. All we could do was to visit him regularly and this we did which, as he had no family contacts, was appreciated by him. He is a man with considerable imagination and talent. He sketches, paints, does carpentry and welding and has a driving ambition to be a novelist. He wrote two or three novels on his own which he posted to me after I had returned to the UK. They were not to my taste being all about vampires, here presented in a sympathetic light, amidst scenes of destruction and horror. However I encouraged him. He was young and any way by which he could imagine or think himself outside of that iron cage that enclosed him was, I thought, bound to be beneficial. I continued to correspond with him for a couple of years after I left Australia until suddenly, without explanation, the letters stopped. Enid tells me he also now refuses to see all visitors. I don't know what that means, except that it can hardly mean anything good for him, and he must still have over ten years left to do. To me it seems so inhuman to lock men up in cages out of all normal contact with friends and people. What we are doing as mature men and women to Joe over twenty five years with shackles and prison bars, seems almost as brutal and cruel as what he did in the passion of youth in fifteen minutes to that old man. An insoluble problem!

'Old Timers'? Village

One pleasant task that falls to me these days is that each Friday afternoon I go to Old Timers Village where I hold a Eucharist for those Anglicans or others inclined to attend. We usually have four or five; we've never reached the double figures! This place is like a small village on the edge of town with a wide variety of accommodation from people living independently in separate bungalows, to those needing sheltered housing who eat in the dining hall, to those needing nursing care. We generally meet in Sheila's sitting room. Soon after I started she announced one Friday she had received the OBE that week but when I made a suitably flattering and gushing response she explained, 'That's only Old Timers' lingo for Over Bloody Eighty!' Why I enjoy going is that nearly all these women have lived in Alice for years and years, since the end of World War II through the long drought in the 40's and 50's, when every tree in the town withered and died and they almost smothered in the heat and desert dust. They watched the steam train puff in once a week on a Friday afternoon, and they watched the army camp and lorry park of the soldiers building a new highway from Alice to Darwin out of a desert track through the wilderness. They had lived through it all and raised their families here, and, while they don't go on about it endlessly, with a little gentle nudging, a discreet question or two, they can be persuaded to tell, with a few dry chuckles, some very surprising experiences.

Palm Valley

This Monday Colin and I drove out to Palm Valley. It is one more idiosyncrasy of the Australian landscape. It is a valley hidden away in the midst of hills of red rock. These rocks are very porous and soak up water like a sponge thus retaining moisture long after the rains have ceased and the Finke River has disappeared below the sands. This has made it possible for a grove of Red Cabbage Palms to survive here from the days before the Ice Age and long after they have disappeared from the rest of Australia and the rest of the world. Thus a truly Jurassic picnic spot and very lovely with it. The last stretch of the track to the valley involves driving up the dry bed of the Finke River where we got completely bogged down in the sand. As we teetered there on the edge of despair, along came the Salvation Army officer from Alice with his wife and family out for a picnic in their four wheel drive and he cheerfully pulled us out of the bog. What a blessing to find oneself living in the ecumenical era!

Border agency 03.12.03

I am in trouble with the bureaucracy as my two year resident permit ran out last month. I had foolishly thought I would only need to send it in to have it re-stamped for another two years, but no, one of the major planks of this government, in this case loyally supported by the opposition, is Boundary Protection by which they seem to mean keeping out as many foreigners as possible. I imagined at first that only applied to dusky-skinned people arriving in boats from Indonesia but not so, they show not the slightest trace of racism in applying their restrictions to all, even unto seventy year old whites from partners in the Commonwealth. If I can't get it solved I may have to move on which I am a little reluctant to do.

Summer time 07.12.03

I wish you could join us for breakfast out on the back porch on some of these December mornings with the sun pouring through the gum tree at the back as we enjoy the last traces of coolness before the day's heat begins in earnest. We fill up the bird bath each day and that, plus the grapes that are ripening on the vine by the back gate, draws a great crowd of green parrots, some days as many as a dozen. These are joined by the little canary-sized birds called honey eaters, flying about like English swallows as they sing and splash in the bath. Of course there are also magpies screeching and throwing their weight about in a very vulgar fashion but, taken altogether, it makes a great start to the day.

Christmas 03

Last night they had their annual Carols by Candlelight in the town park, an old European Christmas tradition transported to the tropics and just as popular here as at home. There must have been about 2000 people present, all races, all sitting on the grass holding candles, babies, bottles of pop, singing carols under a magnificent glowing red sunset that flooded the sky from side to side. Whatever you might say about the Aborigines, of whom there were a good number present, they are no threat to anyone but only to one another. I was thinking you would never get a crowd like that out after dark in the centre of Maseru. People would be too afraid of being mugged or beaten up on their way home in the dark.

30.12.03

Christmas, as usual, was very busy, beginning the week before when Colin and I were invited to the Catholic Presbytery along with a few other priests and sisters. A jolly little clerical assembly. On Christmas Eve we had open house before the midnight mass with mince pies and Christmas cake. It was a lovely service though it still seems a little strange to me to hear the cicadas singing in the background while you are belting out 'O come all ye faithful'. In fact the temperature went down a bit to around 35C over Christmas which was a great relief to all. Because of the heat, I followed Aussie custom and didn't cook a whole turkey; instead I tied two turkey breasts together around macadamia nut stuffing, and accompanied this with a leg of ham on the bone which Colin insists is what he has had (cold) from childhood. Bishop Philip and Joy were here for dinner, plus the hospital chaplain, Barry Fernley and his wife Trish, and the Tucker family. So another little mostly clerical gathering which I enjoyed very much. We had some nice cold salads. Besides the usual coleslaw and potato salads, the chaplain's wife brought one of water melon and onion, drenched in mint sauce – very tasty! I like it here!

Ned Kelly country 16.01.04

I had a week's holiday down at Beechhurst near Wangarata in New South Wales with David Evans and his wife Cecilia. David came to Kelham as a 16 year old lad from Hartlepool and later on joined SSM as a novice for a while. He then went on to work for Bishop Nicholas Allenby SSM in Kuching in Borneo. While there he married Cecilia a very attractive local girl, thereby incurring the displeasure of the Bishop. Later on, after working for Missions to Seamen in Singapore, he was ordained by the Bishop of Bunbury and, several parishes later, he is now Rector of Beechhurst. You would hardly realise when you arrive that you were still in the same country as the Red Centre. It is all green rolling pastures with flocks of sheep, enormous gum trees and gentle rains, a pleasant pastoral air over the whole scene. I got the feel of the place on Sunday after church when I heard one of the women telling David,

'I won't be able to help at the Bring and Buy this week. We are having the Shearers at our place all the week to finish our sheep'. The town of Beechurst itself was the centre of a big gold rush in the 1850's and there are over 2000 Chinese buried in their own cemetery on the edge of town all of who came looking for gold and died before they could get back to China. Let's hope it was not before they got a little gold.

The other drawing card of the place is Ned Kelly of the gold rush era, an Aussie combination of Jesse James and Al Capone, who galloped through the hills wearing an iron helmet to keep him safe from the policemen's bullets. Here they show you the court room where he stood trial and the cell where his dear old mother and mentor was locked up. It is all in a recent novel by Keneally. All this historical angle is worked up by the Tourist Board but it is still a pleasant landscape and a great change from the Alice.

Railways and artists 23.02.04

Great excitement in Alice after I got back when the first train on the first north/south transcontinental line in the world passed through. I was there with most of the rest of the population. There was a band, speeches, and even a camel train to transport the officials to the stand and remind us of all the benefits these officials had conferred upon us. The train left Adelaide on Thursday and should be at the docks in Darwin by Saturday afternoon.

Colin has just come in from a display of Aborigine artwork. This is a growth industry in these parts. It is not so long (post war) since these people discovered how to capture their dreams and aspiration in a style of painting that is uniquely theirs, the so-called 'dot painting'. Some of these painting now are extremely valuable, reaching prices of $3000.00 or even more. There is even a little group of amateur artists that occupy the grass between the church and the rectory though anything less like a group of artists it would be hard to imagine. A half dozen raddled old women with multi-coloured hair in ancient rags that gently pong, sitting on the ground with a few pots of brilliantly coloured acrylic paints, plus an invisible flask of whiskey set out around them and a few brushes in their hands painstakingly filling in the thousands of dots necessary for their latest creation on a long piece of window blind.

———•—•—

From outer space 20.03.04
On our day off today Colin, one of the congregation and I drove out to see Gosse Bluff which is a fair distance beyond Hermansburg. It is the weathered remains of an enormous crater about 20ks in diameter which was created, they say, around thirty million years ago when a meteor of frozen carbon dioxide, ice and dust smashed into the earth at this point, releasing energy one million times more powerful than the Hiroshima bomb and blasting rock from six kilometres down up to the surface to form the core of this enormous crater. The best place to see the extent of it is from the Tyler's Pass Trig station about sixteen kilometres to the north of it. Now of course it is a complete moonscape with no trees or shrubs growing on it. Despite the distance in time the sight of it is still more than awesome as you nervously check the skies to see that all is still OK up there. However, I took along for our lunch at Tyler's Pass a couple of racks of spare ribs. They were succulent and, eaten cold, did much to reconcile us to our own minute place in the history of this land.

———•—•—

A Penal Colony 30.11.04
This week we had our Provincial Chapter at Hobart in Tasmania. Tasmania is a more rugged, wooded, colder and wetter part of Australia with some of the original primeval forest still left standing though much lusted after by the timber companies. As a diversion one day we were taken down to Port Arthur to visit one of the largest of the penal settlements and the first such settlement that I have seen. The site was lovely, surrounded by wooded slopes and sitting at the water's edge. It could accommodate up to 1200 men at any one time and in the years it operated, 1834 – 1877, it was home to some 12,500 men all transported out of England for stealing a sheep or a watch or misbehaviour of all kinds. All

the buildings which are very extensive were constructed by the convicts with bricks they had made on the spot and stone they had quarried.

So construction of more and more buildings was a ready means of keeping the prisoners in employment. They built a large mill which was powered by a huge treadmill on which twenty-four men were kept walking at one time, another solution to the employment problem. You can see the derelict punishment cells where men were locked into solitary confinement for indefinite periods and there was a silent prison, a separate establishment, where no talking or any sound was ever tolerated. An extra dimension of horror was an island named Port Puer (i.e. Boy's Port) where boys from nine years old and upwards, fresh from the streets of London, were incarcerated on the unexplored margins of the known world where they were doubtless subjected to every imaginable abuse. You can also visit the Isle of the Dead where those who at last escaped were allowed to take their rest. I have never been in a place where there was such a brooding atmosphere of evil and brutality and inhumanity, nor do I think that turning the whole place into a kind of Disney world theme park and the 'must see' of the tourist circuit solves any of the problems.

Diggers Rest

Colin's term as Rector comes to an end in July 05 so it looks as if I will be moving down to Diggers Rest near Melbourne. I have enjoyed the holidays I have spent there so far, it is a lovely country spot with temperatures less extreme than in Alice, but I am still having no luck in my application for a permanent residence permit.

I moved in with David Wells and Margaret Dewey at Diggers Rest on the Tuesday after Easter. This priory is not connected to any parish or institutional work and is an hour on the train from Melbourne so I soon found myself looking for some activity to occupy the rather more generous portion of free time that I now have. In the event I turned back to an old friend whom I had met long ago at Kelham. He was a man called John Moschus who lived in sixth century Byzantium. He didn't write theology, instead he travelled widely through Palestine, Egypt, Asia Minor talking to and collecting stories from monks, soldiers, hermits and sea captains. This man loved a good story and he gathered all those he had collected into one book which he called 'Pastures of the Spirit'. In fact it was a kind of Byzantine Readers Digest, full of human interest stories, So I took up the pastime that I had begun at Kelham. I began translating all the stories into English. It proved a happy escape for me on those days when I might have felt small tinges of boredom creeping around the edges.

Looking back over my time in the land of Oz, my overall impression is that on the whole Australia is a land of deserts and rocks and little water, with a climate of droughts, fires and floods. All this makes a very hard life for those who live here, first of all the Aborigines, then the convicts, and lastly the millions of others from every corner of the world who come here looking for a new life and finding it, but not easily.

By the time that we were coming to the end of 2005, the Border Agency had made it quite clear that a person of my advanced age could never expect to be given permanent residence in Australia and so I turned my thoughts to a return to the UK. Here when I applied to the British High Commission I received a warm and welcoming response. All I would need to do was to apply to go back as a 'Returning Resident' and then get the necessary permits after I had arrived in Britain. At the same time Vincent Strudwick, who has been my mate since the first day I arrived at Kelham in 1957, and who had for some years been chaplain to the All Saints convent in Oxford, informed me the sisters there, in the midst of their most recent renovations, had created a new flat in their grounds and if I was willing to apply for residence therein, they (the sisters) would probably say 'yes'. I was, and they did, and since then I have made my home in their grounds. It is ideal for me, close to Vincent and Nina Strudwick, near to the priory at Willen and easily accessible for anyone who may wish to visit me. Perfect!

Epilogue by Vincent Strudwick

This is not the end of Ralph's story. At All Saints Convent with the Sisters of the Poor, Ralph continued to receive visitors, resource the sacramental and devotional life of the Sisters, and enjoy helping out in the 'Steppin'stone' drop-in centre for the homeless on the campus. He befriended the foreign students studying English to whom the Sisters gave hospitality in return for various duties in the Convent and garden – and was always generally 'around' to do unpopular jobs like washing up.

He joined me regularly in attending lectures in the University, and occasionally I prevailed upon him to come to a college dinner afterwards; but that wasn't really his scene.

At one such event, while trying to participate in a conversation with my neighbour, I overheard the following exchange between Ralph and a Professor of Classics:

Professor: When you were in Lesotho, did you meet the King?

Ralph: Sure. Once or twice.

Professor: I taught him Latin you know. I suppose I am the only person here who has taught Latin to a King.

Regularly at Willen Ralph continued to play his part in the thinking that was developing like at 'The Well'; and he even returned to Lesotho to lead a retreat and enjoy the company of the African members of the Society who had recruited and nurtured.

He tells us nothing of this. But in 2010 he resumes the Log.

On the Feast of St Michael and All Angels (September 29th) I celebrated the 50th anniversary of my profession in SSM. Thanks to the kindness and generosity of the All Saints Sisters, we were able to have the Jubilee in their chapel here in Oxford together with the reception and lunch that followed. It was altogether wonderful. The congregation was ample and Jurassic. As I looked across the altar, I could see every layer of my life and ministry represented, from my brother Albert, with whom I had shared a bed when I was seven, to friends from Kelham, Ghana, Sisters from the Order of the Holy Paraclete, and St Etheldreda's, with my Oxford hosts and brothers and sisters from SSM. There were many other personal friends who have so freely journeyed with me and supported me.

Then, three years later, following his stroke and illness, there was another occasion, this time as Willen celebrated the 40th anniversary of its foundation by Ralph with a Eucharist and party at 'The Well'. A hundred people gathered, again at Michaelmas, including friends and former students, as well as local worthies, including the Mayor of Milton Keynes. The preacher, was the bishop of Oxford, The Right Reverend John Pritchard, who for the past seven years had been the Visitor of SSM in England and Europe.

He preached on the promises of God and asked 'What has God promised his religious communities?'

He went on:

'Not permanence, that's for sure. Religious Communities have come and gone. Those in North Africa and Turkey, once the strongest in the world, they have long gone leaving only piles of stones. But the church worldwide is growing incredibly fast in China, Hong Kong, Singapore, Korea, West Africa, South America and so on. Some of our traditional religious communities in this country have gone, to be replaced by different forms of community.

'While for some the job is complete. Faithfulness has been lived, love has been shown, the season is over. In others God is still at work, renewing, raising up, digging over the ground, a new season. Here in SSM we believe in a new season.'

And now we may conclude with Ralph's own words:

If there is one word that characterises these fifty years that have slipped away since the feast of St Michael and All Angels, 1960 when I made my profession in the Society of the Sacred Mission at Kelham, that word would be 'change.' Everything has changed since then. There is a certain irony in that since in 1960 I felt I had come to a place that was above and beyond all change. It looked untouched by time's rude hand. As I sat in the Refectory at breakfast there and looked around at 120 men silently feeding I thought, from the evidence of your eyes, you could be looking at a scene from 1960, or 1950, or 1940, or 1920 or 1910. In every decade they wore the identical habit, ate from the same steel plates, and even the menu with its ever-recurring baked beans, fried bread and kippers had a whiff of eternity about it. Then too every generation faced the same day, divided up into the same four segments, study, prayer, football and physical work, and who would ever think of changing such a satisfying combination? It was just right as it was. However, changes have a way of overtaking you whether you are ready or not. Since 1960, the chapel where I made my profession has become a public dance hall, the college where we worked has been long since closed down, that stalwart band of brothers now includes within its ranks, some women members and even a few families; if the present recruitment trends continue for another decade or so the major ethnic grouping in the Society will be the black Africans. In addition to these visible and objective changes, there have been subtle and important changes in our ideals and aspirations.

We work now, not so much for the conversion of the heathen (especially abroad!) as for the healing of divisions and the creation of one worldwide family. Our ideal is not so much a life of utter purity, as a life laid down in the service of others. We are not so much concerned with reducing the money spent on our own upkeep, as with leaving behind as small a carbon footprint as possible through a life style that is simple and sustainable.

Indeed these fifty years have been a veritable kaleidoscope of ever shifting people, places and policies and yet it would still not be true to say, as I said at the beginning, that everything changes. There are two factors that have remained the same throughout, the same today as they were in 1960. The first is the God who called me then to a completely unexpected and surprising destination. He is the very same God who calls me today to unknown and equally surprising destinies. Secondly, that stumbler who tried amidst doubts and fears to respond to that call in 1960 is the same stumbler who still amidst doubts and fears tries today to respond to a new call, to a new destiny.

It is these two factors, always the same, that give coherence to these fifty years and bind them together into one single story with a plot that is both exciting and intriguing.

Appendix 1

The global changes that Ralph describes, with their impact on the Society of the Sacred Mission, led to changes in structure to match the diversification of culture and work undertaken in different parts of the world. In 1998 the role of 'Director' ceased, and the three Provinces where work was developing were re-named and given greater autonomy. In the spirit of subsidiarity, where decisions are taken at the most local level, the Chapter of each Province, with the Provincial, became the chief authority; while the unity of the Society was guarded by the Provincials' regular consultative meetings in different geographical locations.

The Society had always had a 'Visitor', a bishop who represented the wider church to the Society, and the Society to the church. There now developed a structure with each Province having its own Visitor.

To help the reading of Ralph's text, a short summary of office holders is given.

Visitors to the Society 1972 - 1998

The Rt Revd Denis Wakeling (Southwell)

The Rt Revd David Jenkins (Durham)

The Rt Revd Richard Holloway (Edinburgh)

Directors of the Society

Fr Dunstan McKee (1972 – 1982)

Fr Edmund Wheat (1982 – 1989)

Fr Thomas Brown (1989 – 1984)

Fr Christopher Myers (1984 – 1998)

Provincials in UK since 1972

Ralph Martin 1973 – 1981

Edmund Wheat 1981 – 1991

Rodney Hart 1991 – 1998

The new Provinces were formed: The European Province, the Province of Australia, and the Province of Southern Africa.

The Visitors from this time to the European Province

The Rt Revd Richard Holloway (Edinburgh) 1998 – 2003

The Rt Revd Tom Butler (Southwark) 2003 – 2009

The Rt Revd John Pritchard (Oxford) 2009 – 2014

The Rt Revd Stephen Conway (Ely) 2015

The Provincials from this time of the European Province

Douglas Brown 1998 – 1999

Edmund Wheat 1999 – 2000

Jonathan Ewer 2000 – 2009

Colin Griffiths 2009 –   2014

Jonathan Ewer 2015 (Acting Provincial)

As the Society diversified, so in addition to formal Priories, members gathered round a work, or individual members took on a role for the church while being rooted in a particular Province for their continuing formation and fellowship.

The following list is not meant to be complete or a history, but illustrates some important markers that relate to Ralph's text.

The Mother House at Kelham, together with the theological college, closed in 1973.

Quernmore Park closed in 1991.

Willen Priory and Sheffield were founded in 1973; Willen has been through several transformations and flourishes today as Ralph illustrates. Sheffield closed in 1980.

SSM was at Middlesbrough from 1988 – 1995.

The Society had a presence at St John the Divine in Kennington with several brothers at different times between 1993 and 2005. Fr Robert Stretton SSM joined the staff in 2014 after many years in Lesotho.

In Southern Africa, the priories of the 'old Society' were all closed by 1988, except the Priory in Maseru, which became the focus of a new beginning which Ralph describes.

Fr Michael Lapsley was Provincial in Southern Africa but is now pursuing his itinerant global ministry in the Institute for the Healing of Memories, and as Vice President of the South African Council of Churches.

In the Australian Province, the theological college at St Michael's House, Adelaide had to close after a bushfire in 1983 that destroyed the library, including many books sent from the old Kelham library.

Colin Griffiths pioneered a new house at Alice Springs and Ralph joined him there. Colin later returned to the UK and became Provincial of the European Province in 2009, living at the Well at Willen and developing its work.

Fr Christopher Myers has been parish priest of St John's church, Adelaide for 25 years, and the priory there has served as the Provincial office.

During Ralph's time in Australia, the Visitor was the Most Revd Philip Freier, Archbishop of Melbourne, who with his wife Joy, became a great friend of SSM in its transformations. In 2014 he was elected Primate of the Anglican Church in Australia.

The Japanese Province closed in 1990. Br Andrew Muramatsu SSM still works there, but is attached to the European Province where he did his novitiate in the 1960's.

The dynamism of the changes described in Ralph's log, are reflected in the continuing movement of people and work in the Society.

The present leadership structure is:

The European Province

Visitor: The Rt Reverend Stephen Conway (Bishop of Ely)

Provincial (Acting): Fr Jonathan Ewer SSM

The Southern African Province

Visitor: The Most Reverend Thabo Makgoba (Archbishop of Cape Town)

Provincial: The Very Revd Tanki Mofama SSM (Dean of Maseru Cathedral)

The Province of Australia

Visitor: The Rt Revd Gary Weatherill (Bishop of Ballerat)

Provincial: Fr Christopher Myers SSM

VS

Appendix 2

Building the Community at Willen
An introduction to a seminar by Ralph Martin at Willen Priory 10th December 1977

Today we are going to work on a particular project, or perhaps better, a particular question: 'How do you build a community?' Not just any community in the abstract, but a particular community here. While most of you are not directly part of or involved in this community, yet we felt that by confining ourselves to a particular location, a particular time, and a particular set of problems, we would tie ourselves down to earth, and to a concrete actual situation rather than drifting off into other places and other phantasies. Hopefully in this way we will all benefit from this situation even if we are not ourselves part of it. This means therefore that when we say 'How do you build a community?' we mean 'How do you build a community out of the rough material that is available here in Milton Keynes?' Not, 'How do you build a monastic community?', or 'How would you build one in the twelfth century'?, or even 'How would you build a simple SSM priory', but 'How do you build a complex community made up of various individuals, and also of various small groups already formed, a community that comes from Milton Keynes and is suitable for Milton Keynes for the next few years at least?'.

To give you some idea of what I mean by the complexity of the rough material available, for the benefit of those who don't know us too well, I will give you a breakdown of those who live here at present. Nine work on the site at various jobs, as follows: one is bursar-gardener, one works with the sponsoring committee of the Terminal Care Hospice we hope will be established in the village, one lives in and looks after the retreat house which is a part of the priory complex, one is a housewife and looks after her two small girls, one is general co-ordinator, one looks after the parish of Willen for which we are responsible, one is guestmaster and in charge of cooking, two are retired and so work harder than anyone doing all the jobs no one else has time for. Then there are three who work at jobs outside the priory: one in the Job Centre at Bletchley, one in the Careers Office in Hemel Hempstead, one as the Sector Education minister for the Milton Keynes Christian Council. Then there are four people who do not live in the priory, but who are connected with us in various ways: one works at the Milton Keynes Development Corporation, one is doing a diploma at the School of Library Science at Loughborough, one is Sector Minister for the Board of Social Responsibility for Milton Keynes, and one is a housewife looking after her small family. Finally there are three nuns at the Children's Home in Bedford with whom we have a tentative connection but which we hope will develop into something. In all there are 8 brothers, 2 married couples, 5 single people and 3 nuns.

Given this assortment of people and the assortment is just a cross-section of ordinary life today, can you, should you try, to build a community in which each one can be himself and all can be of use? Since the nucleus of the group is the SSM (Society of the Sacred Mission), it is natural, and I think helpful, that we who belong to the SSM should bring with us from our experience of life together in the Society a certain amount of luggage. One of these bits of luggage which I think is helpful in the present venture and which I now want to unpack is the idea which our founder, Fr Kelly, had about community life. This is the idea which he tried to apply in building up SSM in its early days, and in fact, we could say that Kelham, the large Theological College and the Mother

House of the Society for many years, was one way of working out Fr Kelly's idea, but it was not the only way that that idea could be worked out; Kelham by no means exhausted its possibilities.

If we look at Fr Kelly's original idea about community, we notice that it had three parts, and, in brief, it went like this: He said the SSM existed –

(A) For the service of the Church

(B) By the organised devotion

(C) Of free minded members.

Now we need to take that apart a bit to see what he meant by those brief phrases.

(A) He said that we gather together in a community for the service of the Church, i.e. to be of use, to be of practical use to others. He freely acknowledged that there were all kinds of religious communities, and people joined them for all sorts of reasons: because they wanted to be able to pray more; because they found community life congenial or supportive; because they wanted to enter and to preserve the monastic tradition. All these are legitimate reasons for entering community, but they weren't his idea. The reason he started his society was for service, to be useful to others and it was made of up of people who wanted to give up their lives to be of service to others.

Fr Kelly spoke of it as serving the Church, but he meant Church in the widest terms, not just one party or faction within it, nor one denomination of it, but the whole Christian Church, serving it by assisting it in its mission to all mankind. Whatever brings forward the salvation of man, that is to be served. I think that it is important to get this point clear at the start, because it affects so many questions that follow. For example: Why work in this place rather than that? Try to work in the place where you can best serve the Church and be of most use. Why wear habit or not wear habit? Wear whatever will help you most to be of use to the people you are serving. Why build a complex community with women associates instead of a simple SSM priory? Build that kind of community which can best serve and be of use to the people of this area. That then was the first point of his idea; that was the touchstone. The community exists not for the sake of nurturing or looking after its own members, but for the glory of God, to be of use to other people, to be effective.

(B) The service of the Church and being of use to people is an ideal that many people, thank goodness, follow. But the way in which, according to Fr Kelly, a community should do this, was by organised devotion. By organised devotion, he doesn't mean arranging prayer services at regular intervals. What he did mean, we will understand by taking the words separately and in reverse order. First of all then, devotion. He believed that there were hundreds and thousands of ordinary folks, not especially Catholic, not especially High Church, not especially pious, who wanted to devote their lives to the service of God. And these were the people he started the Society for. The Society was to be the means of bringing these ordinary people together, so that they could support one another, enhance one another, increase the effectiveness of one another, and do in combination far more than any one of them could do in isolation, and do it far more effectively. And that is what he meant by 'organised' devotion: the community was a way of co-ordinating and harmonising what would otherwise be a lot of competent, skilful, devoted individuals who was each fighting a lonely battle on his own. The community then was a kind of spiritual Co-op, whereby lots of ordinary people could combine and so make a difference, and so promote God's glory. But it can't be stressed too much that it was a way of uniting a lot of simple everyday goodness such as we all come across nearly every working day. It would be drawn from all walks of life, and would service all walks of life. Once again this affects all that follows. If it was to be made up of ordinary people, then the way of life, the style of living, the relaxation, and the work undertaken would need to be such that ordinary people could slip into it easily, and do it competently, without feeling that they were either being clamped into a nineteenth-century corset, or expected to perform five miracles each day before breakfast.

(C) Finally the third part of his theory was that this organisation was made up of free minded members. As we have just seen, the purpose of entering the Society was not to give up your individual skills, abilities and strengths, but so that these gifts of yours attended a meeting in London of bishops and principals of theological colleges, which began a series of planned reductions in the number of colleges supported to admit ordination candidates.

In fairness the Commission, which was chaired by Robert Runcie, later Archbishop of Canterbury, did not consider they had 'deleted' Kelham. Their proposal was that the College would have a smaller allocation of English students, increase the number of overseas students from different parts of the Communion, and engage in laity training. See *Runcie: The Making of an Archbishop*, Margaret Duggan (1983).

Ralph worked hard with all of us to grow together into the sort of community that he envisaged. His introduction to one of the 'workshop days' is set out in Appendix 2.

SM magazine, 1973.

But the following April it appears that the objections to him were overcome. In his autobiography Bishop John Brown completes Tola's story by saying that he was now established as the non-stipendiary priest at St Paul's until a replacement for Ralph could be afforded and appointed. *Mainly Uphill: A Bishop's Journey*, John Brown, p.286.

VS

could be enhanced by close combination with others, and better deployed for the benefit of others. For him a community was not a standardised machine with interchangeable parts, it was, as we have already seen, more like a spiritual Co-operative Society, where everyone had invested part of himself, and therefore everyone had a say in the common policy, so that shared convictions could alter and change that pressure for ill which is exerted against us all. Yet, each individual investment was different, drawn from different resources and left in for varying terms of time. And, in fact, each investment could always be withdrawn when the individual decided he could invest it better elsewhere. Thus he envisaged the Society engaged in all sorts of situations, in all sorts of manners of living. Many would work in groups, some as individuals; some groups would be more monastic in style, some more secular, determined by how the job they were doing could be the more effectively done, and determined by the gifts and abilities of those who made it up. In one of his writings Fr Kelly said that a community is 'not so much an organisation as a way of thinking', and by that I suppose he meant a way of thinking as a team, a way of working as a group to develop the capacity of each individual to the full, and to integrate these resources into one harmonious blend moving in one direction, to the advantage of those who are not us.

So then if we look at this idea of Fr Kelly's, I think that it will give us at least a starting point for today's discussions. For his idea gives us what he thought was the Purpose, the Make-up, and the Style of any group that was connected with him. The Purpose – it existed not for the sake of being a community, but to be of use, of use to God, and that meant of use to people. The Make-up – it was not made up of the elite, the pious and the kinky, but of ordinary, everyday people. The Style – not a machine, but a democratic gathering, a spiritual Co-operative of free minded individuals who came together, and stayed together by their own free decision, and worked to a common goal by their common decisions.

Notes by the Editor

12.

13.

14.
15.

1. See *New Dictionary of National Biography*, H. H. Kelly (2
2. Korea.
3. In the traditional orders monks stayed in one place, whil
   Franciscans and Dominicans, were more mobile. Many o
   communities of the Anglican Church in the nineteenth c
   to combine the corporate office of daily prayer with an ac
   ministry.
4. *Leaving Alexandria: A Memoir of Faith and Doubt*, Richar
5. *'Open to the Spirit'*, ed. Colin Craston (1987). Published f
   Consultative Council.
6. *The Tablet*, 21/28 December 1985.
7. J.-P. Migne, *Patrologia Graeca, 87: 2851-3116*.
8. A representation of Christ on the cross, often separating t
   church from the nave.
   At Kelham, it was a bronze sculpture by Sargent Jagger, wl
   the Artillery Memorial in Hyde Park, London. It is now ir
   St John the Divine, Kennington, London where Fr Kelly g
   students.
9. Guiding the life at this time were: 'The Principles', 'The Co
   out the structure of the Society in quasi-legal terms, and tl
   which at Kelham governed the knitty-gritty of daily behav
   based on experience. For example: 'Students may not the l
   a window'.
10. On the list, your 'Department' was posted under its Latin
    (Grub) Domestici (Cleaning) and Sacristani (Preparing th
    were some specials as well, such as 'Hortulani' – cleaning c
    the pigs.
11. Some of us were worried. In 1965, acting for the Warden w

could be enhanced by close combination with others, and better deployed for the benefit of others. For him a community was not a standardised machine with interchangeable parts, it was, as we have already seen, more like a spiritual Co-operative Society, where everyone had invested part of himself, and therefore everyone had a say in the common policy, so that shared convictions could alter and change that pressure for ill which is exerted against us all. Yet, each individual investment was different, drawn from different resources and left in for varying terms of time. And, in fact, each investment could always be withdrawn when the individual decided he could invest it better elsewhere. Thus he envisaged the Society engaged in all sorts of situations, in all sorts of manners of living. Many would work in groups, some as individuals; some groups would be more monastic in style, some more secular, determined by how the job they were doing could be the more effectively done, and determined by the gifts and abilities of those who made it up. In one of his writings Fr Kelly said that a community is 'not so much an organisation as a way of thinking', and by that I suppose he meant a way of thinking as a team, a way of working as a group to develop the capacity of each individual to the full, and to integrate these resources into one harmonious blend moving in one direction, to the advantage of those who are not us.

So then if we look at this idea of Fr Kelly's, I think that it will give us at least a starting point for today's discussions. For his idea gives us what he thought was the Purpose, the Make-up, and the Style of any group that was connected with him. The Purpose – it existed not for the sake of being a community, but to be of use, of use to God, and that meant of use to people. The Make-up – it was not made up of the elite, the pious and the kinky, but of ordinary, everyday people. The Style – not a machine, but a democratic gathering, a spiritual Co-operative of free minded individuals who came together, and stayed together by their own free decision, and worked to a common goal by their common decisions.

Notes by the Editor

1. See *New Dictionary of National Biography*, H. H. Kelly (2005).
2. Korea.
3. In the traditional orders monks stayed in one place, while Friars, like the Franciscans and Dominicans, were more mobile. Many of the revived communities of the Anglican Church in the nineteenth century tended to combine the corporate office of daily prayer with an active apostolic ministry.
4. *Leaving Alexandria: A Memoir of Faith and Doubt*, Richard Holloway (2012).
5. '*Open to the Spirit*', ed. Colin Craston (1987). Published for the Anglican Consultative Council.
6. *The Tablet*, 21/28 December 1985.
7. J.-P. Migne, *Patrologia Graeca*, 87: 2851-3116.
8. A representation of Christ on the cross, often separating the chancel of a church from the nave.
   At Kelham, it was a bronze sculpture by Sargent Jagger, who had sculpted the Artillery Memorial in Hyde Park, London. It is now in the Church of St John the Divine, Kennington, London where Fr Kelly gathered his first students.
9. Guiding the life at this time were: 'The Principles', 'The Constitution' setting out the structure of the Society in quasi-legal terms, and the 'House Rule' which at Kelham governed the knitty-gritty of daily behavioural expectation based on experience. For example: 'Students may not the leave the House by a window'.
10. On the list, your 'Department' was posted under its Latin name; so Cibarii (Grub) Domestici (Cleaning) and Sacristani (Preparing the Chapel). There were some specials as well, such as 'Hortulani' – cleaning out and feeding the pigs.
11. Some of us were worried. In 1965, acting for the Warden who was away,

I attended a meeting in London of bishops and principals of theological colleges, which began a series of planned reductions in the number of colleges supported to admit ordination candidates.

12. In fairness the Commission, which was chaired by Robert Runcie, later Archbishop of Canterbury, did not consider they had 'deleted' Kelham. Their proposal was that the College would have a smaller allocation of English students, increase the number of overseas students from different parts of the Communion, and engage in laity training. See *Runcie: The Making of an Archbishop*, Margaret Duggan (1983).

13. Ralph worked hard with all of us to grow together into the sort of community that he envisaged. His introduction to one of the 'workshop days' is set out in Appendix 2.

14. SSM magazine, 1973.

15. But the following April it appears that the objections to him were overcome. In his autobiography Bishop John Brown completes Tola's story by saying that he was now established as the non-stipendiary priest at St Paul's until a replacement for Ralph could be afforded and appointed. *Mainly Uphill: A Bishop's Journey*, John Brown, p.286.

VS